SPRACHBUND IN THE WEST AFRICAN SAHEL

AFRIQUE ET LANGAGE

Collection fondée par France Cloarec-Heiss,
dirigée par Pascal Boyeldieu

La collection **Afrique et Langage** a pour ambition de permettre aux langues d'Afrique subsaharienne d'être à la fois mieux connues et mieux prises en compte dans les débats théoriques les plus actuels, qu'ils soient d'orientation linguistique, culturelle ou cognitive. Elle se propose d'accueillir des ouvrages qui contribueront à faire connaître le patrimoine linguistique et culturel de ce continent tout autant que des synthèses théoriques. Y trouveront donc naturellement leur place des monographies (grammaires et dictionnaires), des ouvrages concernant le développement linguistique (standardisation, terminologie), des analyses et des éditions de textes littéraires ou de tradition orale, des études ethnolinguistiques présentant des systèmes conceptuels originaux et leurs implications cognitives aussi bien que des travaux ayant trait à l'histoire et à la genèse des langues.

Déjà parus :

1. Bernard CARON (éd.), 2000, *Topicalisation et focalisation dans les langues africaines*, 323 p.
2. Robert NICOLAÏ (éd.), 2001, *Leçons d'Afrique. Filiations, ruptures et reconstitution de langues. Un Hommage à Gabriel Manessy*, 581 p.
3. Guillaume SEGERER, 2003, *La langue bijogo de Bubaque (Guinée Bissau),* 310 p.
4. Zygmunt FRAJZYNGIER, 2003, *Studies in Chadic Morphology and Syntax*, 295 p.
5. Stéphane ROBERT (éd.), 2003, *Perspectives synchroniques sur la grammaticalisation. Polysémie, transcatégorialité et échelles syntaxiques,* 285 p.
6. Pierre PALAYER (et collab.), 2004, *Dictionnaire kenga (Tchad)*, 215 p.
7. Pascal BOYELDIEU & Pierre NOUGAYROL (éds), 2004, *Langues et cultures : terrains d'Afrique. Hommage à France Cloarec-Heiss*, 284 p.
8. Dymitr IBRISZIMOW & Guillaume SEGERER (éds), 2004, *Systèmes de marques personnelles en Afrique*, 216 p.
9. Didier MORIN, 2005, *Prosodie du texte de style oral. L'exemple d'une langue accentuelle : l'afar*, X-219 p.

Sous presse :

10. Pierre PALAYER (et collab.), *Dictionnaire démé (Tchad). Précédé de notes grammaticales*, 490 p.

COLLECTION
AFRIQUE ET LANGAGE
11

Sprachbund in the West African Sahel

Edited by

Bernard CARON & Petr ZIMA

Selaf n° 432

PEETERS
Louvain - Paris
2006

Published with the support of the Grant Agency of the Czech Republic
(Project N° 405-01-1180),

and the assistance of the UMR 8135 (CNRS-INALCO-Paris 7)
« Langage, Langues et Cultures d'Afrique Noire »

D. 2006/0602/37

ISBN: -10 90-429-1745-8 (Peeters Leuven)
-13 9789042917453
ISBN: -10 2-87723-921-7 (Peeters France)
-13 9782877239219

Contents

Foreword

Most of the contributions published in this volume were prepared within the framework of the research project *«Dynamics of Contacts between Populations and Languages - Lexical and Structural Diffusion and the Genealogies in the Sahel»* (Grant Agency of the Czech Republic Project No 405-01-1180) co-ordinated at the Faculty of Humanities, Charles University in Prague in co-operation with the Université de Nice and J. W. Goethe-Universität, Frankfurt-a.-M., and in close co-operation with other centres of research such as CNRS-LLACAN (Paris), Guttenberg Universität (Mainz), Universität Wien, St. Petersburg Universität, etc. At the occasion of the XVIIth International Congress of Linguists (Prague 2003), the proposal of the three co-directors of the project (R. Nicolai, R. Vossen and P. Zima) to organise a special workshop on these problems was accepted by the Scientific Committee of the Congress. It was at this workshop that several of the papers published in this volume were presented and discussed mostly in their preliminary forms. Other papers were presented at a special session of the Biennial Chadic Linguistic Conference which took place at the Faculty of Humanities, Charles University in October, 2003. It was at this occasion that links with Indiana University (Bloomington, USA) were established. The present volume appears in its final form in a close co-operation of the Faculty of Humanities, Charles University, with CNRS-LLACAN, Paris, thanks to the Grant Agency of the Czech Republic.

The purpose of the project was to examine the linguistic situation in the Sahel in view of the recent developments in the study of language contacts, assessing the reality of the Sahel *Sprachbund*. The concept of *Sprachbund*, or 'linguistic area' as a bundle of features common to languages over a geographical area has experienced considerable extention : from phonology and morphology, its domain has been extended to morphosyntax and lexicon. By doing so, the concepts of calquing, typological convergence, relexification and metatypy are being used to characterize the processes witnessed in the study of language contacts.

The following questionnaire regarding the areal distribution of TAM (Tense-Aspect-Mood) paradigms and functions in the Sahel was elaborated and discussed at these working sessions:

1. Is there a Split-Predicative (Subject-Pronoun Complex) or a Verbal Affix Complex TAM marking, or both, or are there transitional phenomena?
2. Is there a SAuxOV, SAuxVO or other word-order?
3. Is there a «classical» negation of TAM paradigms (addition of a negative marker to the positive TAM paradigms) or a «supletive» one (i.e. the existence of fully or partly different TAM markers paradigms in negative constructions)? Are all TAMs or some TAMs concerned, and which ones? Is there any any difference between central and periphery (periphrastic) TAM paradigms?
4. Is there a contrast of modality, such as, minimally, a contrast between indicative and non-indicative paradigms?
5. Is there a relation between 3 and 4? In other words, is negation partly or fully different in indicative and non-indicative forms?
6. Is there a contrast between Pf and Ipf paradigms?
7. Is there a syntactical conditioning of TAMs (as that of relative vs. non relative, focussed vs. non-focussed forms in Hausa or Fula etc.)?

While papers published in Section I of this volume are oriented towards general problems of Sprachbund studies with particular focus on the West African Sahel area, several papers published in section II of this volume represent - directly or indirectly - various sorts of preliminary answers to the concrete problems of the areal manifestation of such verbal phenomena, as formulated above.

In the first paper, P. Zima defines and examines the relevance of the various concepts used in the *Sprachbund* studies. He argues that the theory of relexification developed by creolists and the theory of lexical diffusion linked with the concept of metatypy originating in the Pacific and Amerindian language areas share certain common features. Consequently, "Sprachbund" represents such an idealising extreme generalisation as are such traditional concepts as "dialects", or may be even other -lects.

A. Aikhenvald we examines some problems in language contact, focussing on borrowing patterns rather than forms and discusses the notion of linguistic area. Convergence as a major outcome of long-standing multilateral interaction in language contact is analysed in the light of system-altering and system-preserving changes, and sociolinguistic parameters. She illustrates her study with numerous examples from the the African continent whose linguistic diversity in terms of genetic groupings, areal clusters and Sprachbunds of varied extent and antiquity remains the most challenging testing ground for the comparative method, and for contact linguistics.

R. Nicolaï examines the songhay-mandé situation and argues that, despite certain limited convergence features appearing with particular language contacts, most isomorphic features are to be explained in the light of the process of the constitution of Songhay as an emerging language. Areal convergence features supposed to be the roots of the present affinities are to be considered as a mere heuristic assumption, hoping to explain the existing isomorphisms through a premature generalization of principles experimented elsewhere.

R. Vossen and S. Ermisch examine the phenomena of language retainment and language shift in the Bisa-speaking community in South-Central Burkina Faso. They want to find why the Bisa language has been abandoned by two fifths of the Bisa population whereas neither the Bisa language nor its speakers' identity seem to be affected.

V. Černý *et al.*'s paper deals with the mtDNA sequences of four Chadic populations (Hide, Kotoko, Mafa and Masa) from Northern Cameroon, whose biological samples were collected during anthropological research in the area of their homeland. The paper is trying to examine these molecular genetic observations in the light of recent linguistic and archaeological achievements which consider the Chadic branch in the Afro-Asiatic phylum to be of eastern origin. The analysis of molecular variance, FST genetic distances and phylogeographic analysis revealed that more than half of the Chadic mtDNA sequences of Northern Cameroon can be traced to the region around the Upper and Middle Nile Valley and the Eastern Africa. However, the results show rather important geographical clustering than the correlation of common linguistic classification with molecular genetic data. Moreover, the dating of diversification of a mtDNA cluster specific for the Chadic mtDNA diversification do not coincide with glottochronological and archaeological reconstructions of proto-Chadic settlement in southern part of Chad Basin.

B . Caron studies the pronominal and TAM system of eight closely related Chadic languages spoken in Northern Nigeria : Zaranda, Langas, Dir, Danche, Baraza, Dott, Sigidi and Zaar. Their system has undergone extensive erosion and realignment. As far as TAM systems are concerned, Zaar stands out as oddly original : it has three tone levels, when the others have two; it has ten TAM paradigms that can combine, when the others only have between three and five that don't ; it marks aspect, tense and mood, whereas the others don't express time in their verbal system, the future being a clear case of mood subcategorization. These differences have sociolinguistic origins: the Zaars have come to their present situation by incorporating exogeneous populations which are still identified by the clan system : Angas, Boi, Pyem, Jaar, etc. It has resulted in a complexification of the language which goes against the general assumption that when absorbing a large quantity of foreign population, a language goes through a process of pidginization.

N. Cyffer presents a study of the expression of time in the TAM system of Saharan languages (Kanuri, Teda-Daza and Beria). Comparing earlier studies of Kanuri, such as S.W. Koelle's Kanuri grammar (1854), with its present TAM system, the author establishes the emergence of new sub-categories and a change of meaning and function of TAM categories in course of time. He also observes some vicinity to TAM uses between Kanuri, Hausa and Fulfulde. As these similarities go in line with other similar grammatical patterns (e.g. clause subordination), he proposes that areal contact features had an impact on the Kanuri grammar. In this context the question of linguistic alliances or even 'Sprachbund' comes up.

N. Dobronravin examines the interpretation of Hausa TAM markers in *Littafen nahwowin hausance*, an Arabic-script work written not later than 1907 somewhere in today's Ghana. An early attempt to define parts of speech in Hausa made by a Hausa speaker is discussed. The anonymous amateur linguist used the Hausa word **suna** for both verbs and nouns, and referred to **aiki** ('work ; job ; action') when he wrote about tense, aspect and mood, so practically about Hausa TAM markers. Only in the latter case was the word **aiki** apparently used as a term for a category opposed to **suna**. The split interpretation of Hausa verbs (verbal "infinitive" as a "noun" and the TAM marker as a "verb") is not entirely unanticipated, if one takes into consideration the peculiarities of the Imperfective forms in Hausa, especially in the North-Western dialect cluster.

P. Gottschligg studies the expression of middle voice and syntactic markedness ("relative tenses") in Atlantic languages, and more particularly in Fula, focussing on whether it is a derivational or inflectional category. This article demonstrates that Common Fula middle-voice inflections result from a fusion with a middle derivative, which is still visible in combination with certain other derivatives. He describes various processes of elaboration and simplification in Fula dialects, and attributes these variations to pidginisation in situations where the major contact languages were typologically opposed to the internal developments.

H. Jungraithmayr presents a short history and an overview of the dominant topics of research on the Chadic verb. The description and interpretation of the verbal piece and its characteristic features follow. The sequence of stages in the development of verbal stem types as already outlined by the author in 1978 is being discussed: verb stem inflection, segmental or tonal, is replaced by verb stem immobility and stem-external TAM productivity. The paper concludes by highlighting the most important issues of Chadic verb morphology as well as by hinting at the most urgent needs of future research in the field.

R. Kastenholz studies "Split Predicate Syntax" in Mande languages : invariant particles functioning as auxiliaries, are involved in the constitution of the clause. Inflectional marking and verbal semantics are thus "distributed", i.e. they are expressed by different elements in different syntactic positions. Some languages express near to all grammatical information by means of predicate markers for most, if not all TAM categories (e.g. Bambara, Koranko); in other languages, split predicate syntax is synchronically less prominent or even marginal (e.g. Jɔgɔ, Bɔbɔ). For a number of Western Mande languages, inflectional marking (i.e. to distinguish aspects like *perfective* vs. *imperfective*) is thus not predominantly marked with the predicate markers. It is suggested that, in a diachronic perspective, evidence from this type of languages should be taken into account.

R. Leger & U. Zoch examine the characteristic features of the pronominal systems in the southern Bole-Tangale languages from a synchronic and comparative view, paying special attention to logophoricity. They observe a dichotomy between the geographical northern and southern Bole-Tangale-languages not only in the difference of the grammatical gender in nouns, but also in the closely related pronominal systems. Gender levelling and the appearance of logophoric pronouns in the southern languages can be explained by historical contacts between the Chadic and surrounding Adamawa/Benue-Congo languages. They insist that the idea of expressing logophoricity by using special pronouns is contact induced, not the morphological forms of the pronouns.

In a short note on the Kanakuru TAM system, P. Newman presents a useful summary of his 1974 description of this Chadic language. He establishes some structural features such as the presence of split predicate syntax together with inflection in the verb form, and syntactic markedness in relation with focus, relativization and negation.

Finally, as a conclusion to the volume, P. Zima examines some properties that the TAM verbal/predicate systems in various language groups of the West African Sahel have in common : structural and typological similarities, if not identities, disregarding their different origins, and present/past geographical locations. He proposes that these structural, typological (and sometimes also formal) similarities may be grouped into three complexes, i.e. Split Predicate (or SP+/– Aux) vs Verbal Stem (VS) TAM marking, the Modal dichotomy of contrasting Indicative vs. Non-indicative appearing to have strong ties with the different types of Polarity, i.e. the dichotomy of contrasting Positive vs. Negative paradigms, and last but not least, the syntactic alternation of Neutral vs. Focussed TAM paradigms. He recommends that the questions of their distribution, origins (roots) and present dynamics should be formulated and answered.

The Editors

Sprachbund in the African Sahel : African and General Linguistics – a Mutual Challenge

Petr ZIMA

Charles University, Faculty of Humanities, Praha zimap@cesnet.cz

Abstract

It was only during the most recent decade that the Sprachbund concept and methodology, extended to morphosyntax in general, have been applied to the languages of selected areas of Africa In these contexts, Sprachbund is conceived as a bundle of distinctive features co-existing at all levels of language structures. These distinctive features involve either both forms and functions/meaning or only the functions/meanings: the classical concepts of calquing, or more broadly typological convergence being replaced by more specified concepts of relexification and metatypy. It is argued that the theory of relexification developed by creolists and the theory of lexical diffusion linked with the concept of metatypy originating in the Pacific and Amerindian language areas share certain common features. Consequently, "Sprachbund" represents such an idealising extreme generalisation as are such traditional concepts as "dialects", or may be even other -lects.

Résumé

Ce n'est que pendant la dernière décennie que la notion de "Sprachbund" étendue à tous les niveaux des systèmes linguistiques, la morphologie et la syntaxe y compris, est entrée en vigueur dans la méthodologie linguistique africaine. Dans ce contexte, le Sprachbund est interprété comme un faisceau de traits pertinents qui se manifestent à tous les niveaux des systèmes linguistiques. Ces traits pertinents concernent ou bien les formes et les fonctions/valeurs; ou bien ils ne concernent que les fonctions/valeurs. A l'étape actuelle, les notions de relexification et de métatypie commencent à remplacer celles de calque et de convergence typologique. L'auteur présente la thèse selon laquelle la notion de métatypie, présentée par les linguistes analysant les langues des régions pacifiques et américaines, partage plusieurs traits communs avec la notion de relexification présentée par les créolisants. Dans ce sens, le Sprachbund pourrait représenter une sorte de généralisation comparable à celle du dialecte ou des autres -lectes.

1. The recent wave of uneasy feeling – to put it politely – about classical presentations of genetic and areal classifications of African languages formulated by both general linguists (See e.g. R. M. W. Dixon, 1997: 34; Aikhenvald A. – Dixon, R. M. W., 2001: 9) and linguists specialising in this area (Dimmendaal 2001: 388) has relatively deep roots, both in terms of time and scope. It is true that serious methodological links between the traditional Indo-European linguistic comparativism and research into the languages of Africa have developed since the end of the 19th century, and positive results of the application of diachronic comparative methods are notable in such genetic fields as Bantu, Mande and other sub-branches of Niger-Kordofan, as well as Chadic, Berber, Cushitic and other sub-branches of AfroAsiatic, etc. However, many linguists have felt, and keep feeling, not just since Meinhof's, Klingenheben's, Lukas', but even since Greenberg's and Welmers' times that there are data, casting doubt upon, if not opposing, current African genetic classifications. For several decades, their reactions have been twofold:

1.1. Either these doubts have tempted them to re-shape the current genetic families, branches, sub-branches, etc. While in several cases (Nilo-Saharan, Khoisan) whole families are under doubt, in other cases the internal stratifications of macro-families into branches have been repeatedly re-classified and re-structured: the whole life-work of the Austrian scholar H. G. Mukarovsky followed this line, some aspects of his challenge to traditional comparativism (such as Mukarovsky, 1987) still remaining without competent critical reaction.

1.2. Or, alternatively, all data the genetic character of which was or is in doubt, have been put away outside the genetic-comparative context, and classified as different sorts of loans (and later into their specialising sub-concepts such as loan-translations (calquing) at different levels, «travelling words»/«Wanderwörter», etc.

2. Since Roman Jakobson's and Uriel Weinreich's time, the broader context of language contact and interference has been introduced by general linguists for all the «loan-type» phenomena, and the concept of «Sprachbund» has offered a plausible structural platform for analytical dealing with all these contact and interference phenomena. A handful of early attempts to apply the latter concept to the African language area (Westermann, 1949; Greenberg, 1983), linked as they were with the narrower linguistic concepts of Sprachbund limited to the levels of phonology and lexicon, or with non-linguistic, cultural and ideological factors (Becker, 1948), did not bring any major reshaping of the area in question. Only during the most recent decade have the Sprachbund concept and methodology, extended to morphosyntax in general, been applied to the languages of selected areas of Africa (Sahel, Chad Basin, etc., for details see Cyffer, 2000, 2002, and Zima, 1994, 1998a, 2002.). In these concepts, Sprachbund is conceived as a bundle of distinctive features co-existing at all levels of language structures. These distinctive features involving all levels of the respective structures (i.e. phonology,

morphosyntax and lexicon) consist in non-cognate parallels of genetically unrelated language structures concerning:

a. either *both forms and functions/meaning*: the classical concept of *borrowing*, if conceived in the broadest sense concerning all levels of language structures, could well be kept in use for this purpose
b. or concerning *only the functions/meanings*: the classical concept of *calquing*, or more broadly *typological convergence* if applied to all levels of language structures could again be kept in use for this purpose (Heine-Koteva, 2001); general linguistics, creolistics and certain Amerindian and Pacific linguistic schools have, however, broadened the scope and application of the Sprachbund studies. In fact, they challenge us with the more specified concepts of *relexification* and *metatypy* which should be discussed in the African context.

3. Although unnoticed by many Africanists, the theory of relexification developed recently by creolists of the Lumsden-Lefebvre group (1998, 1999), and the theory of lexical diffusion (originating also from dealing with the Songhay data in Robert Nicolaï's works from the early 1970's until 2003) linked with the concept of metatypy originating in the Pacific and Amerindian language areas (Ross, 1996; Aikhenvald and Dixon, 2001) share certain common features. Speaking strictly in terms of language structures, in both cases we face the usage of phonological patterns of morphemes of one language (whatever their types) in the meanings/functions of another language. These features are certainly *also* characteristic for specific creole situations and may certainly *also* be found in specific cases of sociolinguistic functional patterns linked with emblematic vs. non-emblematic functions, but in my opinion, *these are more general, if not universal structural phenomena of any language contact and interference.*

4. Thus the analytical separation of the concepts of relexification, metatypy and Sprachbund in general has its roots both in misunderstanding the dynamic character of such concepts as the structural phenomena of language, and in mixing linguistic and non-linguistic criteria when analysing language contacts and interference.

4.1. Since Hugo Schuchardt's time, when analyzing creolisation in the past centuries, most scholars have focussed their attention on particular creoles based upon best-known IE language superstrates. Moreover, since Hall's time, most research into creolisation has concentrated on the more or less fully accomplished results of this process, the creoles, disregarding the fact that certain, though often minimal pidginisation and/or creolisation features are inherent in any process of language contacts and interference. Thus, the existence of such creoles as that of Haitian French or Shaba Swahili represent, in their present forms, the results of the same process, the dynamic development of which is inherent, at least in certain of its structural features, in any situation of lasting language contact and interference. In other words, creolisation as a general dynamic structural process is inherent to any more intensive language contact and interference, while the stage of a real «definite» creole system is reached only in certain specific cases.

4.2. Similarly, the Balkan, Indian or the Sahel Sprachbunds represent just extreme cases of long-time cumulated convergence of the respective language structures or even whole clusters of languages. If we define Sprachbund as a bundle of distinctive features and if we methodologically accept the parallelism of Sprachbund development of genetically unrelated languages with that of the genetic isoglosses of languages and dialects, then we must accept the fact that between more ore less clearly definable «Sprachbunds» there is always a rich spectrum of transitional areas, defined perhaps by their interference. Consequently, «Sprachbund» represents such an idealising extreme generalisation as are such traditional concepts as «dialects», or may be even other -lects.

4.3. In this sense, one dangerous misunderstanding must be clarified: no language enters into contact and interference as a simple system, the process of contact and interference is mostly that of two or more stratified structures. Of course, this stratified character of language system is due to many factors, some of them being linguistic and some of them being non-linguistic (social, cultural, or other) in character. While mono-disciplinary understanding of language analysis may involve risks of ignoring the non-linguistic factors, over-estimating multidisciplinarity may involve risks of shortcuts between language structures and non-linguistic factors, such as societies and their cultures. These latter risks apply to the theory dealing with the emblematic vs. non-emblematic character of languages involved in language contacts.

5. To clarify this, let me use as an example contact and interference as reflected in the two genetically unrelated, but geographically and sociolinguistically close languages of the West African Sahel: Hausa and Songhay. In both cases, parallelisms of forms and functions-meanings do appear, but they primarily involve geographically marginal dialects of these dialectally heterogeneous languages. This concerns e.g. the existence of the so-called durative constructions using the morpheme *gà/ga* in the WNW dialects of Hausa on one hand, and the so-called *kìn* habitual in Salaga Dendi Songhay dialect, on the other hand.

5.1. Of course, in the case of the WNW Hausa dialectal imperfective-durative paradigm *sunàa/suwàa/suyàa ga zakkuwaa*, the local, geographically close neighbouring Zarma-Songhay dialectal influence exists, suspected by Paul Newman (2000: 577) to be the main external interference factor influencing the emerging of this dialectal paradigm of Hausa. In my opinion, it should be stressed that this is rather an all-Songhay language influence than a mere Zarma dialectal interference, as the general imperfective *ga/go* markers are displayed by almost all dialects of the southern complex of Songhay dialects in progressive-durative-imperfective (and partly existential and locative) functions. However, looking for external (Songhay) interference factor only does not give an exhaustive analysis of this phenomenon, as this external interference factor is acting, in this case again, in the interplay with the internal structural pressures of the Hausa system itself. As shown earlier (Zima 1998: 139), such constructions may also have been introduced into the WNW Hausa dialects by analogy with the constructions Independent Pronouns + the *gaa/ga* stabilizor + Verbal Noun (i.e. the periphrastic semi locative constructions *sunàa ga zakkuwa* meaning 'they are (at) coming to)'. And such constructions are similarly well documented in several central dialects of Hausa as well.

5.2. The other way round, the case of the habitual verbal paradigm of Songhay marked by *kìn* as reported in the Dendi Songhay dialect of Salaga in Ghana (Nicolaï-Zima, 1997: 32) is only partly comparable with the WNW Hausa *gà* imperfective-durative. While the external pressure of Hausa with its own *kan*-marked habitual forms is also obvious in this case, the possible interplay with the internal pressures of the Songhay system appears only at the *functional level*: as a matter of fact, several periphrastic habitual constructions appear even in other varieties of the Dendi Songhay dialect (as that using *dóónè* = 'to be accustomed', see Zima, 1994a: 32 for the Djougou variety of this Songhay dialect), but none of them may be considered close to the Salaga habitual in *its forms*.

5.3. Thus, in the case of this pair of genetically unrelated, but geographically close languages of the Sahel belt (i.e. Hausa and Songhay) the examples *of areal sharing of both forms and functions* in morphology appear mostly in marginal, «transitional» periphery dialects on both sides of the genetic frontier.

5.3.1. In the case of the habitual verbal paradigm of Songhay marked by *kìn* as reported in the Dendi Songhay dialect of Salaga, we might face the supposed interference of the superstrate lingua franca pattern into the presumed emblematic Dendi substrate. Hausa is clearly the lingua franca for most Dendi-Songhay speakers in Salaga and perhaps in all other Dendi-Songhay speaking regions. At the same time, it must be stressed that this case of a metatypy from the superstrate into the emblematic substrate, might have been supported by parallels in dynamisms in both the substrate and the superstrate verbal systems, several other periphrastic «habituals» appearing in these dialects of Songhay without sharing the parallelism of form with those in Hausa.

5.3.2. In the case of the WNW Hausa dialectal imperfective-durative paradigms, *sunàa/suwàa/suyàa ga zakkuwaa,* and their parallels in forms and functions of the imperfective *ga/go* TAM paradigms of Songhay, they might present a metatypy opposed to the direction postulated by Ross, as Hausa is clearly much more frequently used as a lingua franca by the Songhay-speaking populations in this region, than vice versa. It is of interest here to draw attention to the historian's proposal that major regions of what is now the WNW part of the Hausa-speaking territory, might have been Songhay-speaking territories in the not too distant past, and linguistically «hausanised» only relatively recently (Lange, 1991). On the other hand, rare (but serious) documents exist about certain other areas (Agades) with Hausa prevailing as a sort of revernacularised lingua franca during the last century or more, having replaced Songhay dialects of the northern complex (these latter Songhay dialects having themselves been imposed as revernacularised lingua franca over genetically different languages of a probable AA origin).

6. Thus, dealing with genetically unrelated, but areally close language structures offers clear metatypies comparable to genetically cognate features, displaying parallels both in forms and functions, the direct links of which to creolisation are not always necessarily documentable by clear cases of contemporary creoles. It is possible, however, that their existence supports the role of creolisation as a process inherent to intensive language contacts in the past.

On the other hand, these data inspire a certain caution towards direct and aprioristic identification of the direction of metatypy in the sense lingua franca – emblematic substrate. Either this is not valid at all, or frequent changes of social functions of languages in heteregenous Sprachbund areas produce such structural changes. A. Aikhenvald has recently introduced the concept of *recycling* languages in this perfectly Hallist sense of pidgin-creole-decreolised or vernacular-lingua franca- revernacularised variety lifecycles of languages. Such a theoretical postulate seems plausible, as structural language tendencies develop obviously slower than the sociocultural cycles influencing them. Nicolaï's and Vossen's paper (in this volume) deal with such problems on broader theoretical levels, albeit focussing on different data, those of the possible areal interference and convergence in the large Mande-Songhay region on one hand, and those of territorially limited, but methodically important Mande language islands in the Sahel on the other.

7. The larger the territorial concept of Sprachbund, the more limited its set of distinctive features. And furthermore, the larger the Sprachbund, the older its probable historical depth. And the rarer the parallels in both forms and functions, the more frequent metatypies limited in the classical sense to function-meaning may appear. In the Sahel belt of Africa, the TAM verbal systems appear as very good examples of Sprachbund features. As far as examples of parallels *concerning only functions-meanings* at the morphosyntactic level are concerned, they affect mostly extended areas of very different languages; although research in this field is in its early stages, we believe that several distinctive features affecting their morphosyntactic functions cluster in different regions of the West African Sahel representing thus a transitional belt of «Sprachbunds» analysed not as static phenomena, but as dynamic processes.

References

AIKHENVALD, A. I., 1987, *Strukturno-typologitcheskaya klassifikatsya berberskih yazykov,* Moscow.

AIKHENVALD, A. I., 1996, Areal diffusion in north-west Amazonia: the case of Tariana, *Antropological Linguistics 38,* 73-116.

AIKHENVALD, A. I. and DIXON, R. M. W. (eds), 2001, *Areal Diffusion and Genetic Inheritance. Problems in Comparative Linguistics*. Oxford.

BECKER, H., 1948, *Der Sprachbund,* Leipzig.

CYFFER, N., 2000, Areale Merkmale im TAM System und in der Syntax der saharanischen Sprachen, *Mehr als nur Worte Afrikanistische Beiträge zum 65. Geburtstag von Franz Rottland,* R. Vossen, A. Mietzner, A. Meissner (eds), 159-182, München.

CYFFER, N., 2002, The Lake Chad: a new Sprachbund Boundary? *Lexical and Structural Diffusion*, R. Nicolaï and P. Zima (eds), 27-44, Nice-Praha.

DEGRAFT, M. (ed) 1999, *Language Creation and Language Change,* Cambridge.

DIMMENDAAL, G., 2001, Areal diffusion versus genetic inheritance: an African perspective, *Areal Diffusion and Genetic Inheritance. Problems in Comparative Linguistics,* Aikhenvald, A. I. and Dixon, R. M. W (eds), 358-392, Oxford.

DIXON, R. M. W., 1997, *The rise and fall of languages,* Cambridge.

GREENBERG, J. H., 1983, Some Areal Characteristics of African Languages, *Current Approaches to African Linguistics*, Vol. 1, 3-21, Ivan R. Dihoff (ed), Dordrecht-Cinnaminson.

HEINE, B., REH, M., 1984, *Grammaticalization and Reanalysis in African Languages,* Hamburg.

HEINE, B., KOTEVA, T., 2001, Convergence and Divergence in the Development of African Languages, *Areal Diffusion and Genetic Inheritance. Problems in Comparative Linguistics,* Aikhenvald, A. I. and Dixon, R. M. W. (eds), 393-411, Oxford.

JAKOBSON, R., 1963, Efforts towards a Means-Ends Model of Language in Interwar Continental Linguistics, *A Prague School Reader in Linguistics*, J. Vachek (ed), 481-85, Bloomington.

JUNGRAITHMAYR, H., NICOLAÏ, R. and IBRISZIMOW, D., 1997, The West-Central Sudan and Savanna «Sprachbund». Some Isoglosses in its Favour, *Langues et Contacts de Langues en Zone Sahelo-Saharienne,* Baldi, S. (ed), 109-128, Napoli.

LANGE, D., 1991, Das frühere Kebbi und Mali. Versuch einer historischen Interpretation der Kanta-Traditionen, *Zeitschrift der Deutschen Morgenländlischer Gesellschaft 141,* 1, 139-166.

LEFEBVRE, C., 1998, *Creole Genesis and the Acquisition of Grammar: the Case of Haitian Creole,* Cambridge.

LUMSDEN, J., 1999, Language Acquisition and Creolisation, *Language creation and language change : creolization, diachrony, and development,* DeGraff (ed), 129-158, Cambridge, Mass. : MIT Press.

MANESSY, G., 1995, *Créoles, pidgins, variétés véhiculaires,* Paris.

MUFWENE, S., 2001, *The Ecology of Language Evolution,* Cambridge, U.K.

MUKAROVSKY, H. G., 1987, *Mande-Chadic. Common Stock. A Study of Phonological and Lexical Evidence,* Wien.

MUKAROVSKY, H. G., 1989, Songhai - eine Tschadische Sprache? *Frankfurter Afrikanistische Blätter 1,* 15-29.

NEWMAN, P., 2000, *The Hausa Language. An Encyclopaedic Reference Grammar,* New Haven and London.

NICOLAÏ, R. and ZIMA, P., 1993, Contemporary dialectology as a tool of language classification in Africa: the case of Songhay, *Archív orientální 61,* 179-194, Praha.

NICOLAÏ, R. and ZIMA, P., 1997, *Songhay.* Muenchen.

NICOLAÏ, R. and ZIMA, P. (eds), 2002, *Lexical and Structural Diffusion,* Nice.

NICOLAÏ R., 2003, *La force des choses ou l'épreuve 'nilo-saharienne',* Koeln.

ROSS, D., 1996, Contact-induced Change and the Comparative Method: Cases from Papua-New Guinea, *Comparative Method Reviewed,* M. Durie and M. Ross (eds), 180-217, Oxford.

THOMASON, S. G. and KAUFMAN, T. S., 1988, *Language contact, creolization and genetic linguistics,* Berkeley.

WESTERMANN, D., 1949, *Sprachbeziehungen und Sprachverwandschaft in Afrika,* Berlin.

ZIMA, P., 1994, Quelques remarques concernant le «Sprachbund» et le «Dialektbund» en zone sahelo-saharienne, *Deuxième Table Ronde Internationale du Réseau Diffusion Lexicale en Zone Sahélo-Saharienne*, P. Zima, St. Boušková, and J. Urbanová (eds), 1: 76-84, Praha.

ZIMA, P., 1994a, *Lexique Dendi,* Koeln.

ZIMA, P., 1998, Stabilizers expressing existence, identification and localization in African languages and their roles in the dynamics of their systems, *Language and Location in Time and Space*, Zima, P. and Tax, Vl. (eds), 131-149, Muenchen.

ZIMA, P., 1998a, Localisation in Space and Time and Languages of Different Types and Regions, *Language and Location in Time and Space,* Zima, P. and Tax, V. (eds), 3-10, Muenchen.

ZIMA, P., 2002, Hausa TAM markers analyzed in their dialectal, genetic and areal context, *Lexical and structural diffusion*, Nicolaï, R. and Zima, P. (eds), 265-282.

Reflections on language contact, areal diffusion, and mechanisms of linguistic change

Alexandra Y. AIKHENVALD A.Aikhenvald@latrobe.edu.au

Research Centre for Linguistic Typology, La Trobe University, Melbourne

Abstract

If two languages are in contact, with many speakers of one having some knowledge of the other language, then they typically borrow linguistic features back and forth - habits of pronunciation, significant sounds (phonemes), grammatical categories, vocabulary items, and even grammatical forms. Borrowing typically extends over all or most of the languages in a geographical region, so that we get large-scale linguistic diffusion, defining the region as a 'linguistic area'. One of the hardest tasks in comparative linguistics is distinguishing between similarities due to genetic inheritance and those due to borrowing. In this paper, we look at recurrent problems in language contact, focussing on borrowing patterns rather than forms and discussing the notion of linguistic area. Convergence as a major outcome of long-standing multilateral interaction in language contact is analysed in the light of system-altering and system-preserving changes, and sociolinguistic parameters. The African continent - with its linguistic diversity in terms of genetic groupings, areal clusters and Sprachbunds of varied extent and antiquity - remains the most challenging testing ground for the comparative method, and for contact linguistics.

Résumé

Si deux langues sont en contact, et qu'un grand nombre de locuteurs de l'une ont une certaine connaissance de l'autre, ils échangent alors des traits linguistiques tels que des habitudes de prononciation, des sons pertinents (phonèmes), des catégories grammaticales, des éléments de vocabulaire et même des formes grammaticales. Si les emprunts couvrent de manière significative toutes ou la plupart des langues d'une région géographique, l'on obtient une diffusion linguistique à grande échelle aboutissant à l'identification de la région comme une 'aire linguistique'. L'une des tâches les plus ardues en linguistique comparative consiste à distinguer les similarités dues à l'héritage génétique de celles dues à l'emprunt. Dans cet article, nous examinerons les problèmes récurrents dans les situations de contacts de langues en insistant sur les modèles d'emprunt plutôt que sur les formes empruntées, afin de cerner la notion d'aire linguistique. La convergence en tant que résultat d'une interaction multilatérale de longue durée est analysée en fonction des changements qui modifient ou préservent les systèmes, ainsi que des paramètres sociolinguistiques. Le continent africain – avec sa diversité linguistique en termes de groupements génétiques, d'agrégats aréaux et de *Sprachbunds* de dimension et d'âge variables – reste le terrain d'expérimentation le plus stimulant pour la méthode comparatiste et pour l'étude du contact des langues.

1. INTRODUCTORY REMARKS

Languages can resemble each other in the categories, constructions and types of meaning they use, and in the forms they employ to express these. These similarities may be due to universal properties: for instance, all languages have clausal negation, or a way of expressing a command, or of forming a question. Two languages can share the same form by pure coincidence. The Korean word for 'two', pronounced as [du], bears a chance similarity to Latin *duo* 'two' (also see Aikhenvald and Dixon 2001a: 1-2). Similarities of these kinds tell us nothing about the history of languages.

If two modern languages descend from a common ancestor, both may retain features of this shared 'proto-language'. Their similarities are then due to genetic inheritance. Genetically related languages often develop similar categories – this process, termed 'drift' by Sapir (1921: 147-170), is also known as 'parallel development' (LaPolla 1994).

If two languages are in contact, with many speakers of one having some knowledge of the other language, then they typically borrow linguistic features back and forth – habits of pronunciation, significant sounds (phonemes), grammatical categories, vocabulary items and even grammatical forms. Borrowing typically extends over all or most of the languages in a geographical region, so that we get large-scale linguistic diffusion, defining the region as a 'linguistic area'.

It has long been recognised that one of the hardest tasks in comparative linguistics is distinguishing between similarities due to genetic inheritance and those due to borrowing (cf. the classic debate between Sapir and Boas). As Dench (2001: 113) put it, 'making the argument for an innovation shared by virtue of a period of common development is never easy. I take it for granted that a statement of shared inheritance as explanation for a shared feature should only be made once all other possible explanations for the shared feature have been exhausted. These other possibilities will include accidental similarity in form, borrowing and genetic drift.'

We now look at recurrent problems in language contact, focussing on borrowing patterns rather than forms (§2). In §3, we discuss the notion of linguistic area. Some outcomes of long-standing multilateral interaction in language contact are outlined in §4.

2. LINGUISTIC DIFFUSION AND BORROWING

Before we proceed, a few terminological remarks are in order. The term 'borrowing' is used here in its broad sense, as 'the transfer of linguistic features of any kind from one language to another as the result of contact' (Trask 2000: 44).[1] Linguistic diffusion is understood as the spread of a linguistic feature across a geographical area or as borrowing within a linguistic area. Within an area, diffusion can be unilateral (when it proceeds from one source) or multilateral (when it involves several sources). Another alternative term for linguistic diffusion is interference, defined as the transfer of features from one's first language into one's second language (cf. Trask 2000: 169). Unlike diffusion, interference applies to cases of individual bilingualism and second language acquisition.

It is useful to distinguish between borrowing – or diffusion – of forms and of patterns. Diffusion or borrowing of forms is also known as direct diffusion. For instance, Baale, a South-West Surmic language, borrowed an aspectual particle *wa* 'just now, recently' from Tirma and Chai, languages of the South-East branch of the same family (Dimmendaal 2001: 363). Indirect diffusion, sometimes also called 'transfer of patterns' (Heath 1978), involves developing a new category or a new term of a category, to match a pattern in the source language. For instance, a language can develop a system of noun classes, switch-reference or evidentiality out of its own formal resources. In Luo, a Nilotic language, heads of endocentric compounds are developing into noun class prefixes as a result of influence from the neighbouring Bantu languages (Dimmendaal 2001: 382); see Cyffer (2002: 41) for similar examples in Kanuri.

Indirect diffusion may be manifested in identical derivations and structurally similar idioms, such as compounds which literally mean 'breast mouth' and 'house leg' and translate as 'nipple' and 'wall' respectively, in both Baale and Tirma and Chai. In each case the absence of a particular pattern in a closely related language is an indicator of its areal origin: thus, nominal compounds found in both Baale and Tirma-Chai are absent from Baale's closest relatives, the Didinga-Murle languages from the South-West subgroup of Surmic (Dimmendaal 2001: 363).

Prosodic features are particularly prone to diffusion in language contact. Jungraithmayr (2000: 93) reports that 'the employment of tone in verb-aspectual systems', prominent in Benue-Congo, Adamawa-Ubangi and other Niger-Congo languages spoken next to Chadic languages, made its way into Chadic. As a result, in southeastern fringe Chadic languages such as Tumak and Zime, which are in contact with Niger-Congo languages, the perfective-imperfective opposition is marked by tone change, as shown in Table 1. The use of tones for marking aspects is remarkably similar to that found in Niger-Congo languages, such as Gbaya, an Ubangian language from the same area as the southeastern fringe Chadic. Eastern

[1] A recently suggested alternative to this term is 'code-copying' (see Johanson 2002). Borrowing ought to be distinguished from 'the alternative use of two languages either within a sentence or between sentences' (Clyne 1987: 740). This covers code-switching and code-mixing. See Hill and Hill (1986: 348), for a differentiation 'between meaningful and appropriate code-switching [i.e. which follows established conventions and practices – A.A.] and disorderly usage of the type which has been called «code-mixing»'.

Chadic languages spoken outside the contact area mark this same opposition by ablaut, or vowel change, as does Mubi, shown in the last row of Table 1.

Table 1. Contact induced use of tone for aspect marking in Chadic languages

LANGUAGE AND ITS AFFILIATION	GLOSS	PERFECTIVE	IMPERFECTIVE	MARKING
Tumak (southeastern Chadic)	'die'	**má** (high tone)	**ma** (mid tone)	tone
Zime (Batna) (southeastern Chadic)	'die'	**mát** (high tone)	**mat** (mid tone)	tone
Gbaya (Ubangian, Niger-Congo)	'see'	**zɔ̀k** (low tone)	**zɔ́k** (high tone)	tone
Mubi (eastern Chadic)	'die'	**màát**	**mùwáát**	ablaut

The use of ablaut for aspect marking has hardly ever been borrowed into any Niger-Congo language (with a possible exception of Laal, an Ubangian language which seems to have traces of Chadic-type vowel alternations in verbal morphology: Jungraithmayr 2000: 94). This illustrates, in a nutshell, how different linguistic features vary in their 'proneness' to diffusion. We have seen, in Table 1, that the functions of tones may diffuse. Alternatively, types of tonal distinctions can spread within an area. Kastenholz (2002) provides ample discussion of how different dialectal areas of Mande have developed different numbers of tonal distinctions (from two to four), depending on the languages they are in contact with.[2]

Only a careful examination of the diffusion of linguistic features between genetically unrelated and typologically different languages in varied situations of language contact allows us to determine tendencies and preferences in contact-induced grammatical change (though this does not have to involve establishing straightforward 'hierarchies' of borrowability).

Both direct and indirect diffusion may involve simultaneous gain (of new morphemes and patterns) and loss (of old morphemes and patterns). Or it may involve creating new patterns which coexist with the old ones, together with new rules for the distribution of old patterns.

The distinction between diffusion of forms and diffusion of patterns is crucial, since linguistic communities differ with respect to their acceptance of loan forms. Some adopt loan forms on a large scale, while others consider using 'foreign' importations as a token of unacceptable language-mixing. One Arawak language, Tariana, has a prohibition against borrowing forms from its neighbours, while Resígaro – another Arawak language spoken in a different region – borrows them freely (see Aikhenvald 2002: 5-6). As Heine and Kuteva (2001: 410) put it, 'it may happen that people borrow a comparative or a reflexive morpheme from another language but [...] they are more likely to borrow conceptual templates, like event schemas'.

[2] The diffusability of prosodic features (including tone and accent type) has also been illustrated by Matisoff (2001), using the material of South-East Asian languages.

3. LINGUISTIC AREAS

The concept of linguistic area, or Sprachbund, is central to the notion of diffusion. A linguistic area is generally taken to be a geographically delimited region including languages from at least two language families, or different subgroups of the same family, sharing significant traits (most of which are not found in languages from these families or subgroups spoken outside the area).[3] Languages within an area must share a fair number of distinctive diagnostic traits (also see Emeneau 1956; Sherzer 1973: 760; and discussion in Tosco 2000).

The main problem is how to locate the diagnostic traits, especially when at least some shared features – or similarities – between contiguous languages can be explained by accident, universals, genetic factors (that is, in a situation where the languages in contact are related), etc. As shown in the masterly study of Mesoamerica as a linguistic area by Campbell, Kaufman and Smith-Stark (1986: 535-6), not all shared features have the same 'weight': 'highly «marked» exotic, or unique shared traits weigh more than does material that is more easily developed independently, or found widely in other languages'. Since 'meaningful linguistic areas are the historical products of linguistic diffusion, the stronger linguistic areas are those whose shared traits can be shown to be diffused – and cannot be ascribed to a common ancestor, to chance, or to universals'. Thus, a highly frequent phenomenon – such as for instance verb-final constituent order, the existence of nasalised vowels, or the presence of a perfective-imperfective opposition in the aspectual system – would not be assigned as much weight as a more exotic, unusual characteristic. An example of such an exotic feature is the suppletive formation of negative and positive paradigms found in Mande languages (Zima forthcoming; Kastenholz 2002), as well as in Songhay and in Hausa (Zima forthcoming).

Drastic changes in the use of syntactic constructions (as is, for instance, the case for infinitives in the languages of the Balkans) or in morpheme shape in the languages within an area could be seen as a highly distinctive trait, indicative of areal diffusion. Such features could be unusual for a subgroup or a family, without being typologically 'exotic'. For instance, Chadic languages in contact with Kwa languages have developed a Kwa-like monosyllabic word-structure (Jungraithmayr 2000: 94). Cross-linguistically, having monosyllabic lexemes is not unusual. But this feature is not found in Chadic languages outside the contact area. Since the source of diffusion (from Kwa to Chadic) can be easily established, this feature can be assigned special weight. Along similar lines, the reciprocal is marked with a suffix on a verb in Oceanic languages on the northwest coast of West New Britain,

---

[3] An alternative use of the term 'linguistic area' just for bilateral interaction between languages, reserving the term 'Sprachbund' for multilateral areas, was proposed by Thomason and Kaufman (1988); this, however, goes against the mainstream terminological consensus: see Zima (2000a; 2002).

rather than with a prefix, as in Oceanic languages elsewhere. By itself, this is not an exotic feature. However, the languages of West New Britain share it with their (unrelated) neighbour, a Papuan language Anêm; an obviously diffusional origin of this trait makes it a distinctive diffusional characteristic of the area (Thurston 1987: 79-80).

A typologically well-attested property cannot by itself be considered area-defining. However, the way properties cluster can be area-specific. In a classic paper, Campbell, Kaufman and Smith-Stark (1986) single out four morphosyntactic features characteristic of the Meso-American area:

(a) nominal possession of the type his-dog the man;
(b) relational nouns (that is, body part nouns used as markers of spatial relationships);
(c) vigesimal numeral systems;
(d) non-verb final basic word order which may correlate with the absence of switch reference;
(e) numerous 'pan-Meso-American' formations, e.g. 'knee' as 'head of the leg', or 'boa-constrictor' as 'deer-snake'.

Along similar lines, a combination of properties defines the multilingual linguistic area of the Vaupés River Basin in Brazil and Colombia with languages belonging to genetically unrelated Tucanoan and Arawak families. These include:

(i) nasalisation as a prosodic feature;
(ii) four to five evidentials marking the way in which the speaker has acquired the information (whether seen, heard, inferred, assumed, or learnt from someone else);
(iii) numerous classifiers used with demonstratives, numerals and in possessive constructions;
(iv) small systems of genders in verbal agreement;
(v) nominative-accusative profile;
(vi) one locative case covering direction ('to'), location ('in, at') and source ('from');
(vii) numerous identical formations, e.g. 'father of goods' = 'rich man'.

None of these properties is restricted to Meso-America or to the Vaupés area. The way in which they occur together is area-specific. Similarly, none of the properties given for Mainland South-East Asia as a linguistic area (see Matisoff 2001; Enfield 2001) is unique; however, the way they go together accounts for the existence of a 'pan-South-East Asian' area. The 'clustering' of features may be significant, while the features themselves are not necessarily so.

The question of how many features are sufficient to delimit an area (see Haig 2001) relates to the 'weight' of each individual feature, and to the ways in which the properties cluster together. Areas can be created on 'different levels'; that is, in a particular linguistic situation one might expect more areal diffusion in one type of linguistic feature than in another. The great majority of the shared features of Standard Average European are syntactic, while one of the most salient features of the South-East Asian languages is their 'monosyllabicity' and 'tone-proneness' (hence the term *Tonbund*, 'tonal area': Matisoff 2001). And see Jakobson (1938), on the idea of a 'phonological' Sprachbund in Eurasia.

The problems with establishing genetically inherited versus diffusional features in North-American Indian languages north of Mexico have been analysed in Sherzer (1976), and Bright and Sherzer (1976). For Australia, problems of this kind have been analysed by Dixon (2002). To disentangle various types of similarities between related languages, a fine-grained reconstruction on the level of individual subgroupings is needed, as is the case with Indo-European languages in the Balkan linguistic area. Otherwise one would never be able to go beyond just saying that 'Sprachbund situations are notoriously messy' (Thomason and Kaufman 1988: 95).

When closely related languages are in constant contact, additional complications arise. Teasing apart the effects of diffusion, genetically inherited phenomena and the possible outcomes of parallel development is often a daunting – and an almost impossible – task. Languages which have never been in contact or never formed a linguistic area can share diffused properties if they have borrowed the features independently from the same or a similar source. This was probably the case for numerous Ethio-Semitic languages which share similar features, taken from shared Cushitic substrata (Tosco 2000).

4. CONVERGENCE IN AREAL DIFFUSION

Intensive contact within a linguistic area tends to bring about the gradual convergence of languages whereby the conceptual categories of one language are replicated in another. Borrowing a conceptual template rather than a morpheme brings about the enrichment of patterns in a target language. The diffusion of evidentiality distinctions in the Vaupés River Basin area in northwest Amazonia resulted in languages developing detailed means of marking the ways of information acquisition, allowing one to be precise in the statements made. Along similar lines, Abbi (2002) demonstrated how Santhali and Kharia, Munda languages from India, have adopted new means of causative formation from the neighbouring Indo-Aryan languages, in addition to the previously existing ones, evolving complex rules of different causative choices for different verb types.

Alternatively, languages may simply lose the patterns absent from other languages in the same area. Jungraithmayr and Leger (2002) showed how Southern Bole-Tangale languages (Chadic) are losing nominal plurals and the morphological distinctions between transitive and intransitive verbs, which are absent from the neighbouring Central Jukunoid and Adamawa languages. Southern Bole-Tangale languages are also restructuring their gender system: many erstwhile masculine nouns are shifting to the formally unmarked feminine class, thus reducing the functional load of gender differentiation. Jungraithmayr and Leger (2002: 84) hypothesise that this is 'a last stage of development [...] towards the total loss of gender', another category not found in either Central Jukunoid or Adamawa.

Within a linguistic area, the multilateral diffusion of linguistic features often goes together with creating new types of categories which may lack an exact match in any language within the area. Their contact-induced changes involve a variety of mechanisms including (see Aikhenvald 2002):

(a) Reanalysis, i.e. a historical process whereby a morphosyntactic device acquires a different structure from the one it originally had, with little or no change to its surface form or semantics. A number of verbs in Udi (a Northeast Caucasian language) – which originally contained noun class agreement markers – were reanalysed as simple stems, as part of the process of losing the noun class system (Harris and Campbell 1995: 66-7).
(b) Reinterpretation, or extension, of already existing morphemes and categories, whereby they start being used in a variety of new contexts (see Harris and Campbell 1995: 66-7).
(c) Grammaticalisation, that is, 'the development from lexical to grammatical forms and from grammatical to even more grammatical forms' (Heine and Kuteva 2002: 2), as is the case for the development of proximative aspect using the verb 'become' in Nandi, a Nilotic language, under the influence of the Bantu language Gusii (Kuteva 2000). (Further examples of contact-induced grammaticalization of lexical items have been described by Bisang 1996 and Matisoff 1991, for South-East Asia.)
(d) Grammatical accommodation, defined as morphosyntactic deployment of a native morpheme on the model of the syntactic function of a phonetically similar morpheme in the diffusing language, that is, the language which is the source of diffusion. This is also known as 'shift due to phonetic similarity' (Campbell 1987). Watkins (2001: 58) shows how the influence of the Hittite imperfective marker *-ske-* on Eastern Ionic Greek resulted in the development of an imperfective meaning by the homophonous Greek morpheme. In Pipil, a Uto-Aztecan language (Campbell 1987: 263-264), a marker of possession *-pal* was originally a relational noun, as in *nu-pal* 'mine', *mu-pal* 'yours' and so on. On the basis of similarity with Spanish *para* 'for, in order to', this morpheme can now appear without any prefixes and have the meaning of 'in order to, so that', being used to introduce a subordinate clause (see similar examples in Aikhenvald 2002: 225-6).

These mechanisms are closely linked. Both reanalysis and grammatical accommodation most often go together with reinterpretation of categories and forms. Whether grammaticalisation and reanalysis are to be considered separate mechanisms remains a matter for debate (see Harris and Campbell 1995: 92, for a summary). While it can be argued that every instance of grammaticalisation involves reanalysis, reanalysis can occur without grammaticalisation. This provides justification for distinguishing the four processes outlined above.

Language contact may bring about gradual convergence resulting in structural isomorphism, whereby the grammar and semantics of one language are almost fully replicated in another (cf. Gumperz and Wilson 1971; Nadkarni 1975; Friedman 1997). This process has also been defined as metatypy by Ross (2001: 146), implying 'reorganisation of the language's semantic patterns and «ways of saying things», and the restructuring of its syntax'. An example of structural isomorphism comes from two languages in contact within the Vaupés River Basin linguistic area. Example (1) is from Tariana, an Arawak language, and (2) is from Tucano, a Tucanoan language. Example (3) comes from Baniwa, an Arawak language closely related to Tariana, but spoken outside the Vaupés area. The Baniwa morphemes are obviously cognate to Tariana, but the categories and the meanings expressed are very different.[4]

Tariana

(1) **paita** **di-ñha-yena-naka**
one+NUM.CLASS.ANIMATE 3sgnf-eat-pass,go.by/do.little.by.little-PRESENT.VISUAL
'One (person) is eating little by little' (I see him)

Tucano

(2) **ni'kɨ́** **ba'â-tiha-mi**
one+NUM.CLASS.ANIMATE eat-do.little.by.little-PRESENT.VISUAL.3person.sg.masc
'One (person) is eating little by little' (I see him)

Baniwa

(3) **apaite** **li-ñha** **li-dʒena**
one+NUM.CLASS:MASCULINE 3sgnf-eat 3sgnf-pass/go.by
'One (man) is eating too much'

Firstly, unlike Tariana and Tucano, Baniwa has no obligatory tense and evidentiality. Secondly, Tariana and Tucano have a numeral classifier for animate referents, while the Baniwa form cognate to Tariana refers to male humans. And thirdly, the same etymon, Tariana *-yena* and Baniwa *–dʒena* 'pass, go by', has developed different meanings in the two languages: in Baniwa, it means 'exceed, do too much', and in Tariana, it means 'do little by little'.

All the Tucano categories are replicated in Tariana. Consequenly, the same interlinear gloss applies to both (1) and (2), with just one difference. While Tucano

[4] Abbreviations are: masc - masculine; nf - nonfeminine; NUM.CLASS - numeral classifier; sg - singular.

is exclusively suffixing, Tariana maintains a few prefixes (inherited from Proto-Arawak). Unlike Tariana, Tucano marks person with portmanteau morphemes fused with evidentiality and tense. This illustrates an instance of almost complete convergence, resulting from intensive areal diffusion.

Linguistic convergence does not always result in the creation of identical grammars, nor in the straightforward projection of categories from one language into another. That is, structural and conceptual isomorphism and the creation of almost identical grammatical and semantic structures (illustrated by Friedman 1997, among others) are not universal outcomes of language contact. Languages in contact often maintain their distinct typological profiles.

Convergence may involve at least three kinds of processes, each with a distinct outcome:

(i) Convergence can result in the adoption of new patterns by all languages. New patterns coexist with the old ones, and new rules for their distribution are developed. (This is somewhat comparable to the creation of etymological doublets – i.e. different words borrowed at different times which develop different meanings in the recipient language, e.g. English *chief* and *chef*, both from French *chef*.) The isomorphism of grammatical structures is not complete since each language preserves its own 'typological profile' alongside the adoption of a 'foreign' one. An example of this is the linguistic area of the Vaupés River Basin – we have seen, in examples (1) and (2), how Tariana has adopted the categories found in Tucanoan languages, and at the same time maintained its own prefixing structure.

(ii) Alternatively, convergence can result in creating a new common grammar, which combines features of both systems in contact – a compromise between the structures. Grammatical isomorphism may be almost complete. An example is the language contact situation between Yucuna, an Arawak language, and Retuarã, from the Tucanoan family. Neither language qualifies as 'typically Arawak' or 'typically Tucanoan'; in actual fact, each language has adopted features from the other, creating a new common ground. So, for instance, Retuarã has acquired a few prefixes, while Yucuna lost the Arawak active-stative split system originally expressed with a combination of pronominal prefixes and suffixes.

Convergence of types (i) and (ii) presupposes the lack of any relationships of dominance or diglossia (in terms of a high language-low language relationship) between the languages in contact: that is, no language (or community of language speakers) has more prestige than their neighbours.

(iii) Convergence can also involve the adoption of the structure of another language and concomitant loss of categories which have no equivalent in the other language. The necessary condition for this is a relationship of dominance between languages. This kind of convergence involves the loss of patterns and is often accompanied by the attrition and obsolescence of the 'minority' language. It results in morpheme-for-morpheme intertranslatability between the languages in contact. Thus, numerous endangered languages undergo restructuring under the influence of the majority language, as was the case with Arvanitika Albanian (Tsitsipis 1998) restructured under the influence of the dominant Greek; and with Resígaro, a moribund Arawak language from northeastern Peru, under the influence of the dominant Bora (a Bora-Witotoan language) (Aikhenvald 2002: 5-6; 269).

In all these cases convergence involves system-altering changes and restructuring of at least one of the languages in contact. A head-marking language can acquire dependent-marking properties; a suffixing language may acquire prefixes (and lose suffixes); an active-stative language may acquire nominative-accusative properties.

The very idea of such restructuring and concomitant system-altering changes goes against the oft-quoted 'structural compatibility requirement'. In its strong form, this requirement states that grammatical borrowing (viewed broadly) can operate only between similar systems (cf. Meillet 1914: 84, 87; Moravcsik 1978; Weinreich 1953: 25 etc.). This claim holds only as a tendency (as demonstrated by Harris and Campbell 1995, and also Haig 2001). Examples of the three types of convergence – discussed above – show the ways in which languages come to be structurally similar due to areal diffusion, notwithstanding the original differences in their grammar.

Many more questions concerning linguistic convergence arise. How does the diffusion of features start, and what are the sociolinguistic and purely structural factors which may or may not enhance it? Which features are more – and which are less – prone to diffusion? How does a language community adopt certain linguistic features as 'emblematic' of their ethnicity? And – a particularly important question, especially relevant for areas of the world known to have been populated for tens of thousands of years (such as Africa or Australia) – can extensive language contact over a lengthy period of time, with features and forms being borrowed back and forth, obscure pre-existing genetic relationships? As Dench (2001: 113-114) put it, 'it may not be possible to show conclusively for any particular innovation that it results from genetic inheritance rather than that it is motivated by contact with another language. If enough such cases occur, then the suspicion we might attach to any putative inherited innovation will mount and we should become increasingly sceptical of any suggested genetic classification.' In Dench's words, 'we should leave open the possibility that all questions may turn out to be undecidable'.

Only in-depth studies, based on first hand data, will enable us to formulate sensible inductive generalisations concerning the ways in which genetically unrelated or distantly related languages become similar due to prolonged contact, multilingualism and borrowing. Such studies have been accomplished for just a few places in the world; examples include the Balkan linguistic area (e.g. Joseph 1983; Friedman 1997 and references therein), India (e.g. Emeneau 1980; Masica 1976), the East Arnhem Land and the Daly River regions in Australia (Heath 1978; Dixon 2002: 674-9), the Vaupés linguistic area in north-west Amazonia (Aikhenvald 2002). Within Africa, arguments have been put forward in favour of considering a wide area around the Lake Chad as a Sprachbund (Cyffer 2002).

With its linguistic diversity in terms of genetic groupings, areal clusters and Sprachbunds of varied extent and antiquity, the African continent remains the most challenging testing ground for the comparative method, and for contact linguistics. As Zima (2000a: 3) put it, quoting an ancient Latin inscription, *ex Africa semper aliquid novi.*

References

ABBI, A., 2002, Restructuring grammars in contact situations: a case of causative constructions in endangered languages, *International Journal of Dravidian Linguistics* XXXII, 69-80.

AIKHENVALD, A. Y., 2002, *Language contact in Amazonia,* Oxford, OUP.

AIKHENVALD, A. Y. and DIXON, R. M. W., 2001a, *Introduction*, Aikhenvald and Dixon (eds), 1-26.

AIKHENVALD, A. Y. and DIXON, R. M. W. (eds), 2001b, *Areal diffusion and genetic inheritance: problems in comparative linguistics,* Oxford, Oxford University Press.

BISANG, W., 1996, Areal typology and grammaticalization: Processes of grammaticalization based on nouns and verbs in East and Mainland South East Asian languages, *Studies in Language* 20, 519-98.

BRIGHT, W. and SHERZER, J., 1976, Areal phenomena in North-American Indian languages, *Variation and change in language. Essays by W. Bright,* pp. 228-68, Stanford, Stanford University Press.

CAMPBELL, L., 1987, Syntactic change in Pipil, *International Journal of American Linguistics* 53, 253-80.

CAMPBELL, L., KAUFMAN, T. and SMITH-STARK, T., 1986, Meso-America as a linguistic area, *Language* 62, 530-70.

CLYNE, M., 1987, Constraints on code-switching – How universal are they?, *Linguistics* 25, 739-64.

CYFFER, N., 2002, *The Lake Chad: a new Sprachbund boundary?*, Nicolaï and Zima (eds), 27-44.

DENCH, A., 2001, *Descent and diffusion: the complexity of the Pilbara situation*, Aikhenvald and Dixon (eds), 105-33.

DIMMENDAAL, G. I., 2001, *Areal diffusion versus genetic inheritance: an African perspective*, Aikhenvald and Dixon (eds), 358-92.

DIXON, R. M. W., 2002, *Australian languages: their origin and development,* Cambridge, Cambridge University Press.

EMENEAU, M. B., 1956, India as a linguistic area. *Language* 32, 3-16.

EMENEAU, M. B., 1980, *Language and linguistic area,* (Collection of papers, ed. Anwar Dil), Stanford, Stanford University Press.

ENFIELD, N. J., 2001, *On genetic and areal linguistics in mainland Southeast Asia: parallel polyfunctionality of 'acquire'*, Aikhenvald and Dixon (eds), 255-90.

FRIEDMAN, V. A., 1997, One grammar, three lexicons: ideological overtones and underpinnings in the Balkan Sprachbund, *CLS* 33, 23-44.

GUMPERZ, J. J. and WILSON, R., 1971, Convergence and creolization. A case from the Indo-Aryan/Dravidian Border in India, *Pidginization and creolization of languages,* edited by D. Hymes, 151-68, Cambridge, Cambridge University Press.

HAIG, G., 2001, *Linguistic diffusion in present-day Anatolia: from top to bottom,* Aikhenvald and Dixon (eds), 195-224.

HARRIS, A. and CAMPBELL, L., 1995, *Historical Syntax in cross-linguistic perspective,* Cambridge, Cambridge University Press.

HEATH, J., 1978, *Linguistic Diffusion in Arnhem Land,* (Australian Aboriginal Studies: Research and Regional Studies #13), Canberra, Australian Institute of Aboriginal Studies.

HEINE, B. and KUTEVA. T., 2001, *Convergence and divergence in the development of African languages*, Aikhenvald and Dixon (eds), 393-411.

HEINE, B. and KUTEVA, T., 2002, *World lexicon of grammaticalisation,* Cambridge, Cambridge University Press.

HILL, J. and HILL, K. C., 1986, *Speaking Mexicano. Dynamics of syncretic language in Central Mexico,* Tucson. The University of Arizona Press.

JAKOBSON, R. O., 1938, Sur la théorie des affinités phonologiques des langues, *Actes du Quatrième Congrès International de Linguistes,* 48-59, Copenhagen, Einar Munksgaard.

JOHANSON, L., 2002, *Structural factors in Turkic language contacts,* London, Curzon.

JOSEPH, B. D., 1983, *The Synchrony and Diachrony of the Balkan Infinitive. A study in areal, general and historical linguistics*, Cambridge: Cambridge University Press.

JUNGRAITHMAYR, H., 2000, *Chadic – a network of genetic and areal relationships*, pp. 90-98 of Zima (ed).

JUNGRAITHMAYR, H. and R. Leger, 2002, *Loss, shift and growth in Southern Bole-Tangale languages*, pp. 79-90 of Nicolaï and Zima (eds).

KASTENHOLZ, R., 2002, *"Samogo" language islands, and Mande-Senufo (Gur) interference phenomena*, pp. 91-110 of Nicolaï and Zima (eds).

KUTEVA, T., 2000, Areal grammaticalisation: the case of the Bantu-Nilotic borderland, *Folia Linguistica* XXXIV, 267-83.

LAPOLLA, Randy J., 1994, Parallel Grammaticalizations in Tibeto-Burman Languages: Evidence of Sapir's "Drift", *Linguistics of the Tibeto-Burman Area,* 17: 61-80.

MASICA, C., 1976, *Defining a linguistic area: South Asia,* Chicago: University of Chicago Press.

MATISOFF, J. A., 1991, Areal and universal dimensions of grammatization in Lahu, *Approaches to Grammaticalization*, vol. 2, edited by Elizabeth C. Traugott and Bernd Heine, pp. 383-453, Amsterdam, John Benjamins.

MATISOFF, J. A., 2001, *Genetic versus contact relationship: prosodic diffusibility in South-East Asian languages*, pp. 291-327 of Aikhenvald and Dixon (eds).

MEILLET, A., 1914, Le problème de la parenté des langues, *Scientia* 15/35.

MORAVCSIK, E., 1978, Language contact, *Universals of human languages*, vol. 1, edited by Joseph H. Greenberg, Charles A. Ferguson and Edith A. Moravcsik, pp. 93-123, Stanford, Stanford University Press.

NADKARNI, M. V., 1975, Bilingualism and syntactic change in Konkani, *Language* 51, 672-83.

NICOLAÏ, R. and P. ZIMA, 2002, (eds), *Lexical and structural diffusion. Interplay of internal and external factors of language development in the West African Sahel,* Publications de la Faculté des Lettres, Arts et Sciences humaines de Nice et de la faculté des Etudes Humaines, Université Charles de Prague.

ROSS, M. D., 2001, *Contact-induced change in Oceanic languages in northwest Melanesia*, pp. 134-66 of A. Y. Aikhenvald and R. M. W. Dixon (eds).

SAPIR, E., 1921, *Language,* New York, Harcourt, Brace & World.

SHERZER, J., 1973, Areal linguistics in North America, *Current trends in linguistics*, 10, edited by T. Sebeok, pp 749-95, The Hague, Mouton.

SHERZER, J., 1976, *An areal-typological study of American Indian languages north of Mexico,* North-Holland Linguistic Series, 20, Amsterdam, North-Holland.

THURSTON, W. R., 1987, *Processes of change in the languages of northwestern Britain,* Canberra, Pacific Linguistics.

THOMASON, S. G. and T. Kaufman, 1988, *Language Contact, Creolization and Genetic Linguistics,* University of California Press, Berkeley, Los Angeles, Oxford.

TOSCO, M., 2000, Is there an "Ethiopian Linguistic area"?, *Anthropological Linguistics* 42: 329-65.

TRASK, L., 2000, *The dictionary of historical and comparative linguistics,* Edinburgh, Edinburgh University Press.

TSITSIPIS, L. D., 1998, *A linguistic anthropology of praxis and language shift. Arvanitika (Albanian) and Greek in Contact,* Oxford, Clarendon Press.

WATKINS, C., 2001, An Indo-European linguistic area and its characteristics: ancient Anatolia. Areal diffusion as a challenge to the comparative method?, pp. 44-63 of Aikhenvald and Dixon (eds).

WEINREICH, U., 1953, *Languages in contact,* New York, Linguistic Circle of New York.

ZIMA, P., 2000a, *Areal and genetic factors in language classification and description: Africa south of the Sahara*, pp. 2-3 of Zima (ed).

ZIMA, P., 2000b, (ed), *Areal and genetic factors in language classification and description: Africa South of the Sahara,* Munich, Lincom Europa.

ZIMA, P., 2002, *Hausa TAM markers analyzed in their dialectal, genetic and areal context: interplay of internal and external factors*, pp. 265-81 of Nicolaï and Zima (eds).

ZIMA, P., forthcoming, *Sprachbund, metatypy, diffusion and creolisation (African and general linguistics: a mutual challenge).*

Aires de convergence, mirages et perspectives : le cas de « l'aire songhay-mandé »[1]

Robert NICOLAÏ

Institut Universitaire de France, Université de Nice nicolai@unice.fr

Abstract

The existence of typological affinities between the Mande languages and the Songhay complex are well-known, and this "relationship" is worth looking into for several reasons. It will give us a better general knowldege of the languages of this region of West Africa, their dynamism, and the theoretical insights they imply. The elementary question confronting all those looking for the roots of this sort of isomorphism is: are these affinities really the result of areal convergence?

Taking into account the results of the most recent achievements of research in the genealogical ties of Songhay, the author answers this question in the negative way. According to him, despite certain limited convergence features appearing with particular language contacts, most isomorphic features are to be explained in the light of the process of the constitution of Songhay as an emerging language.

Areal convergence features supposed to be the roots of the present affinities are to be considered as a sort of heuristic assumption, wishing to explain the existing isomorphisms through a premature generalization of principles experimented elsewhere.

Résumé

L'existence de ressemblances typologiques entre les langues mandé et songhay est bien connue et cette « parenté » mérite qu'on s'y intéresse à la fois pour une meilleure connaissance des langues de cette région de l'Afrique occidentale, pour celle des dynamiques qui les ont affectées, pour l'intérêt théorique que sa spécificité suscite et pour sa valeur d'exemplarité. La question « naïve » qui se pose porte sur ce qui permet d'expliquer l'isomorphisme constaté : s'agit-il là du résultat d'un phénomène de convergence aréale ?

Je répondrai à la question en prenant en compte les derniers résultats de recherche concernant les apparentements généalogiques du songhay et en montrant que, contrairement aux apparences, nous n'avons pas affaire ici à un phénomène de convergence linguistique. L'isomorphisme s'explique très simplement grâce à l'hypothèse de la constitution du songhay en tant que langue émergente, ce qui n'empêche bien évidemment pas la manifestation de phénomènes de convergence limités sur certains points entre les langues en contact.

---

[1] Ce texte reprend sous une forme largement modifiée l'essentiel du contenu de « Songhay-mande convergence area : questions and frames », sous presse in : Heine/Nurse (eds), *Africa as a linguistic area/Areal typology and African languages*, Cambridge Univ. Press.

> On conclura au plan de la méthode en constatant que la « convergence aréale » ici supposée n'est, dans le cas étudié, pas autre chose qu'un pseudo-objet, « logiquement » construit sur la base des projections « heuristiques » du chercheur qui souhaitait « trouver » une explication de l'isomorphisme constaté à travers une généralisation « à l'aveugle » des principes expérimentés par ailleurs.

L'existence d'une « parenté typologique » entre les langues mandé et songhay n'est pas un fait nouveau, elle a été soulignée par de nombreux auteurs[2] et l'on parle parfois à son endroit de convergence linguistique ou de *Sprachbund* ; toutefois l'étude des langues en contact ne conduit pas nécessairement à interpréter ainsi les isomorphismes[3] qui semblent soutenir cette hypothèse. Cette « parenté typologique » mérite donc qu'on s'y intéresse, au moins pour sa valeur d'exemplarité.

Dans ce but, il importe en premier lieu de rappeler l'état de la question en ce qui concerne l'apparentement du songhay, car il détermine en grande partie le détail de l'étude qui suivra. Le rattachement du songhay à la famille nilo-saharienne, affirmé par la *doxa* greenbergienne (1963), a été tout d'abord controversé (Lacroix : 1969, Nicolaï : 1990) puis apparemment « confirmé » par des études générales concernant l'ensemble de la famille nilo-saharienne (Bender : 1995, Ehret : 2001) sans que les auteurs de ces synthèses soient d'accord entre eux sur la place à lui attribuer dans l'arborescence de la famille. La dernière étude en date (Nicolaï 2003)[4] critique de façon détaillée l'ensemble des travaux incluant le songhay dans le nilo-saharien et entend montrer que les résultats atteints sur ce point sont inacceptables à ce jour, et que cela résulte à la fois des modèles et méthodes choisis, de leurs présupposés, de la nature des données et des *a priori* de recherche. Ainsi la proposition d'apparentement du songhay au nilo-saharien ne saurait plus être conservée si l'on entend 'apparentement' dans son acception classique de filiation généalogique et par 'nilo-saharien' une famille (ou un *phylum* à vocation de famille) de langues généalogiquement apparentées organisées selon un schéma arborescent.

---

[2] Dont Greenberg (1963) (langues SOV *versus* SVO), Houis (1971) (langues économiques), Heine (1975) (appartenance au 'type B'). »

[3] J'appelle 'isomorphisme' la relation que l'on peut établir entre deux langues qui ont les mêmes structures, ou entre deux structures sémantiques d'ordre différent présentant des relations combinatoires identiques. L'isomorphisme relève du constat, il ne préjuge en rien d'une direction ou d'un phénomène de diffusion qui « expliquerait » le parallélisme formel ou structural. Il ne concerne pas un trait (une isoglosse) donné(e) mais un faisceau, homogène ou non, de traits (isoglosses).

[4] Pour synthétiser on pourrait résumer ainsi les étapes : 1) le songhay est donné comme 'langue isolée' (Westermann) puis typologiquement rapproché du mandé (Delafosse) ; 2) affiliation du songhay au nilo-saharien (Greenberg, 1963) ; contestation de cette affiliation par P.-F. Lacroix (1969) ; 4) première hypothèse « créole » touareg mandé (Nicolaï, 1990) ; réaffirmation de l'apparentement nilo-saharien (Bender, 1995, Ehret, 2001) ; 6) deuxième hypothèse « créole » évolution d'une *lingua franca* chamito-sémitique (Nicolaï, 2003).

L'analyse des données a orienté l'étude vers une recherche d'hypothèses où l'importance du poids lexical chamito-sémitique dans cette langue trouverait une explication. On a pu montrer que ce lexique potentiellement chamito-sémitique que les *a priori* des études antérieures n'avaient pas permis d'identifier[5] est important et qu'il n'est pas uniquement confiné aux emprunts arabes ou à des effets ponctuels de diffusion à partir des langues de contact, mais qu'il touche un vocabulaire central ; qu'il concerne non pas des unités lexicales isolées mais des champs lexicaux dans toute leur complexité, souvent dans le détail de leur structuration. Finalement le songhay est « redirigé » vers le domaine chamito-sémitique, *mais* sans qu'il soit question pour autant de le situer dans un rapport généalogique avec les langues de cette famille. La conclusion est que, sous réserve d'approfondissements, le songhay apparaît comme le résultat de l'évolution complexe d'une probable *lingua franca*, d'une variété véhiculaire ancienne de langue (dont la nature précise, berbère, sémitique plus ou moins ancien, éthio-sémitique ou autre, est encore à établir). Cette variété, pas nécessairement homogène elle-même, probablement simplifiée, se serait stabilisée après que des populations originellement de langue non chamito-sémitique se la fussent appropriée. *A priori*, deux hypothèses sont possibles et ne peuvent pas être départagées à ce stade :

- soit une *lingua franca* disparue en tant que telle, après avoir eu une action modificatrice importante aurait très fortement relexifié une autre langue régionale existante, constituant ainsi le songhay ;
- soit la *lingua franca* en question « était » ce qui est aujourd'hui le songhay. Dans ce cas, ce serait tout simplement sa *nativisation* qui aurait constitué la langue.

En conséquence, du point de vue linguistique, la structure typologique du songhay, sa parenté sémantico-lexicale mais aussi morpho-syntaxique avec les langues mandé du nord est donc peut-être (probablement ?) « *autre chose* » que le résultat d'un procès de convergence linguistique. Il n'y a pas nécessairement ici, comme je le préciserai, le type de phénomène qu'on retient sous le terme de *Sprachbund*, bien que le contact continu puisse accentuer la convergence apparente dans l'aire considérée et finalement *surimposer* à cet « *autre chose* » initial une dynamique de *Sprachbund*. L'hypothèse de *constitution de langue* qu'illustrent les faits songhay est cohérente avec les critères généralement reconnus pour le développement de pidgins stabilisés, de même qu'elle rend compte de la parenté lexicale concernant le vocabulaire fondamental, alliée à l'impossibilité (la difficulté ?) d'établir correctement des correspondances phonétiques strictes.

---

[5] Il n'est pas possible dans ce cadre de présenter les données et analyses qui justifient ces hypothèses, cependant, l'on pourra se référer à Nicolaï (2003) pour la présentation extensive et détaillée, et à Nicolaï (2004a, 2004b) pour une présentation plus synthétique.

Corrélativement le statut de véhiculaire qui est encore aujourd'hui le sien, la diversité anthropologique des populations qui l'emploient, la cohérence de cette réalité avec ce que l'on sait du monde médiéval africain sont des indices historiques en accord avec cette hypothèse, laquelle peut aider à mieux comprendre les trois faits suivants :

1. *La diversité concernant les sources chamito-sémitiques mises en rapport avec le lexique songhay.*

On peut s'attendre à ce qu'une probable lingua franca à base chamito-sémitique fonctionnant entre l'Afrique « blanche » et l'Afrique « noire » ait intégré les apports lexicaux que son usage aura nécessité : du couchitique à l'égyptien ; de l'arabe au berbère. Les données connues sur la lingua franca méditerranéenne nous donnent l'exemple d'une variabilité lexicale dans le temps (vénitien, génois, provençal, etc.) qui souligne une dynamique proche et montre que les modifications peuvent être relativement rapides.

2. *L'importance de la diffusion lexicale concernant le vocabulaire chamito-sémitique partagé entre le songhay et les langues négro-africaines voisines.*

Si une (utilisation de l'arabe, du berbère ou d'une autre variété X en tant que) lingua franca telle celle dont je suppose l'existence préalable ici a effectivement existé, alors il faut s'attendre à ce que de nombreuses entrées de son lexique aient été incorporées dans les langues voisines du mandé nord-ouest tout autant que dans le wolof, dans les langues sahariennes et dans bien d'autres, y compris dans les langues « réellement » (?) nilo-sahariennes ! Une telle dynamique peut expliquer l'importance du lexique « ancien » et partagé qu'atteste l'étude de la diffusion lexicale dans l'ensemble de l'espace géographique ouest-africain. Cela permet aussi de rendre compte des rapprochements qui ont pu être faits par ailleurs avec le mandé ou le tchadique (cf. Creissels, 1981 ; Mukarovsky, 1987 ; Nicolaï, 1977a, 1984 ; Zima, 1988).

3. *La « morphologisation » de la forme pidginisée dans les cadres typologiques prédominants de l'espace mandé versus la « lexification » d'une forme de langue mandé*[6]. C'est ce phénomène particulier que traduit l'isomorphisme songhay-mandé dont le tableau ci-joint montre l'importance. En effet, la structure morphosyntaxique du songhay est plutôt simple et typologiquement proche des langues mandé.

---

[6] Cf. Creissels, 1981 ; Lacroix, 1969 ; Nicolaï, 1977, 1984, 1990, pour des remarques concrètes sur la présence de morphèmes référés au mandé. Pour une vue plus développée, l'on se réfèrera à Nicolaï (à paraître, in : Heine & Nurse).

Le plan morphosyntaxique.

On trouvera ci-dessous, sous forme de tableau, les points essentiels sur lesquels portent l'isomorphisme constaté entre songhay et mandé.

Tableau de l'isomorphisme

Formation des mots : dérivation et composition	Globalement, les procédés de dérivation sont comparables dans les deux groupes de langues qui connaissent également une composition très productive organisée selon les mêmes schémas formels ; le procédé de réduplication est aussi très productif.
Détermination des substantifs.	Les différents procédés de la détermination des substantifs sont souvent parallèles et il en va de même de l'organisation des syntagmes de détermination avec les deux ordres inversés : {Complétant + Complété}, {Qualifié + Qualifiant}.
Enoncé prédicatif.	Les formes de l'énoncé prédicatif {S Aux O V Cpl} présentent d'évidentes affinités, il y a aussi des affinités sur de nombreux points du système TMA et de la conjugaison négative.
Les modalités de la grammaticalisation à partir du lexique.	En mandé comme en songhay, les morphèmes relateurs de circonstant sont suffixés au lexème et pour certains d'entre eux, sont également dérivés à partir de formes lexicales en usage dans la langue, phénomène qui dépasse largement le cadre des langues du contact.
Organisation sémantique et structuration sémiotique.	Nombreux parallélismes de découpage conceptuel[7].

Conclusion partielle.

1) Si l'on prend retient une perspective typologique telle celle référée à l'ordre des mots proposée par Heine (1975), songhay et mandé peuvent être catégorisés comme étant de type B2 (Manding), sauf pour le songhay occidental et septentrional qui, connaissant l'ordre SVO, relèvent du type B1. Le tableau ci-dessous rappelle la nomenclature des traits retenus par Heine pour caractériser ce type et montre l'importance des structures effectivement partagées entre songhay et mandé :

[7] Cependant, sous réserve d'une étude plus approfondie, ces affinités dans le découpage et la catégorisation sémantique semblent le plus souvent être partagées par tout l'espace occidental africain et donc, ne pas caractériser uniquement le rapport songhay-mandé.

Tableau des Structures partagées songhay-mandé

1) S-V	8) N-Num	20) V-PronO ; PronO-V
2) S-V-O ; S-O-V	9) Pos-N	21) T-V
3) S-V-Loc	10) N-Dem	23) PronA-PronO
5) N-Post	14) Pos-Adj	24) PronA-T
6) Gen-Nom	15) V-Adv	26) T-PronO
7) N-Adj	19) PronA-V	

2) L'homogénéité typologique des structures morphosyntaxiques est cependant troublée dans l'espace songhay par le fait bien connu que cette langue connaît les deux ordres des énoncés SOV et SVO ; parallèlement l'on remarque que les dialectes qui montrent l'ordre SVO sont ceux du songhay occidental, c'est-à-dire ceux qui sont situés au contact des langues mandé (de type SOV) tandis que les dialectes privilégiant l'ordre SOV en sont apparemment plus éloignés[8].

Le plan phonético-phonologique.

Tout autant, et peut-être davantage qu'au plan morphologique la phonologie et la phonétique manifestent l'existence d'un isomorphisme important entre songhay et mandé mais il est intéressant de noter que (en l'état des connaissances) ce domaine présente aussi une variation dialectale peut-être plus importante que celle attestée au plan morphosyntaxique. Il est ainsi possible d'identifier une stratification des différenciations phonético-phonologiques qui contribue sur quelques points à estomper l'isomorphisme reconnu. Ces modifications, qu'il est en partie possible d'organiser dans une chronologie relative, résultent toutes de situations de contact spécifiques et peuvent être mises en rapport avec le contexte d'usage censé les avoir entraînées. Pour certains dialectes elles ne concernent que des points limités (cf. marensé, zarma) tandis que pour d'autres, tels le dendi ou le songhay septentrional, elles impliquent un véritable changement de type linguistique. Les situations de contact sont diverses, et sans être exhaustif je relève[9] :

- abandon de leur langue première au profit d'un véhiculaire tout en restant dans leur espace socioculturel initial pour les populations berbères qui parlent le songhay septentrional (cf. apparition[10] des consonnes uvularisées (**ṣ, ẓ, ṛ, ḷ, ṇ, ṭ, ḍ**) des consonnes spirantes (ɣ, x), de la consonne occlusive [**q**] ainsi que de la voyelle brève centralisée [ə]) ;

---

[8] Cf. Gensler, 2004, sous presse pour des considérations et des questions sur ce fait, voir aussi Nicolaï (2003) pour des éléments de réponse à la question posée.
[9] On peut se référer à Nicolaï (1980a, 1987, 1989) pour des descriptions détaillées.
[10] Dans le songhay, mais non pas dans le répertoire linguistique des locuteurs de cette langue, qui ont toujours possédé, en parallèle, une langue berbère !

- modification d'une variété véhiculaire en pays dendi à travers son usage par des populations utilisant des langues d'un autre type (type syllabique CV fortement prédominant ; opposition de degré entre les voyelles moyennes qui n'est réalisée nulle part en songhay sauf à Djenné, perte de l'opposition entre les liquides **l** et **r** ; présence d'occlusives labiovélaires) ;
- diffusion de quelques traits de la langue dominante dans l'usage vernaculaire de communautés songhay minoritaires dans les villages marensé du Burkina Faso (spirantisation de l'occlusive vélaire sonore) ;
- rétention probable d'une articulation labiovélarisée (**k**^{w}, **g**^{w}) en zarma sous l'effet d'un contact continu avec les populations hawsa.

On trouvera ci-dessous illustrés les principaux isomorphismes phonético-phonologiques de l'espace songhay-mandé.

Le phonème /p/. Il s'agit d'un phonème défectif dans l'inventaire de nombreuses langues d'Afrique occidentale où il fonctionne uniquement dans des idéophones, des interjections et dans quelques verbaux-nominaux qui partagent tous un trait sémantique d'expressivité[11] ; comportement qui est la règle générale pour la plupart des dialectes songhay et qui est très répandu en mandé[12]. Le phénomène concerne donc à la fois l'expressivité dans la langue (idéophones, exclamations) et l'organisation du sous-système consonantique ; en effet si, en songhay, l'on prend la peine de mettre en rapport cette « absence de **p** » en tant que corrélat potentiel de /**b**/ avec les caractéristiques combinatoires reconnues dans la langue et l'inventaire du paradigme des consonnes possibles en position de coda où, à part /**b**/, ne sont possibles que des consonnes sonantes, alors on remarque que /**b**/ fonctionne comme les sonantes {**m, w, r, l, y, n, ŋ**} et non pas comme une occlusive bruyante corrélative d'un phonème sourd plus ou moins défectif. Ce fonctionnement est corroboré en songhay par de nombreuses variations intra et interdialectales entre {**m, w, b**} (Nicolaï : 1977b) et il est probablement commun à l'ensemble des langues considérées.

A priori donc, ce qui est aréal ici, ce sont deux phénomènes conjoints : l'utilisation d'une forme phonétique particulière en tant que trait expressif et une caractérisation structurale des sous-systèmes phonologiques[13].

---

[11] Cf. Houis, in : *Afrique et langage* 1, 1974 : 35.

[12] Il existe des langues qui ne souscrivent pas à ce schéma, ainsi en soninké où Diagana (1984) note que **p** est en distribution complémentaire avec **h** après nasale, il ne semble pas avoir le même statut. Voir aussi l'utilisation du **p** géminé en songhay (Nicolaï : 1981b).

[13] Parallèlement, notons qu'il serait utile d'approfondir ce qu'il en est au niveau aréal de cet autre « phonème marginal » / **h**~/ que j'interprète en songhay comme un phonème post-nasalisé (2001c) mais qui, à part la transcription de certains emprunts arabes, reste cantonné à des lexèmes à fonction plus ou moins onomatopéiques ou interjective. Je crois avoir remarqué – mais sans les avoir étudiés – des 'parallélismes' en bambara, cf. **hɔ̃n** « tiens !, prend ! ».
Enfin, d'autres traits phonologiques sont partagés par le songhay et au moins certaines langues mandé voisines comme le soninké. Il semble en être ainsi des règles de la gémination des consonnes

L'absence d'opposition **s** ~ **z** *en songhay occidental.* Tous les dialectes songhay connaissent l'opposition /**s**/ ~ /**z**/, à l'exception du songhay occidental qui sur ce point s'aligne sur la typologie de nombreuses langues mandé nord (soninké, bambara, dyula, soso, malinké, maninka, mandinka, bobo, ...) – certaines situées au contact direct du songhay ou dans un espace contigu mais d'autres géographiquement plus éloignées[14].

La comparaison interdialectale permet d'établir qu'en songhay occidental /**z**/ s'est confondu avec /**j**/ qui, lui-même, est le résultat de la phonologisation d'une variante palatalisée des occlusives vélaires. Par ailleurs, la confusion généralisée entre les sons [z] et [j] qui affecte ce dialecte ne semble pas répondre à une nécessité interne et n'entre pas dans les schémas les plus courants de l'évolution phonétique. En effet, l'étude des contextes ne permet pas de conclure à une simple palatalisation : le phénomène n'est lié ni à la présence d'un trait vocalique [+antérieur], ni à celle d'un trait [+haut], ni au contact d'une semi-voyelle /**y**/ et aucun autre contexte palatalisant ne peut être retenu comme déclencheur. De plus la confusion n'est pas symétrique car la fricative sourde /**s**/, corrélative de /**z**/, ne se confond pas avec l'occlusive palatalisée /**c**/ corrélative de /**j**/, parfois réalisée comme une affriquée ; quant au phonème /**ʃ**/, peu fréquent, il n'est jamais confondu avec cette occlusive palatalisée et ne possède pas non plus de correspondant sonore /**ʒ**/. Ce que nous observons est une déphonologisation entraînant de véritables confusions lexicales : ainsi on confondra en songhay occidental les lexèmes **ji** « *huile* » (***gi**) et **ji** « *nager* » (***zi**), le tout impliquant une re-caractérisation de la série des fricatives par rapport à l'opposition de sonorité.

En conséquence on supposera que c'est à travers son contact avec les populations parlant des langues mandé-nord-ouest que le songhay occidental a acquis ce trait typologique particulier bien répandu dans la zone, et on l'interprétera comme un fait de diffusion localisé, parallèle à celui qui *a priori* aurait permis en dendi le passage des consonnes labiovélarisées {**kw, gw, ŋw**}, aux consonnes labiovélaires {**kp, gb, ŋm**} répandues dans la zone kwa[15]. Finalement, il s'agirait d'un phénomène limité, peut-être même récent[16].

La défectivité de /**r**/. On constate que dans l'ensemble de tous les dialectes songhay /**r**/ n'est que très rarement attesté en position initiale. De façon plus ou moins forte selon les dialectes cette défectivité se manifeste au travers d'une ten-

---

à l'intérieur des mots, de la possibilité de réalisation d'une consonne syllabique nasale en position initiale de mot, du type de la structure syllabique et peut-être aussi des règles de combinaison des consonnes en position interne. Autant de phénomènes qui touchent à la fois à l'inventaire des phonèmes et aux propriétés structurales des systèmes.

[14] Bien que des réalisations de [z] soient possibles en tant que variantes, cf. en bambara (Dumestre : 1994).

[15] Mais là, sans avoir aucune incidence sur l'inventaire des phonèmes. cf. Greenberg (1983) et Nicolaï (1990) pour un commentaire sur cette dernière diffusion.

[16] Cf. Nicolaï (1980b). Notons encore que l'absence de cette confusion dans la variété de songhay occidental utilisée à Araouane plaide aussi pour en faire un phénomène tardif.

dance à restructurer les emprunts comportant cette initiale, soit par l'adjonction d'un élément prothétique (cf. la forme songhay (kaado) **òróggò** « *manioc* », issue du hawsa), soit par métathèse ; parallèlement le même phénomène affecte une partie importante des langues mandé (soninké, mandinka, bozo, etc.).

Ce caractère est strictement formel et il ne semble pas possible de le lier à un phénomène particulier : il n'est pas marqué par l'expressivité comme celui concernant /**p**/ et il n'est pas limité à une frange de contact géographiquement définie comme c'est le cas pour la confusion **s** ~ **z**.

Autres rapprochements. Mais l'isomorphisme phonologique songhay-mandé va largement au-delà de ces trois caractères et il est d'autant plus intéressant qu'il permet de délimiter une aire qui semble trouver sa frontière à l'intérieur même de l'espace mandé, entre le mandé de l'est et mandé du nord-ouest[17] ; le tableau de la page 46, qui reprend pour le mandé les données de Vydrine 2003, illustre la proximité typologique du songhay et du mandé nord-ouest face au mandé de l'est.

Hypothèse du « véhiculaire substrat »

Je propose tout d'abord la synthèse suivante :

1) On reconnaît l'existence d'un isomorphisme phonologique entre les langues mandé et songhay et les rapprochements sont plus particulièrement nombreux avec les langues du sous-ensemble nord-ouest du mandé.
2) L'analyse détaillée de quelques uns des traits retenus montre qu'ils ne peuvent pas tous être renvoyés à une même dynamique : l'isomorphisme manifesté témoigne donc dans sa constitution d'une *stratification* dont l'analyse est encore à faire pour l'essentiel.
3) La reconnaissance de ce phénomène de *stratification* qui montre que dans le faisceau de traits caractérisant l'isomorphisme, certains dépassent l'aire considérée tandis que d'autres introduisent des frontières à l'intérieur des entités (songhay ou mandé) comparées, suggère qu'une comparaison globale qui ne dépasserait pas une lecture « écrasée » des faits, ne permettrait pas de rendre compte de la dynamique qui s'est manifestée, tout en « indiquant » cependant quelque chose de l'évolution des langues qui partagent l'espace géographique retenu.

[17] Je retiens sous le terme 'mandé du nord-ouest' l'ensemble des langues {soninké , azer, bozo (Tieyaxo, Hainyaxo, Tyema-Cewe), sorogama, bobo-fing ; Manding (bamana, maninka, jula, marka dafin) ; West manding (kagoro, xasonka, Kita maninka)}. C'est sur cet ensemble de langues que Vydrine s'appuie pour distinguer entre les deux entités est-ouest en rapport avec le faisceau d'isoglosses phonologiques utilisé dans le tableau que je reprends dans le texte. C'est grâce au travail de cet auteur que j'ai pu affiner mon analyse.

MANI-BANDAMA	WEST MANDE	SONGHAY
monosyllabisme (CV, CLV)	schéma dissyllabique prédominant	schéma dissyllabique prédominant
systèmes à 9 voyelles ou plus, harmonie vocalique +AFT, -ATR, +nasal	systèmes à sept voyelles (5 voyelles dans le mandingue de l'ouest et le soninké ; 6 voyelles dans le maninka de Kita)	systèmes à 5 ou 7 voyelles
absence de phonèmes nasals consonantiques	présence de consonnes nasales ; finales nasales non syllabiques correspondant dans certaines langues à la nasalité des voyelles précédentes	présence de consonnes nasales ; existence de finales nasales
système très réduit de consonnes internes dans le mot	systèmes plus ou moins riche de consonnes internes au mot, particulièrement dans le nord	système consonantique complet en position interne dans le mot
homorésonance	pas d'homorésonance	
pas de voyelles longues	opposition de longueur en position non finale (dans de nombreuses langues) ; en toutes positions en mandinka	opposition de longueur en toutes positions
3 à 5 niveaux tonals	typiquement : deux tons ; transition vers les systèmes accentuels (mandinka, kagoro, certains dialectes jallonke) ; systèmes à trois tons allant vers des systèmes à deux éléments (Kpellé)	typiquement : deux tons (haut et bas) + montant et descendant analysables comme la combinaison des tons simples ; transition vers les systèmes accentuels (songhay septentrional) ; absence de contrastes prosodiques en songhay oriental et occidental

Or on peut aller plus loin en s'attachant au détail des faits : ainsi la mise en évidence d'une frontière à l'intérieur du domaine mandé est importante en raison du lien typologique plus étroit qu'elle permet d'établir entre mandé nord-ouest et songhay[18]. La question du rapport entre ces deux groupes de langues se profile alors sous un jour nouveau car la conjonction entre l'hypothèse concernant la constitution du songhay en tant que résultante d'un contact avec une forme véhicularisée de langue chamito-sémitique telle que je l'ai proposée et le constat de Vydrine (2000) à propos de la différenciation phonologique interne dans l'espace mandé ouvre une voie d'explication qui risque d'être à la fois moins simple et plus intéressante.

Dans cette perspective, une première hypothèse (qui, trivialement, ne ferait appel qu'à l'influence réciproque des langues en contact) serait de supposer que le songhay aurait pu avoir une action sur les langues mandé nord-ouest, expliquant de cette façon la différenciation constatée en mandé. Mais cela présuppose que l'on admette l'existence préalable, et ancienne (!), d'un « songhay » doté d'un système phonologique identique à celui qu'il présente aujourd'hui pour qu'il ait pu influencer le mandé dans cette direction ; ce qui n'est pas impossible mais laisse de côté aussi bien l'hypothèse que j'ai avancée (2003) quant à sa formation non-généalogique que celle que j'ai évincée quant à sa « filiation nilo-saharienne » ! Par ailleurs, au plan quantitatif, la disparité entre les langues en présence ne plaide pas, *a priori*, en faveur d'une telle hypothèse.

La voie d'explication la plus intéressante est plutôt celle qui met le phénomène en rapport avec l'hypothèse de la constitution du songhay à partir du contact avec un véhiculaire chamito-sémitique. On se demandera alors si songhay et mandé nord-ouest – tous les deux ensemble – ne devraient pas à cet ancien véhiculaire chamito-sémitique supposé les traits partagés et/ou « convergents » qu'atteste la comparaison typologique de leurs systèmes phonologiques actuels. Selon l'hypothèse que j'ai développée, cette forme chamito-sémitique véhicularisée aurait effectivement conduit à la constitution du songhay ; mais dans le même temps, il se serait manifesté un contact différencié dans l'espace saharo-sahelien entre ce véhiculaire et l'ensemble des langues du contact, introduisant dans les langues voisines mandé nord-ouest cette modification particulière dans leurs systèmes phonologiques[19] qui permet aujourd'hui de les distinguer des autres groupes de langues mandé (Mani-Bandama).

---

[18] Vydrine (2003) conclut ainsi son analyse : 1) *The gulf between the Mani-Bandama and the West Mande languages in what concerns their phonological structure types turns to be not as wide as it may seem. West Mande languages reveal the traces of some archaic features (9 or 10 vowel system with vocal harmony; the absence of nasal consonant phonemes; the possibility of a syllabic nasal in word-final position; the mechanism of homoresonance; the contrast of fortis/lenis consonants) which make the Proto-Western-Mande close to the Mani-Bandama phonological type and allows a reconstruction of the Proto-Mande type close to the Proto-Volta-Congo model.* 2) *In the Mande group, the phonological type of language proves to depend much more on areal rather than genetic factors. This factor should be seriously taken into account in the proto-language reconstruction.*

[19] Au même titre que l'on constate dans le lexique des langues de cette région, une présence importante de lexèmes que je réfère à cette source chamito-sémitique (cf. **bâa** aimer, vouloir ; **bàkà** mettre qqch. à tremper, platée ; **bisa** devancer, etc.) ; voir Nicolaï (2003) pour une étude détaillée.

Ici, afin de conforter la vraisemblance d'une hypothèse nouvelle, il est intéressant de vérifier s'il existe par ailleurs des cas où une telle simplification typologique est effectivement attestée dans des langues dont la phonologie était, sans ambiguïté, originellement chamito-sémitique, au point de les faire aboutir à des structures typologiquement sans aucun lien avec leur configuration initiale, telles celles qui sont aujourd'hui répandues dans les langues mandé, par exemple. De tels cas existent et l'arabe en fournit une très bonne illustration si l'on s'intéresse au niveau de simplification phonologique qu'atteint l'arabe tchadien (variété véhiculaire de l'arabe). En comparaison avec l'arabe classique cette langue possède un système phonologique simplifié voisin de celui que connaît le songhay : un système vocalique identique à cinq voyelles avec une opposition de longueur et trois degrés d'aperture ; un système consonantique qui, après avoir perdu la quasi-totalité de ce qui fait la spécificité des systèmes consonantiques sémitiques (interdentales, emphatiques, uvulaire, pharyngales) (Jullien de Pommerol, 1997 : 118-120), est aussi devenu comparable au système consonantique songhay.

arabe tchadien					arabe classique									songhay				
lab	*ap*	*pal*	*vel*	*glot*	*lab*	*int-dent*	*ap*	*emph*	*pal*	*vel*	*uv*	*phar*	*glot*	*lab*	*ap*	*pal*	*vel*	*glot*
*p[20]	t	*tc	k	’			t	ṭ		k	**q**		’		t	*c	k	
b	d	j	*g		b		d	ḍ	ğ					b	d	j	*g	
f	s	c	x	h	f	**t̮**	s	**ṣ**	š	**ḫ**		**ḥ**	h	f	s	(š)		h
	z					**d̮**	z	**ḍ̮**		**ġ**		‘			z			
m	n	*ɲ			m		n							m	n	*ɲ	*ŋ	
	r						r								r			
	l						l								l			
w		y			w				y					w		y		

La réduction du système tchadien est parallèle à celle que l'on peut constater dans le recouvrement du songhay par les langues chamito-sémitiques lorsqu'on introduit dans un rapport global (compte tenu des limites de la connaissance que nous avons de la stratification des phénomènes)[21] les entrées songhay dont l'origine chamito-sémitique est probable avec leurs correspondantes actuelles en arabe ou en berbère.

C'est une réduction de cette nature que l'on pourrait supposer avoir conduit à l'état de langue effectivement reconstructible aujourd'hui au plan phonologique pour l'ensemble des langues songhay, pour peu que l'on fasse abstraction des différences induites par l'adjonction de certains phonèmes des langues de substrat et de certaines évolutions phonétiques conduisant à des phonologisations postérieures ou à la stabilisation d'oppositions faiblement représentées (cf. **c**, **g**, **ɲ**, **ŋ**).

[20] L'astérisque ne signale pas une reconstruction mais un phonème absent de l'inventaire de l'arabe classique. les flèches conduisant à *g dans la partie 'songhay' du tableau montrent la direction la plus régulière des évolutions conduisant à l'actualisation de /g/.
[21] Cf. Nicolaï 2003 : 285 (cf. d >> ẓ, ḍ, d, ḏ, ṭ ; k > > q, k, ḫ, ġ, (ḥ) ; etc.).

On remarquera de plus que l'absence des phonèmes labials /**p**/ et /**v**/ en songhay que montre le tableau « retient » le parallélisme structurel avec l'arabe ; corrélativement, on conçoit que certaines caractéristiques spécifiques partagées entre mandé et songhay telles que la défectivité de /**r**/ initial ou encore la présence de systèmes tonals, soient explicables à partir des systèmes phonologiques mandé.

Effet de perspective : le système prosodique songhay.

On a généralement considéré que le songhay possédait « originellement » un système tonal, lequel aurait disparu en songhay oriental et occidental, et j'ai présenté (1981a, 1982) au niveau dialectologique ce phénomène en établissant un système de règles qui traitait l'affaiblissement du système en termes de neutralisations tonales et de règles de contraintes. De façon classique, je « décrivais » alors les modalités de transformation d'un système tonal ; cette description était bien évidemment fondée sur l'hypothèse que le songhay préalable à la dialectisation possédait bien un système tonal et impliquait, en conséquence, le procès de disparition que je présentais pour rendre compte des faits occidentaux et orientaux manifestant de sa disparition.

Or, dans le nouveau contexte ici créé par l'hypothèse du « *véhiculaire substrat* », cette analyse, sans être infirmée, perd son évidence ! En effet, si le songhay résulte effectivement de ce véhiculaire supposé dont la base est donnée comme « chamito-sémitique » alors il ne possédait pas de système tonal « à l'origine ». La présence du système tonal (comparable au système actualisé aujourd'hui en mandé nord-ouest) est une résultante complexe de la constitution de la langue et en conséquence, il n'est pas évident du tout que le songhay occidental et le songhay oriental qui ne possèdent pas de système tonal et qui sont géographiquement les voisins immédiats des populations chamito-sémitiques du contact « *aient perdu* » ce système[22] : ils peuvent très bien ne l'avoir jamais acquis et celui-ci ne s'être imposé / conservé que dans les variétés plus méridionales[23]. On rendrait ainsi compte de l'absence du système tonal non pas par l'effet d'un amuïssement du système tonal au contact de l'arabe (sans autre justification que celle induite par le constat empirique de cette absence) mais, tout simplement, à travers la reconsidération de l'ensemble de la situation de contact, en « admettant » que dans l'espace qui est devenu celui du songhay oriental et occidental, la structure prosodique initiale du véhiculaire substrat supposé n'a pas été réinterprétée dans le moule structural de la prosodie mandé.

---

[22] Ces deux groupes dialectaux sont aussi ceux qui sont géographiquement frontaliers des langues chamito-sémitiques (hassaniyya, arabe, touareg).

[23] Notons cependant que dans les langues méridionales qui connaissent un système tonal, tout particulièrement dans le stock posé comme « emprunt arabe » mais aussi au-delà, on peut identifier à travers la présence d'un ton modulé, généralement montant, la trace d'une consonne irréalisable dans le système phonologique songhay (cf. zarma : **lěebù** "être paralysé » (ˤyb) ; **sǎy** « semer à la volée, couler (liquide), verser » (šˤy)) ce qui pourrait servir à affiner les hypothèses.

De cette présentation je tire les enseignements suivants :

- Au plan structurel les systèmes phonématiques songhay et mandé nord-ouest forment un ensemble quasi homogène lequel ressemble beaucoup au système « simplifié » que connaît aujourd'hui l'arabe tchadien ;
- le processus évolutif, attesté, qui a conduit le système phonématique arabe à sa réduction en arabe tchadien est cohérent avec celui, suggéré, qui aurait pu se développer à partir d'une variété véhiculaire chamito-sémitique préalable pour conduire au système songhay ;
- la division interne au songhay entre les langues possédant un système tonal et les autres pourrait s'expliquer en référence avec cette variété véhiculaire chamito-sémitique préalable tout autant que par un phénomène d'amuïssement tardif dû au contact ;
- cette même variété véhiculaire chamito-sémitique pourrait également avoir imposé – bien que de façon moins prégnante – sa « marque » sur d'autres langues régionales, ce qui expliquerait de nombreux effets de contact : traces lexicales en wolof, traces lexicales en mandé et modifications structurelles au niveau du système phonologique en mandé nord-ouest.
- L'évolution uniforme n'est probablement pas une donnée a priori de la nature évolutive des langues : c'est seulement une donnée a priori des modalités de représentation des « praticiens de la recherche » que sont les linguistes qui, eux, opèrent a posteriori ! En conséquence, les résultats construits en y faisant appel peuvent tout aussi bien être conformes à la réalité, ou bien ne l'être pas.
- Les a priori les mieux partagés donnés en préalable à la description des dynamiques linguistiques peuvent conduire à des analyse trompeuses : ce que montre la confrontation de mon ancienne analyse du système prosodique songhay avec l'hypothèse ici proposée.
- Corrélativement, on constate que l'on trouve toujours – au niveau instrumental – un système de règles, conforme à la théorie du moment, pour « décrire » le procès évolutif supposé (que celui-ci ait eu une réalité effective ou pas !).

En conclusion sur ce point, nous avons affaire à la fois :

- à un « domaine empirique » qui exemplifie une transformation entre des systèmes qui étaient donnés *a priori* comme appartenant à des types réputés sans commune mesure ;
- à un « modèle d'explication » qui est justifié de contrevenir à « l'apparente sagesse » de ne s'en tenir qu'à des hypothèses d'évolution fondées sur des postulats uniformitaristes ; « sagesse » qui est obérée par l'arbitraire de ses propres présupposés et par l'effet de clôture qu'ils induisent.

Synthèse

Ce tour d'horizon achevé, une synthèse s'impose : si l'on s'en tient aux isoglosses l'ensemble des comparaisons que j'ai présentées permet de dire ce qui suit :

1) Il existe des rapports entre de nombreux aspects de la typologie des langues songhay et mandé qui se manifestent à travers une série de rapprochements à tous les niveaux : phonologie, morphologie, catégories morphosyntaxiques, ordre des mots, sémantique, structuration lexicale.
2) Les lignes d'isoglosses ne se constituent pas en faisceaux homogènes ; plusieurs d'entre elles coupent à travers les entités 'mandé' (cf. Vydrine, 2000) ou 'songhay' (SOV/SVO ; **s~z**) tandis que d'autres s'étendent largement au delà de ces deux ensembles de langues (cf. fonction de /**p**/). De telles différences suggèrent que ce n'est pas une seule et unique dynamique qui conduit à la « massification » du phénomène observé. Effet qui, ici, « *crée* » un *pseudo-objet* d'étude, construction *a posteriori* effectuée par le chercheur. Sa pertinence, et la pertinence de son étude ne va donc pas de soi pour la connaissance linguistique ; elle doit donc être préalablement justifiée[24]. Notons que l'idée simple (et probablement *trop* claire !) de la diffusion selon le vieux modèle de la théorie des ondes est tout aussi problématique.
3) Si les aires des langues de type Manding (B2) que Heine (1975) a proposées correspondent aujourd'hui à deux espaces géographico-linguistiquement distingués (Sénégal-Niger et Dosso-Nikki), le fait de pouvoir considérer que le songhay occidental de type (B1) devait posséder antérieurement le type B2 et qu'il a évolué sous l'effet de contraintes fonctionnelles sociolinguistiquement déterminées permet de justifier l'hypothèse d'une étape préalable unifiée concernant l'aire des langues de type Manding et peut-être, en se fondant sur la typologie phonologique, de placer la « centralité » de cette aire à l'ouest de la zone mandé, dans la zone songhay proprement dite et dans celle du contact songhay-mandé.
4) Les structures des langues songhay dont les structures s'écartent du type Manding (B2), telles celles du songhay occidental et du songhay septentrional, peuvent concrètement s'expliquer par des évolutions subséquentes à cet état 'initial'.

L'incidence de l'hypothèse généalogique.

L'exemple du contact songhay-mandé aura montré, là où la documentation historique reste incertaine et avant d'élaborer des hypothèses sur la nature des

[24] Corrélativement, sa pertinence va de soi pour une étude des modalités de rationalisation *a posteriori* mises en œuvre par les chercheurs. Voir aussi Nicolaï (2000) pour des remarques sur la dimension construite et *a posteriori* de la mise en évidence des aires de convergence ou d'affinités linguistiques. Cf. également, Campbell (2002).

isomorphismes structuraux, l'importance qu'il y a à s'intéresser aux domaines linguistiques sensibles à l'histoire et à ses contingences tels le lexique[25]. Ainsi tant que le songhay était *donné* comme une langue nilo-saharienne et que l'on a *tenu pour acquis* cette proposition, l'on en a 'logiquement' *inféré* que mandé et songhay appartenaient à deux entités généalogiques distinguées. De ce fait l'on se plaçait dans une configuration satisfaisante pour interpréter 'logiquement' l'isomorphisme constaté comme le résultat d'une convergence entre deux groupes de langues en contact intense, et il y avait lieu de penser que sa dynamique pouvait être décrite grâce à quelques « opérations » cognitives simples telles, par exemple, celle de métatypie[26]. Mais cela n'a de sens qu'autant que les présupposés sont justifiés : à savoir, lorsque nous avons bien affaire à l'évolution de langues généalogiquement distinguées et supposées, initialement, avoir été typologiquement différentes. Or j'ai mentionné que l'hypothèse du rattachement du songhay au nilo-saharien est remise en question ; en conséquence, si la contestation est bien justifiée, la « forme » du songhay d'aujourd'hui a de fortes chances de traduire *autre chose* qu'un simple effet d'évolution convergente ou, à tout le moins, la convergence n'est qu'un élément secondaire pour son explication.

Je rappelle ici qu'en s'en tenant (pour l'instant !) à l'idée précédemment mentionnée de l'existence d'une probable *lingua franca* à l'origine de la constitution du songhay, deux hypothèses s'offrent qui ne sauraient être départagées en l'état des connaissances : soit une *lingua franca* disparue en tant que telle, après avoir eu une action modificatrice importante aurait très fortement relexifié une autre langue régionale préexistante (une variété du mandé en l'occurrence) « constituant » ainsi le songhay, soit la *lingua franca* en question « était » ce qui est aujourd'hui le songhay[27] ; dans ce dernier cas, ce serait tout simplement la nativisation de cette *lingua franca* qui aurait « constitué » cette langue.

---

[25] J'ai noté en effet que l'approche lexico-sémantique était « méthodologiquement (?) » laissée aux marges de l'étude des aires de convergence, sans doute parce que le caractère non-systématique souvent attribué aux dynamiques lexicales semble être, *a priori*, peu compatible avec la rigueur affichée des considérations morphosyntaxiques ou phonologiques.

[26] La métatypie, notion reprise de Ross (1997 : 241) est ainsi présentée : « The class of language changes which is diagnostic of contact induced change includes (a) the reorganization of language's semantic patterns and 'ways of saying things', and (b) the restructuring of its syntax [...]. This reorganization and restructuring is truly diagnostic of contact-induced change only if we can show that new patterns bring the language closer to a putative inter-community language. I have coined the term 'metatypy' for this reorganization and restructuring [...], as this kind of language change leads to a metamorphosis in structural type ». Elle résulte d'une généralisation à partir de la notion de calque, elle est censée traduire des habitus et induire une homogénéité qui conduit à une simplification dans la communication et c'est peut-être une opération fondamentale de « copiage » dans le procès d'élaboration des aires de convergence.

[27] Il s'ensuit qu'en l'absence de travaux complémentaires, toute proposition qui tendrait à rendre compte du songhay comme d'un créole abrupt *versus* une forme de langue caractérisée par un emprunt lexical lourd aurait de fortes chances d'apparaître à la fois prématurée et illégitime. Toutefois il importe de mentionner l'effort de synthèse éclairant que l'on trouve dans Wolff, E. & Alidou, O. (2001) qui a le mérite de présenter la problématique des langues « mixtes » puis d'organiser et de mettre en perspective les hypothèses et débats autour de la question de la nature 'créole' du songhay.

Mais, quelle que soit l'issue des recherches futures il n'est déjà plus possible d'interpréter les isomorphismes auxquels le songhay participe comme le simple résultat de l'évolution de langues qui seraient données comme « originellement » distinctes et qui se seraient typologiquement rapprochées les unes des autres à travers des siècles ou des millénaires de contact et de plurilinguisme, ou d'une autre variante de cette « explication » princeps.

La stratification des isoglosses.

Après avoir reconnu « globalement », la réalité de l'isomorphisme, l'étude de sa stratification conduit à remarquer que les dynamiques structurelles qui concernent les différents sous-systèmes de la langue sont différemment déterminées par les facteurs contraignants de l'évolution :

- les dynamiques phonologiques semblent être plus sensibles aux effets du contact que les dynamiques morphosyntaxiques;
- les dynamiques morphosyntaxiques semblent être plus sensibles aux phénomènes fonctionnels de simplification résultant de l'emploi véhiculaire de la langue;
- la structure lexicale apporte des informations utiles du point de vue historique et du point de vue de la constitution généalogique de la langue.
- etc.

Corrélativement les fonctionnalités des langues (qui, elles aussi, évoluent dans le temps) engendrent des dynamiques susceptibles de modifier les configurations initiales. Ainsi dans le contact songhay-mandé, l'on remarquera une accentuation du phénomène de convergence apparente sur certains points, par la *surimposition* d'une dynamique de *Sprachbund* comme le suggère l'étude détaillée de la stratification géographique et linguistique des traits partagés manifestés par les isoglosses (cf. la confusion localisée **s/z** en songhay occidental) ou bien, à l'inverse, son *masquage* sur d'autres points par l'introduction d'évolutions subséquentes déterminées par des fonctionnalités impliquant des processus de simplification (cf. l'abandon de l'ordre SOV en songhay occidental et septentrional). Il importe donc de focaliser l'étude sur les phénomènes de stratification car leur non prise en compte, et la saisie « écrasée » qui s'ensuit pourrait conduire à des interprétations erronées.

Du point de vue méthodologique enfin, l'on pourrait s'interroger sur l'intérêt des critères / traits retenus par rapport à l'aire décrite et sur la nécessité de les organiser : dans quelle mesure peut-on identifier des critères / traits (des isoglosses ?) capables de caractériser l'aire songhay-mandé dans sa spécificité ? Est-il possible de proposer des principes permettant de distinguer cette aire en tant que telle sur la base de caractères bien définis ?

Il n'y a pas d'isoglosses spécifiques qui soient limitées uniquement à l'aire songhay-mandé[28] et c'est toujours à un faisceau conjoncturel de traits que l'on a affaire[29]. La recherche d'une caractérisation de l'aire se manifeste seulement par la sélection *a posteriori* de quelques traits que l'on aura retenus de façon *ad hoc*, uniquement pour identifier l'état de fait que l'on croit reconnaître ; il s'agit donc là d'une opération « classificatoire » que l'on fait *nécessairement* et qui conduit à une représentation caractérisée de son « objet ». Aller au-delà, partir du constat de l'émergence de cette représentation pour tenter d'en faire un « outil heuristique » (« instrumentaliser » les (faisceaux d')isoglosses !) risque d'être maladroit ; de même qu'il serait naïf de lui attribuer une valeur « catégorielle » sous peine de circularité. L'actualisation d'un isomorphisme peut résulter de facteurs variés qui n'ont pas nécessairement quelque chose à voir avec ce que l'on entend habituellement par phénomènes de convergence ainsi que l'étude de l'aire songhay-mandé a pu le montrer.

Références

BENDER, L., 1995, *The Nilo-Saharan Language. A Comparative Essay*, München.

CAMPBELL, L., 2002, *Areal Linguistics : a closer Scrutiny*, 5th NWCL, International Conference: Linguistic Areas, Convergence, and Language Change, University of Manchester.

CREISSELS, D., 1981, De la possibilité de rapprochements entre le songhay et les langues Niger-Congo (en particulier Mandé), *Nilo-Saharan,* Th. Schadeberg & M.L. Bender (éds.), pp. 185-199.

DELAFOSSE, M., 1901, *Essai de manuel pratique de la langue mandingue*, Paris, Leroux.

— 1924, Langues du Soudan et de la Guinée, *Les langues du Monde*, 2 vols. Paris.

DIAGANA, O., 1984, *Le parler soninké de Kaédi, syntaxe et sens*, Thèse de Doctorat d'Etat, Paris V-Sorbonne

DUMESTRE, G., 1994, *Le bambara du Mali: essais de description linguistique*, Paris.

EHRET, Chr., 2001, *A Historical-Comparative Reconstruction of Nilo-Saharan*, Köln.

GENSLER, O., 2004, «Two marked» areal features in Songhay syntax: Implication for prehistory, International Symposium « Area Typology of West Africa », Leipzig, B. Comrie & E. Wolff (éds.), *JWAL Special Issue* 30.2

GREENBERG, J., 1963, *The Languages of Africa*, The Hague.

— 1983. « Some areal characteristics of African Languages », I.R. Dihoff (éd.), *Current Approaches to African Linguistics* (Vol.1), pp. 3-21.

HEINE, B., 1975, Language typology and convergence areas in Africa, *Linguistics*, 144, pp. 27-47.

HOUIS, M., 1971, *Anthropologie linguistique de l'Afrique noire*, Paris.

[28] Être ou non un système tonal, posséder une structure post-positionnelle ou prépositionnelle, marquer la possession inaliénable par simple juxtaposition, etc. Bien évidemment aucun de ces critères n'est spécifique. Mais le faisceau (arbitraire ou caractérisé par des dépendances internes entre les traits retenus), lui, est spécifique.

[29] Ou bien lorsqu'une isoglosse semble être plus spécifique (cf. la défectivité de /**r**/) elle caractérise un phénomène ponctuellement utile par sa contingence, mais dont l'intérêt, du point de vue général n'est pas évident.

HOUIS, M., 1974, A propos du phonème /p/, *Afrique et langage* 1, pp. 35-38.

JULLIEN DE POMMEROL, 1997, *L'arabe tchadien. Emergence d'une langue véhiculaire*, Paris.

LACROIX, P.-F., L'ensemble songhay-jerma. Problèmes et thèmes de travail, *Actes du 8e Congrès SLAO*, Abidjan, 24-28 mars 1969, pp-99.

MUKAROVSKY, H., 1987, Songhai und Westtschadisch (ohne Hausa), *Actes, Fünfter Internationaler Kongress für Hamito-Semistik*, Wien, Current issues in Linguistics Theory, Amsterdam.

NICOLAÏ, R., 1977a, Sur l'appartenance du songhay, *Annales de la Faculté des Lettres de Nice*, N° 28, Nice : pp. 129-135.

— 1977b, Réinterprétation et restructuration en zarma-songhay, *Bul. IFAN*, 39b2, pp. 432-455, Dakar.

— 1980a, Le songhay septentrional (études prosodiques), *Itinérances en pays peul et ailleurs*, vol. 1, Société des Africanistes, pp. 261-289, Paris.

— 1980b, Notes sur les lexiques songhay du 19ème siècle et sur les attestations des Tarikh, *Afrika und Übersee*, n°64-2, pp. 235-256.

— 1981a, *Les dialectes du songhay (contribution à l'étude des changements linguistiques)*, Paris.

— 1981b, Problèmes de dynamique linguistique : la restructuration du système sonantique songhay, *Travaux du Cercle Linguistique de Nice*, n°2, pp. 95-116, Nice.

— 1982, Problèmes de dynamique linguistique : recherches en prosodie songhay, *Studies in African Linguistics*, XIII, 3, pp. 273-322, Los Angeles.

— 1984, *Préliminaires à une étude sur l'origine du songhay (matériaux, problématique et hypothèses)*, Berlin.

— 1987, Is Songhay a creole language ?, G. G. Gilbert (éd.), *Pidgins and Creole Languages, Essays in Memory of John E. Reinecke,* Honolulu , University of Hawaii Press, pp. 469-484.

— 1989, Revernacularisation et déterminismes évolutifs : les exemples du songhay septentrional et du dendi, *Current approaches to African Linguistics*, vol. VI, Foris, pp. 100-114, Dordrecht.

— 1990, *Parentés linguistiques (à propos du songhay)*, Paris.

— 2000, *La traversée de l'empirique, essai d'épistémologie sur la construction des représentations de l'évolution des langues*, Paris.

— 2001, Voyelles nasales ou consonnes aspirées nasales en songhay (approche de la marginalité), *Proceedings 2nd World Congress of African Linguistics*, E. Wolff & O. Gensler (éds.), Köppe Verlag, Köln, 2000, pp. 359-372.

— 2003, La force des choses ou l'épreuve nilo-saharienne, *Questions sur les reconstructions archéologiques et l'évolution des langues*, Köln.

— 2004a, Aux marges de l'espace chamito-sémitique : songhay et diffusion aréale, *Faits de langues, Les langues chamito-sémitiques (afro-asiatiques)*, éds. A. Mettouchi & A. Lonnet.

— 2004b, Songhay-mande convergence area : questions and frames, Heine/Nurse (éds.), *Africa as a linguistic area/Areal typology and African languages*, Cambridge Univ. Press.

ROSS, M., 1997, Social networks and kinds of speech-community event, R. Blench & M. Spriggs (éds.), *Archeology And Language I*, pp. 207-261, London – New York.

VYDRINE, Valentin. 2003. Areal and genetic features in West Mande and Mani Bandama (East Mande) phonology: in what sense did Mande languages evolute? *Journal of West African Languages* XXX.2 : 113-126.

WESTERMANN, D., 1927, *Die Westlichen Sudansprachen*, Berlin.

WESTERMANN, D., Bryan, M. A., 1952, *Languages of West Africa*, Londres.

WOLFF, H. E., Ousseina Alidou, 2001, On the Non-Linear Ancestry of Tasawaq (Niger). Or : How « mixed » Can a Language Be ?, *Sprache und Geschichte in Afrika* 16/17 : 523-574.

ZIMA, P., 1988, Songhay, Hausa and Chadic (preliminary Notes on Lexical Affinities), *Progressive Traditions in African and Oriental Stidies; Asia, Africa, Latin America*, 21, pp. 185-192.

Du contact au changement de langue : l'isolement singulier du bisa (mandé-est)

Rainer VOSSEN & Sonja ERMISCH Vossen@em.uni-frankfurt.de

Université Johann Wolfgang Goethe de Francfort sur le Main

Abstract

The paper focusses on the phenomena of language retainment and language shift in the Bisa-speaking community in South-Central Burkina Faso.

Language is closely related to cultural identity. Thus, the abandonment of a people's mother tongue in favour of a dominating neighbour language often results in the loss of cultural identity. In this respect, Bisa seems to be a special case: although surrounded by Gur languages, neither the Bisa language nor its speakers' identity seem to be affected.

It should be noted, however, that language retainment and language shift constitute the edges of a developmental continuum and that changes within a language take place only gradually. It is therefore very unlikely that the two fifth of former Bisa speakers who abandoned their mother tongue and shifted to another language did so without passing through different stages. To support this assumption we have to find out how these different stages look like and by which features gradual shift can be characterized.

Résumé

L'objectif de cet article est de traiter des questions de conservation et de changement de langue chez les Bisa dans le centre sud du Burkina Faso.

Une langue est toujours étroitement liée à l'identité culturelle des locuteurs. De ce fait, pour une communauté linguistique, l'abandon de la langue maternelle au profit d'une langue majoritaire voisine signifie dans la plupart des cas une perte de son identité culturelle. Le bisa constitue sur ce point un cas spécial : bien que ses locuteurs soient entourés par des locuteurs de langues gur, ni la langue ni la culture bisa ne semblent être sérieusement affectées.

Il faut noter toutefois que les phénomènes de conservation et de changement de langue constituent les points extrêmes d'un développement linguistique continu et que les changements qui s'opèrent dans une langue ne se font que de façon graduelle. Il est de ce fait assez invraisemblable que les deux cinquièmes des ex-locuteurs du bisa qui ont abandonné leur langue maternelle au profit d'autres langues l'aient effectué sans être passés par un certain nombre d'étapes. Pour défendre cette affirmation il est nécessaire de définir ce que sont ces étapes et par quelles caractéristiques le changement graduel peut être marqué.

1. Remarque préliminaire

Dans une publication antérieure (pour des détails voir Vossen & Keuthmann 2002) le bisa (Burkina Faso, Afrique Occidentale) avait été présenté sous la notion d' « îlot linguistique » . Dans le présent article nous essayerons tout d'abord de présenter brièvement les questions de conservation et de changement de langue dans la communauté bisa, puis de mettre les deux thèmes en corrélation.

2. Bisa, un îlot linguistique ? Traces linguistiques et spéculations historiques

De nos jours, les historiens ont de la peine à reconstruire le parcours historique des Bisa au-delà des limites chronologiquement tangibles de l'occupation coloniale et de la domination Mosi. Il en résulte des suppositions et des spéculations plus ou moins plausibles dont la quintessence est résumée par Faure (1996 : 51) comme suit :

> Le peuple bissa est né progressivement d'absorption d'autochtones, de conquérants et de migrants. De ce fait, chercher les origines lointaines des Bissa n'a pas de sens pour contribuer à l'histoire de l'appropriation du sol dans la région.

Dans une perspective géo-historique, où des reconstructions d'une genèse ethno-linguistique s'avéreraient indispensables, les preuves linguistiques de la géographie dialectale en pays bisa (voir carte 1) témoigneraient d'un poids historique et d'une aire géographique beaucoup plus importants. Ce que Faure considère comme une absorption progressive, une assimilation constante des autochtones, des envahisseurs et des immigrés, apparaît au niveau linguistique comme une césure dialectale des variétés occidentales lébri et leré. La question de savoir quand et où ces « strates archaïques » se sont formées peut être clarifiée au mieux si l'on arrive à identifier les acteurs de cet amalgame ethno-linguistique.

A présent cette question a à peine plus de sens qu'une spéculation. Middleton (1997 : 113), dans sa présentation d'un synopsis géo-historique d'événements plus complexes qui sont à la base de la dispersion linguistique et culturelle mandé, a fortement insisté sur la signification historique et régionale des migrations – qui se sont effectuées parfois des siècles durant – des branches sud et ouest du « noyau mandé » dans le cours supérieur du fleuve Niger. Ces « Mandé périphériques » – parmi lesquels les ancêtres des Bisa actuels du Burkina Faso et du Ghana – s'installèrent parmi des populations non locutrices du mandé. Ils étaient en quête permanente de sols propices à la culture de céréales d'origine soudanaise, inconnues jusqu'alors de leurs « hôtes » autochtones. Selon McNaughton (1988 : xix) ce serait de cette manière qu'une véritable diaspora se constitua, et ce sont exactement ces groupements périphériques de locuteurs du mandé qui réalisèrent un transfert culturel considérable dans la savane ouest africaine. « Leur habileté de négociants tout autant que l'autorité sociale et culturelle de leurs nombreux lignages d'érudits musulmans leur offrirent un statut assez élevé » (Middleton 1997 : 113 ; traduit de l'anglais). Les Dioula, qui peuvent être considérés comme un élément de liaison parmi eux, eux-mêmes des négociants réputés, ont continué l'islamisation de la région. En un mot : « Il y a absolument eu un grand mélange historique entre ces groupes [de Mandé périphériques] parmi eux et entre eux et leurs voisins non-mandé » (loc. cit., traduit de l'anglais).

Même sur la base d'une brève esquisse de la dispersion mandé comme celle-ci il est possible de s'imaginer le cadre confus et complexe d'une évolution dans laquelle, entre autres, le rôle historique factuel des Bisa, de leurs ancêtres et probablement d'autres groupes contemporains qui ont dû contribuer à la formation de l'actuelle identité ethnolinguistique bisa, reste largement non élucidé. Face à ces problèmes historiques, Ki-Zerbo (1981 : 180f) avance, plutôt résigné, que toute tentative de reconstruction du « rayon de dispersion des Mandé » sur la base de « données fiables » paraît quasiment impossible, vue la complexité des événements et la diversité des populations impliquées. La reconstruction de l'histoire pré-coloniale bisa ne fait à cet égard pas d'exception ; mieux, la recherche de leur origine doit être mise en corrélation avec celle de leurs cousins Samo dans le nord sur la base des traditions orales encore assez vivaces (cf., p.ex., Prost 1950 : 9f).

Ce que Ki-Zerbo trouve incomplet dans l'histoire des migrations mandé et des mouvements sociaux en général est justement souligné par Faure (1996 : 36) avec une référence particulière au Bisa : comment serait-il possible d'écrire l'histoire des Bisa avant 1800 étant donnée la rareté de sources linguistiques, des traditions orales et des documents historiques ? Il est possible – comme Faure l'a déjà envisagé – de suivre un chemin de reconstruction indirecte par les études anthropologiques régionales d'éléments culturels, les rapports entre les Bisa et les Mosi et, en même temps de démêler les interpénétrations et amalgames entre les deux cultures occasionnés par l'histoire. Ceci est d'une grande importance pour l'histoire politique recente de l'émergence de la communauté Bisa comme facteur régional de pouvoir ; cela permettra en plus d'éclaircir l'antagonisme entre les Bisa et les Mosi tout autant que l'interférence partielle des Bisa par leurs puissants voisins qui se reflète dans l'aire de distribution du dialecte barka. Plusieurs auteurs (p. ex. Tauxier 1924 : 170 et Prost 1953 : 1336) ont attiré notre attention sur cette différence entre les Bisa indépendants du temps pré-colonial au sud-ouest (Leré) et les Bisa sous domination Mosi dans la région du Tenkodogo (Barka). Non élucidée reste cependant la question des populations autochtones – Faure (1996 : 50) les appelle « proto-Bissa » – qui ont occupé originellement la région. Que la diaspora Bisa du peuple mande d'avant la confrontation avec les Mosi ait occupé un territoire plus étendu que la récente distribution linguistique ne le suggère, a déjà été souligné par Prost (1950 : 7). Il est question ici d'un territoire dont l'étendue va au-delà de Manga dans le sud et jusqu'à Boussouma (près de Kaya) et Boulsa dans le nord, créant ainsi le « pont » avec l'actuelle région Samo (voir carte 2).

Même si Balima (1996 : 56ff) définit les Bisa, tout autant que les Samo, les Bobo et les Gourounsi comme des populations autochtones « géronto-démocratiques » du Burkina Faso pour les mettre en contraste avec les populations « autocratiques » Mosi et Gourma, la question demeure de savoir comment l'existence des communautés périphériques de locuteurs mandé peut être expliquée dans l'histoire générale de la dispersion des Mandé. Les difficultés des historiens à retracer l'histoire bisa au-delà de la période de contact avec les Mosi sont à cet effet assez évidentes.

La distribution du bisa permet de faire des spéculations sur les ancêtres de cette communauté linguistique en ce qui concerne leur large implication dans des interactions politiques et économiques bien avant la conquête Mosi. Nous avons fait état auparavant de l'étroite relation génétique des langues bisa et samo qui suggère l'existence antérieure d'un continuum dialectal vers le nord. En plus, même les limites sud du territoire bisa actuel ne sont pas clairement définies puisque les quelques rares et disparates agglomérations disséminées tout au long de la frontière du Ghana actuel et bien au-delà à l'intérieur du pays sont occupées par des locuteurs du bisa et du kusal. A voir ces communautés, qui sont toutes linguistiquement mélangées, il est bien possible d'imaginer une extension bien profonde du territoire bisa d'alors vers le sud. Etant donnée cette expansion évidente dans le passé de ces groupes dialectaux, on peut émettre l'hypothèse que les ancêtres de la population Bisa actuelle ont été impliqués dans le négoce auprès des routes commerciales pré-coloniales : le commerce de l'or de la zone de Koumassi et plus au nord le long de la Volta noire en direction de Dienne ; concomitamment le commerce outrancier d'esclaves, frappant en particulier la région de Bouna ; enfin le commerce de cola et de l'or des rives ouest de la basse Volta via le Niger à l'est jusqu'à Kano et sans oublier la vente du sel en provenance de la basse Volta blanche.

3. Le bisa comme résultat d'une hybridation linguistique ?

Comme cela a déjà été mentionné, il y a au sud du territoire bisa, dans la zone de transition avec le kusal, une confusion géo-linguistique remarquable, plutôt inattendue vue la netteté des autres zones de démarcation entre les Bisa et leurs voisins mosi, locuteurs des langues gur. C'est là, dans l'extrême sud-ouest du pays bisa précisément où, selon notre interprétation des données phonologiques et lexicales, la strate la plus « archaïque » du continuum dialectal bisa doit se situer. Ceci étant, l'affirmation plutôt inopinée de Dittmer (1975 : 503) selon laquelle le bisa « ne serait rien d'autre que du kusasi mandéïsé » mérite d'être mentionnée. Une telle hypothèse ne peut être cependant soutenue par des arguments linguistiques ou extra-linguistiques convaincants. Toutefois on ne peut exclure d'une manière générale l'idée d'une mandéïsation linguistique ou d'autres formes de mélanges linguistiques ou culturels.

Il est de ce fait légitime de chercher une explication à travers l'interprétation des (présumés) îlots linguistiques identiques au bisa comme étant le résultat d'un processus linguistique graduel d'hybridation ou de changement. La question d'une relation non linéaire a été récemment soulevée par Wolff & Alidou (2001) dans le contexte des dialectes songhay. En effet, il est possible que, dû à des circonstances historiques complexes, un « problème comme les interférences étendues » entre des systèmes linguistiques arrive à un tel point « qu'un mélange linguistique dépourvu de toute relation génétique en soit le résultat » (Wolff 1979 : 45). Un tel mélange linguistique apparaît surtout à travers des contacts de langues assez intensifs, à grande portée et d'une longue durée. Un tel scénario s'offre d'ailleurs clairement si l'on considère la dispersion linguistique et culturelle du mandé en général, si l'on tient compte de la situation spécifique du contact entre le mandé et le gur – dans le cas spécifique du bisa et du moré – et surtout si l'on tient compte de la question, encore ouverte, de la relation linguistique entre le mandé et le songhay (Mukarovsky 1966, Nicolaï 1989 ; voir aussi Kastenholz 1991/92 et Köhler 1975 : 342). Pour le cas du bisa (plus précisément du « proto-bissa ») cependant l'éventualité d'un mélange culturel et linguistique n'a pas encore été envisagée.

4. Hybridation linguistique et changement de langue : quelques questions essentielles

Dans un contexte linguistique d'hybridation et de changement les questions suivantes semble être impératives pour le bisa :

(1) Pourquoi la langue bisa a-t-elle été abandonnée par à peu près les deux cinquièmes de la population bisa alors que l'identité bisa a été conservée ?
(2) Y-a-il des preuves de l'existence de variétés bisa pidginisées ou même créolisées qui puissent être liées à un processus graduel de changement de langue ? Quels facteurs du « model gradualiste » de créolisation peuvent être retrouvés dans les variétés du bisa ?
(3) Où et pourquoi s'amorce le processus de changement de langue ?
(4) Quels traits grammaticaux du bisa peuvent être rattachés aux langues environnantes ?

Sur la question (1) : Pourquoi la langue bisa a-t-elle été abandonnée par à peu près deux cinquièmes de la population bisa alors que l'identité bisa a été conservée ?

Une langue est étroitement liée à l'identité culturelle de la communauté qui la parle. Ainsi, l'abandon par un peuple de sa langue maternelle au profit d'une langue voisine dominante résulte le plus souvent de la perte de l'identité culturelle. Le bisa semble à cet effet être un cas spécial : bien qu'entouré par les langues gur, ni la langue bisa ni l'identité de ses locuteurs ne semblent être affectés.

On doit prendre en considération toutefois le fait que les phénomènes de maintien ou de changement de langue constituent les aboutissements d'une évolution continue et que les changements dans une langue s'opèrent seulement de manière graduelle. Il est de ce fait très improbable que les deux cinquièmes de Bisa ayant abandonné leur langue maternelle au profit d'une autre langue (spécialement le moré) aient dû le faire sans passer par des étapes successives. Nous ne disposons malheureusement d'aucune preuve qui nous permette de documenter ces étapes et les traits caractéristiques de ce changement graduel.

Sur la question (2) : Y-a-il des preuves de l'existence de variétés bisa pidginisées ou même créolisées qui puissent être liées à un processus graduel de changement de langue ? Quels facteurs du « model gradualiste » de créolisation peuvent être retrouvés dans les variétés du bisa ?

Etant donné que les pidgins apparaissent dans des situations d'intenses contacts de langue, les variétés en question doivent se trouver dans les zones frontalières entre les communautés parlant bisa et leurs voisins locuteurs de langues gur. Un facteur important qui vient à l'idée est la notion de simplification. Pour faciliter la communication, les locuteurs dépouillent leurs langues de tous les traits qu'ils considèrent comme assez spécifiques. Il en résulte un jargon qui, en soi, n'est plus intelligible pour les locuteurs de la « forme originale » da la langue. Selon Sebba (1997, basé sur Mühlhäusler 1986), le développement d'un pidgin comprend quatre étapes :

1. *l'étape du jargon* qui est caractérisée par une grammaire et un vocabulaire assez instables,
2. *l'étape d'hybridation* tertiaire qui est caractérisée par une stabilité croissante et une extension du lexique ; à cette étape le pidgin sert de moyen de communication entre deux groupes ne parlant pas la langue cible originale (ou lexificatrice) ;
3. *l'étape de pidgin stable* pendant laquelle le pidgin développe ses propres normes de grammaire, de lexique et de prononciation ; et
4. *l'étape d'un pidgin étendu* dans laquelle les fonctions du pidgin et ses domaines d'emploi sont si bien étendus qu'il peut à présent être employé comme une lingua franca.

La créolisation peut apparaître durant l'étape d'expansion ou plus tôt. Le schéma d'évolution selon Sebba (1997 : 133) est le suivant :

- Phonologie : la longueur des mots et la complexité structurelle s'accroissent.
- Morphologie : la morphologie dérivationelle prend de l'importance ; en plus, il peut y avoir des éléments de morphologie flexionnelle.
- Syntaxe : la grammaticalisation des catégories majeures, des « règles de déplacement », la subordination relative et les complémentiseurs peuvent émerger.

- Lexique : le lexique se développe à travers les extensions métaphoriques, la multifonctionnalité des items lexicaux et le développement de la morphologie dérivationelle.
- Extension des possibilités de choix stylistiques au fur et à mesure que les fonctions de la langue s'élargissent.

Si le mécanisme de pidginisation et de créolisation joue un rôle dans le cas du bisa il sera possible de découvrir des variétés bisa qui sont moins complexes que d'autres. En plus il pourrait y avoir des variétés bisa si éloignées du parler « original » qu'elles ne devraient plus être compréhensibles pour les « vrais » locuteurs bisa.

Il demeure cependant un autre problème assez sérieux lié à l'absence d'une variété standardisée du bisa ou de l'une de ses langues avoisinantes, qui est indispensable pour la description des traits de simplification, qu'ils soient d'ordre phonologique, morphologique, lexical, syntaxique ou sémantique. Pour ce qui est de la complexité, aucune des variétés ne peut être considérée de façon décisive comme plus complexe que les autres, et en plus, il y a intelligibilité mutuelle entre toutes les variétés bisa.

Sur la question (3) : Où et pourquoi s'amorce le processus de changement de langue ?

Concernant les deux cinquièmes de la population bisa actuelle qui n'ont plus la maîtrise de cette langue, on peut déduire que ceci est le résultat d'un processus de changement de langue relativement récent (de seulement quelques générations). Cette conclusion se fonde sur une observation qui donne la vague impression que ce changement n'a pas (encore) eu un grand impact, si jamais il y en a eu, sur la langue en tant que symbole de l'identité bisa. Bien que nous ne soyons pas absolument sûrs de ce qui a engendré le changement de langue, il ne semble pas être exagéré de voir une corrélation entre le territoire bisa à prédominance mosi et la large majorité de Bisa, non locuteurs du bisa, qui y résident.

D'un point de vue historique ou diachronique on peut émettre l'hypothèse que la langue bisa en elle-même a vu le jour à travers un processus de créolisation dans lequel le « proto-bissa », la langue des Mandé nouvellement venus dans la région et le « pré-bissa » (signifiant une ou plusieurs langues autochtones d'un stock inconnu) ont dû être imbriqués.

Sur la question (4) : Quels traits grammaticaux du bisa peuvent être attribués aux langues environnantes ?

Cette question demeure entièrement ouverte. Elle ne peut être résolue que dans le cadre d'une coopération étroite des spécialistes des domaines mandé, gur, songhay et probablement d'autres langues de la région.

Références

BALIMA, S.-A., 1996, *Légendes et histoire des peuples du Burkina Faso*, Paris , J.A. Conseil.

DITTMER, K., 1975, Die Obervolta-Provinz. Dans : H. Baumann (éd.), Die Völker Afrikas und ihre traditionellen Kulturen. IIème partie: Ost-, West- und Nordafrika, *Studien zur Kulturkunde*, 35, Wiesbaden, Franz Steiner, 495-542.

FAURE, A., 1996, *Le pays bissa avant le barrage de Bagré. Anthropologie de l'espace rural,* Paris & Ouagadougou, SEPIA – A.D.D.B.

KASTENHOLZ, R., 1991/92, Comparative Mande studies : state of the art, *Sprache und Geschichte in Afrika* 12/13 : 107-158.

KI-ZERBO, J., 1981, *Die Geschichte Schwarz-Afrikas,* Wuppertal, Peter Hammer.

KÖHLER, O., 1975, Geschichte und Probleme der Gliederung der Sprachen Afrikas. Dans : H. Baumann (éd.), Die Völker Afrikas und ihre traditionellen Kulturen. Ière partie : Allgemeiner Teil und südliches Afrika, *Studien zur Kulturkunde*, 34, Wiesbaden, Franz Steiner, 305-337.

MCNAUGHTON, P. R., 1988, *The Mande Blacksmiths. Knowledge, power, and art in West Africa,* Bloomington & Indianapolis : Indiana University Press.

MIDDLETON, J., 1997, Mande, J. Middleton (éd.), *Encyclopedia of Africa South of the Sahara,* Tome 3, New York, Charles Scribner's Sons ; Simon & Schuster Macmillan, 113.

MÜHLHÄUSLER, P., 1986, Pidgin and Creole Linguistics. Oxford: Basil Blackwell. (Expanded and revised edition, 1997, *Westminster Creolistics Series* 3, Londres, University of Westminster Press.)

MUKAROVSKY, H. G., 1966, Zur Stellung der Mandesprachen, *Anthropos* 61 : 679-688.

NICOLAÏ, R., 1989., Songhay et mandé, *Mandekan* 18 : 69-80.

PROST, A., 1950, La langue bisa. Grammaire et dictionnaire, *Etudes voltaïques*, 1, Ouagadougou.

PROST, A., 1953, Notes sur l'origine des Mossi, *Bulletin de l'IFAN* 15 : 1333-1338.

SEBBA, M., 1997, Contact Languages – Pidgins and Creoles, *Modern Linguistic Series,* London, Macmillan.

TAUXIER, L., 1924, *Nouvelles notes sur le mossi et le gourounsi*, Paris, Larose.

VOSSEN, R. & K. KEUTHMANN, 2002, The notion of language island and the case of Bisa in Burkina Faso (West Africa), R. Nicolaï & P. Zima (éd.), *Lexical and Structural Diffusion. Interplay of internal and external factors of language development in the West African Sahel,* (CORPUS – Les Cahiers, 1.), Nice, Université de Nice–Sophia Antipolis, 215-242.

WOLFF, H. E., 1979, Sprachkontakt und Ethnizität : sprachsoziologische Anmerkungen zum Problem der historischen Interpretierbarkeit genetischer Sprachbeziehungen, *Sprache und Geschichte in Afrika* 1 : 143-173.

WOLFF, H. E. & O. ALIDOU, 2001, On the non-linear ancestry of Tasawaq (Niger). Or : how 'mixed' can a language be ?, *Sprache und Geschichte in Afrika* 16/17 : 523-574.

CARTE 1 : LA SITUATION GÉO-LINGUISTIQUE DU BISA

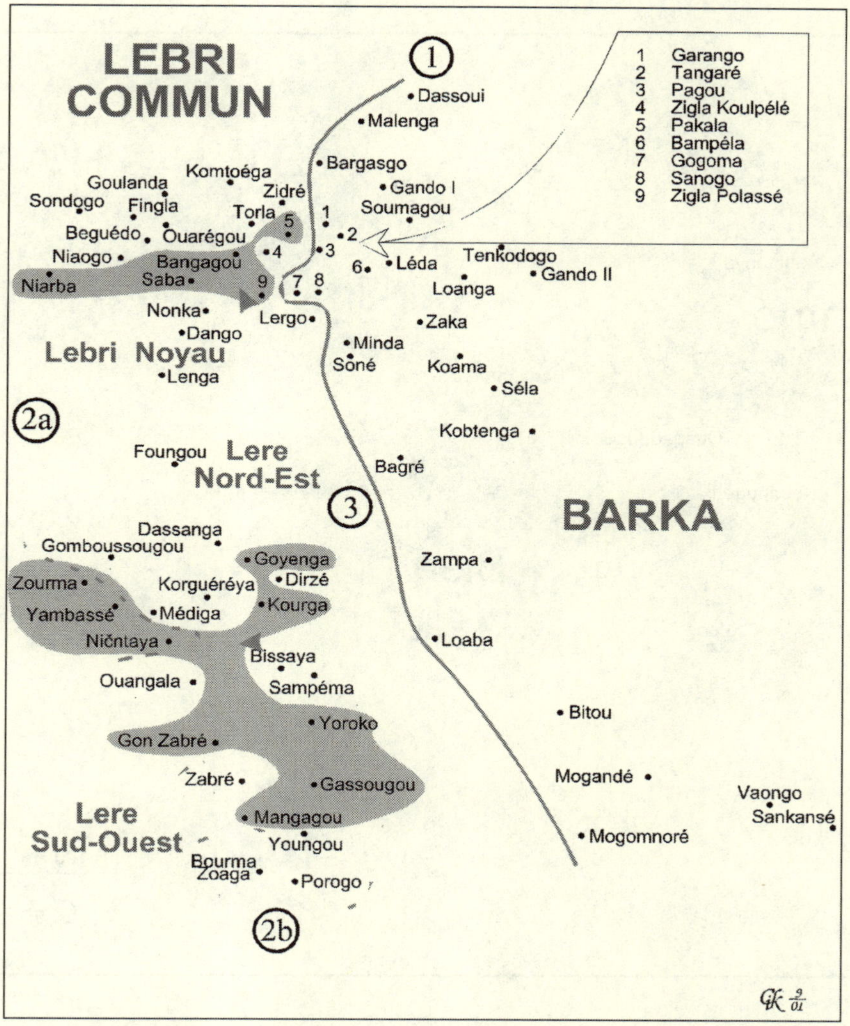

CARTE 2 : LE TERRITOIRE DES BISA
AVANT LA CONFRONTATION AVEC LES MOSI

Molecular genetics relationships of Chadic populations from Northern Cameroon in peri-Saharan Area

Viktor ČERNÝ cerny@arup.cas.cz

Department of Anthropology & Environment, Institute of Archaeology, Czech Academy of Sciences, Letenská 4, 118 01 Prague 1, Czech Republic

Martin HÁJEK

Department of Anthropology & Environment, Institute of Archaeology, Czech Academy of Sciences, Letenská 4, 118 01 Prague 1, Czech Republic

Radek ČMEJLA

Institute of Hematology and Blood Transfusion, U nemocnice 1, 128 20 Prague 2, Czech Republic

Jaroslav BRŮŽEK

Laboratoire d'Anthropologie, University Bordeaux I, Avenue des Facultés, 33 405 Talence, France

Dana ŽÁKOVÁ

Institute of Hematology and Blood Transfusion, U nemocnice 1, 128 20 Prague 2, Czech Republic

Markéta BROMOVÁ

Department of Anthropology & Environment, Institute of Archaeology, Czech Academy of Sciences, Letenská 4, 118 01 Prague 1, Czech Republic

Radim BRDIČKA

Institute of Hematology and Blood Transfusion, U nemocnice 1, 128 20 Prague 2, Czech Republic

Abstract

This paper deals with the mtDNA sequences of four Chadic populations (Hide, Kotoko, Mafa and Masa) from Northern Cameroon, whose biological samples were collected during anthropological research in the area of their homeland. Data collection was based on a strict geographical sampling strategy; the ethnic affiliation of the individuals playing only a secondary role. However, the ethnonyms are retained here for the purposes of comparing the aforementioned groups with other populations living in the peri-Saharan area. None of the examined Chadic populations displays a departure from the normal mismatch distribution pattern, and the null hypothesis of expansion event cannot be rejected. By analysis of FST genetic distances the authors observed that except Mandenka all populations living west of the inland delta of the Niger as well as in North Africa show an important genetic differentiation from the Central and Eastern African groups. The analysis of molecular variance, FST genetic distances and phylogeographic analysis revealed that more than half of the Chadic mtDNA sequences of Northern Cameroon can be traced to the region around the Upper and Middle Nile Valley and the Eastern Africa. This observation is highly surprising if we consider the present-day geographical distance (at about 2,000 km) separating these two groups. This paper is trying to show these molecular genetic observations in the light of recent linguistic and archaeological achievements which consider the Chadic branch in the Afro-Asiatic phylum to be of eastern origin. However, our results show rather important geographical clustering than the correlation of common linguistic classification with molecular genetic data. Moreover, the dating of diversification of a mtDNA cluster specific for the Chadic mtDNA diversification do not coincide with glottochronological and archaeological reconstructions of proto-Chadic settlement in southern part of Chad Basin. In this respect, two different types of estimations of mutation rate are discussed here. A continuous and well-defined geographic sampling strategy of the different genetic polymorphisms of native populations of sub-Saharan Africa is further needed as it is the only way of understanding differentiation of mtDNA sequences in micro-regional scale.

Resumé

Cet article analyse les séquences de l'ADN mitochondrial de quatre populations tchadiques (Hidé, Kotoko, Mafa et Masa) du Cameroun septentrional, dont les échantillons biologiques ont été rassemblés pendant la recherche anthropologique dans le pays. L'échantillonage de données a été basé sur une stratégie de prélèvement géographique stricte ; l'affiliation ethnique des individus jouant seulement un rôle secondaire. Cependant, les ethnonymes sont maintenus ici afin de comparer les groupes mentionnés ci-dessus à d'autres populations vivant dans le secteur péri-Saharien. Aucune des populations tchadiques examinées dans le travail ne s'écarte du modèle normal de distribution, et l'hypothèse nulle de l'événement d'expansion démographique ne peut pas être rejetée. Par analyse des distances génétiques de FST nous avons observé que sauf les Mandenka toutes les populations vivant à l'ouest du delta intérieur du Niger aussi bien qu'en Afrique du Nord montrent une différentiation génétique importante par rapport aux groupes africains centraux et orientaux. L'analyse de la variance moléculaire (AMOVA), les distances génétiques de FST et les analyses phylogéographiques ont révélé que l'origine d'un grand nombre des séquences de l'ADN mitochondrial des populations tchadiques vivant aujourd'hui au Cameroun du Nord peut être située dans la région autour de la vallée supérieure et moyenne du Nil ou en Afrique orientale. Cette observation étonne fortement si nous considérons la distance géographique actuelle (environ 2000 kilomètres) séparant ces deux régions. Cet article essaye d'examiner ces observations de la génétique moléculaire à la lumière des résultats linguistiques et archéologiques récents qui envisagent aussi une origine orientale des langues tchadiques (dans le phylum Afro-Asiatique). Cependant, nos résultats montrent que les groupements géographiques des séquences mitochondriales sont plus importants que les groupements basés sur les classifications linguistiques courantes (méthodes génétiques). D'ailleurs, les dates de diversification des branches mitochondriales revelées chez les populations tchadiques ne coïncident pas avec les reconstructions glottochronologiques des langues proto-tchadiques. À cet égard, deux types différents d'évaluation du taux de mutation de l'ADN mitochondrial sont discutés ici. Néanmoins, une stratégie continue d'échantillonage strictement géographique des populations indigènes de l'Afrique sahélo-soudanienne est nécessaire car c'est la seule manière de comprendre la diversité et la différentiation des séquences de l'ADN mitochondrial à l'échelle microrégionale ou bien encore en confrontation avec les nouvelles méthodes de classification linguistique.

Biochemical and molecular genetic applications in the study of the genetic relationships of various world populations present an archaeogenetic perspective which enables reconstruction of the demographic history and migration pattern at a continental (cf. Cavalli-Sforza et al., 1994; Haeseler et al., 1996), regional (cf. Rickards et al., 2000; Calafell et al., 2000) or even microregional (cf. Manni and Barrai, 2000) scale. The genetic structure of every population contains traces of significant demographic events such as reduction (bottleneck effect), expansion, or absorption of foreign elements (Rogers and Harpending, 1992; Harpending et al., 1993; Relethford, 1998a; Excoffier and Schneider, 2000).

In comparison to other world populations, sub-Saharan populations show a very high degree of genetic diversity in almost all genetic polymorphisms. This was proven during the research undertaken more than a decade ago, and according to a number of authors it can be taken as confirmation of the monophyletic theory and of the African origin of the genetic diversity of contemporary humans (Cann et al., 1987; Vigilant et al., 1991; Tishkoff et al., 1996 but see also Templeton, 1993a, 1993b; Relethford, 1998b). The inhabitants of the Savanna/Sudan belt of Africa are well differentiated from the Pygmies and the Bantu in the south and from the Berbers and Arabs in the north (Excoffier et al., 1987; Cavalli-Sforza et al., 1994), but their mutual relationships are not yet clearly understood.

Recent articles dealing mainly with phylogeographic analysis of sub-Saharan L-types haplogroups revealed many important demographic events in the history of African continent (Watson et al., 1996, 1997; Krings et al., 1999; Torroni et al., 2001; Mateu et al., 1997; Alves-Silva et al., 2000; Rando et al., 1998; Bandelt et al., 2001; Pereira et al., 2001; Salas et al., 2002). However, molecular diversity of the populations living in specific geographic environments is not yet much understood as few samples have been secured in geographically well-defined localities. The geographic origins of the sequences obtained from hospital's patients which are used in such studies are currently deduced from the ethnic affiliations which the donors claim. The samples we analyze here were collected in Northern Cameroon during field examinations by the authors of this article (VC and JB).

The main goals of this paper are to report new mitochondrial DNA (mtDNA) sequences of Chadic speaking populations from Northern Cameroon, to analyze their genetic diversity and to establish their relationships within the peri-Saharan area. Particular attention has been paid to the populations of the Savanna/Sudan belt where the so called Aquatic civilization based on the farming of sorghum and pearl millet developed approximately 8,000-6,000 years ago (Newman, 1995). The Neolithic strategy was, however, accompanied by herding of domestic animals, particularly cattle. These cultural and economic developments were connected according to some linguists with the migration of Chadic or proto-Chadic speakers westwards from the Upper Nile region to the Southern Chad Basin (Blench, 1999; Ehret, 1995).

THE SETTLEMENT OF THE SOUTHERN CHAD BASIN

The Chad Basin can be considered as center of gravity of Central Africa (Holl, 2002). Excavations of its southern part have revealed a huge quantity of archeological sources documenting cultural changes and human movements tightly connected with the changing environment of Lake Chad during past climatic phases (Connah, 1981; Maley, 1981; David and MacEachern, 1988). Permanent settlement is associated with the Early Holocene 8,000-5,000 BP development and the beginnings of Neolithic economy (Rapp, 1984; Delneuf, 1998; Marliac et al., 2000; Holl, 2002). The earliest evidence of Holocene settlement in the Chad Basin is Dufuna in the Upper Yobe valley along Komadugu Guna river in Northern Nigeria. This site provided at the same time the oldest boat (8,000 BP) on the African continent (Breunig, 1996).

The first known Neolithic site is that of Konduga in Nigeria, dated to 6340 ± 250 BC, which has yielded a polished stone industry and ceramics decorated with combed incisions. Subsequent Neolithic records provided many different items such as potsherds decorated with comb impressions, terra-cotta figurines of *Bos sp.*, polished stone axes, ovicaprine bones and even bones of perhaps already domesticated cattle (David and Sterner, 1987, 1989). Later, after the retreat of Lake Chad in the second millennium BC, artificial hillocks resembling tells gradually appearing in lower lying areas announce the beginning of better documented Late Holocene settlement. The archeological data attest permanent or at least semi-permanent villages or dry season camps whose subsistence pattern suggests a combination of livestock breeding, hunting, mollusc-collecting and fishing (Holl, 2002). From the end of the first millennium BC slag appears in archaeological contexts, this being evidence of metallurgy. It is interesting that alongside those groups of inhabitants who began to adopt these technological advances, traditional Neolithic communities survived at the feet of the rocky massifs (Marliac et al., 2000).

Subsequently, rather interior small-scale migrations appeared after the turn of the century. A turning point in terms of settlement pattern came in the 5th-6th centuries AD as an expansion took place across the Chadic plain east of the Mandara Mountains. Waves of infiltrating immigrants are believed to have arrived, mainly from the northeast, and their descendants should be found according to some ethnologists among some groups living east of the Mandara Mountains (Seignobos, 2000). Other populations penetrated into the area in the 7th-11th centuries AD in the face of the expansionism of great state formations, particularly Kanem empire north-east of Lake Chad. In the 15th century there was further immigration into the region from the east by those escaping the Baguirmi kingdom that laid east of the rivers Logone and Shari. In the 15th-17th centuries further and stronger waves of immigrations occurred in the Southern Chad Basin, associated with the expansionism of the Bornu empire situated west of Lake Chad and profiting from the slave trade. Last reported migration is connected with the fall of «Sao» culture (Gronenborn, 1996, 1998; Gronenborn and Magnavita, 2000).

All samples that we obtained in Northern Cameroon come from peoples speaking one of Central Chadic languages. The glottochronological reconstruction of the Chadic languages based on 100 words of Swadesh's list (Barreteau and Jungraithmayr, 1993) has shown that the earliest split in Chadic language group occurred around 4,500-4,100 BP between the Eastern, Central, Southwestern and Northeastern branches. The divergence between the Southwestern and North-eastern branches was further accelerated by the recent expansion of the Nilo-Saharan Kanuri language during the last millennium. According to the recent developments and re-formulations of different methodological approaches it is now accepted that we can rely on the relative chronology of this diversification rather than on absolute dating (Tourneux, personal communication).

MATERIAL AND METHODS

Subjects

The biological samples were obtained from unrelated individuals of local origin attributing themselves to four different ethnic groups belonging to the Chadic branch of the Afro-Asiatic linguistic phylum (Ruhlen, 1987; Barreteau and Dieu, 2000). Two types of environment have been visited in Northern Cameroon. While the Mafa and the Hide – «*les montagnards*» live in the Mandara Mountains, the Masa and the Kotoko «*les riverains*» live in the vicinity of the Logone and Chari rivers respectively (Figure 1).

The sample of Hide was collected at Tourou village on the Cameroon-Nigerian border. The Hide form today a very small ethnic group counting approximately 8,000 people (Hallaire, 1991) and from a linguistic point of view are classified to the South sub-branch of Central Chadic languages. The Mafa sample was collected in Soulede village, which lies approximately 60 km east of Tourou, not far from Mokolo. The village (or rather more densely populated area) can be considered as a center of Mafa speaking territory which regroups some 130,000 inhabitants (Martin, 1970). The Mafa are today the most numerous ethnic group of the Mandara Mountains. Like the Hide, they can be classified linguistically as belonging to the South sub-branch of Central Chadic languages. The third sample has been collected in three close villages (Holouf, Kala Kafra and Maltam) near Kousseri on the border of Cameroon and Chad. The area is inhabited by the people known as Kotoko who are considered in some ethnographic and archaeological literature as direct descendant of above mentioned Sao culture (Griaule, 1943; Lebeuf, 1969; Lebeuf and Lebeuf, 1977; Jansen and Gauthier, 1983). They speak different languages or dialects of the Northern sub-branch of Central Chadic languages (Barreteau and Dieu, 2000). The fourth sample has been secured approximately 200 km southward in four villages in the vicinity of Yagoua also on the Cameroon-Chad border (De Garine, 1964). The inhabitants of these villages speak Masa which, like Hide and Mafa, belongs to the Southern sub-branch of Central Chadic languages which are mainly spread along the Middle Logone river (Barreteau and Dieu, 2000).

We have collected the buccal swabs from non-related volunteers. This type of biological examination is not invasive or painful and provides a sufficient amount of genetic material for our study. This work has been undertaken with the help of local assistants - speakers of all above mentioned Chadic languages. Great attention has been paid not to include maternally related individuals in the study; only adult and health peoples have been examined.

Molecular genetic analysis

The buccal swabs were stored in sterile tubes containing 800µl lysis buffer (50mM Tris pH 8.0, 50mM EDTA pH 8.0, 50mM sucrose, 100mM NaCl, 1% SDS). DNA was isolated from 200µl of the lysis buffer by the QIAquick PCR purification kit (QIAGEN) columns and stored in 70µl of distilled water.

The first hypervariable segment (HVS-I) of the mtDNA control region (D-loop) was amplified between nps 15,975 and 16,421 using the primers L15995 (5'-CTC CAC CAT TAG CAC CCA AAG) and H16401 (5'-TTG ATT TCA CGG AGG ATG GTG) in a total volume of 25µl by PCR. Amplification conditions were as follows: initial denaturation at 94°C for 5 mins. followed by 35 cycles of 94°C for 50 secs., 51°C for 30 secs. and 72°C for 45 secs. Final extension step was 72°C for 5 mins. The quality of the amplicons was estimated visually on a 1.5% agarose gel and re-isolated from it by QIAquick gel extraction kit (QIAGEN) according to manufacture procedures. The samples were subsequently sequenced by application of BigDye Terminator chemistry. The samples containing the length heteroplasmy (most of that containing homopolymeric cytosine stretch from positions 16184 to 16193) were completed by the sequencing of the opposite mtDNA strain.

The coding region of mtDNA where mutations are less frequent but evolutionary more important was analysed by enzymatic digestion of PCR products. The polymorphisms were recorded as present or absent after their electrophoretic separation in 1% agarose gel. Only phylogenetically most important polymorphisms determined by the recently published African mtDNA studies (Alves-Silva et al., 2000; Pereira et al., 2001; Salas et al., 2002) were investigated in this study. We analysed the 3592 *Hpa*I site enabling us to differentiate between the L1 and L2/3 haplotypes, the 16390 *Ava*II site differentiating the L2 and L3 haplotypes (some of them can be read also from the chromatograms) and 2349 *Mbo*I site differentiating the L3e haplotypes which are particularly important in Central Africa/Sudan region (Bandelt et al., 2001).

Statistical analysis

Chromatograms have been viewed by Chromas 1.5 software where only the sequences between nps 16,030 to 16,370 (341bp) according to the Cambridge Reference Sequence (Anderson et al., 1981) have been considered. This segment has been chosen according to the length of the already published African sequences (Watson et al., 1996; Rando et al., 1998; Krings et al., 1999; Côrte-Real et al., 1996; Brakez et al., 2001; Graven et al., 1995). The alignment has been undertaken by BioEdit Sequence Alignment Editor 5.0.9. version (Hall, 1999) and exported subsequently to the TextPad 4.6.2. Editor.

Standard diversity indices were analyzed for each population by means of ARLEQUIN software package (Schneider et al., 2000). Gene diversity h_S and its sampling variance $V(h_S)$ were calculated according to Nei (1987: p180), defining the probability of two randomly chosen haplotypes in the sample being different. Subsequently, the mean number of differences between all pairs in the sample D_{ii} with its total variance $V(D_{ii})$ were calculated (Tajima, 1983, 1993) along with nucleotide diversity π and its variance $V(\pi)$ - or in other words, the probability of two randomly chosen homologous nucleotides being different (Tajima, 1983; Nei, 1987: p257). The irregularities of mismatch distributions (distributions of nucleotide pairwise differences) were tested by the significance of raggedness index (Harpending, 1994).

The mtDNA sequences of the Chadic speaking populations from Northern Cameroon were then compared with the published and available African mtDNA sequences of 22 populations. They were chosen according to the aims of the present study, which is to analyze the genetic relationships of Chadic peoples from Northern Cameroon and establish their possible biological origin in peri-Saharan area.

At the inter-population level the analysis of molecular variance (AMOVA) has been applied. We have joined the populations into six larger geographic groupings: Chadic (Hide, Kotoko, Mafa and Masa), Central (Kanuri, Fulbe, Hausa, Yoruba, Songhai and Tuareg), Western (Serer, Wolof, Mandenka, Mauritanian and Saharawi), Eastern (Nilotic, Somali, Kikuyu, Nubian and Turkana), North-western (Moroccan Arabs, Moroccan Berbers, Berbers from Souss valley and Mozabite Berbers from Ghardaia oasis) and North-eastern

(Egyptians from Lower Egypt and Egyptians from Upper Egypt). Subsequently, we have investigated how the proportion of genetic variance is distributed among the groups, among the populations within the groups and within the populations.

FST genetic distances between the populations were calculated using the pairwise difference method, and 1,000 permutations were used to compute statistical significance at the level of 0.05 (Weir and Cockerham, 1984). To visualise these FST distances between the populations the multidimensional scaling analysis (MDS) in STATISTICA 5.5 software (StatSoft) and the neighbour-joining tree in PHYLIP software packages were employed. The stress factor of the MDS analysis indicates whether the model based on the matrix of bilateral distances is sufficiently robust and really reflects mtDNA similarities and dissimilarities among the groups. This analysis can be considered as an alternative to the factor analysis.

Subsequently, we established the phylogenetic relationships of Chadic mtDNA haplotypes by the application of the reduced median network in the Network 3.1 software (Bandelt et al., 1995, 1999). Because the HVS-I comprises also mutations with extremely high mutation rate (so called hot spots or recurrent mutations), we were obliged to bring down their weights. The identification of these hot spots was done according to the recent knowledge (Forster et al., 2002) as well as according to experiences we obtained during the construction of the networks. On the other hand, we have increased the weights of the evolutionary more stable mutations in coding region two times.

RESULTS

All 341bp (nps 16,030-16,370) long mtDNA sequences of HVS-I control region (Anderson et al., 1981) were analyzed for 108 maternally unrelated individuals of four Chadic speaking populations from Northern Cameroon (25 Hide, 32 Mafa, 19 Kotoko and 32 Masa). Among the homologous positions we observed 89 polymorphic sites at the analysed segment. In total, only 1 individual (Hide 45) had the same sequence in the analyzed segment as that referred to by Anderson et al. (1981) and can be thus classified to haplogroups R, U, H, HV or H. Of the 93 substitutions there is a transition bias (70 transitions versus 23 transversions), which is also frequently observed in other human populations (Watson et al., 1996). No indels have been detected out of the homopolymeric cytosine stretch (nps 16184-16193) and the resulted length heteroplasmy was not considered in further analyses.

The main statistical parameters of mtDNA diversity of all 26 populations are listed in Table 1. From the gene (h_s) and nucleotide (π) diversities as well as from the mean number of pairwise differences (D_{ii}) some sort of order appears. Compared with the other sub-Saharan populations, the Chadic group (0.981; 0.025 and 8.426 for h_s, π and D_{ii} in average respectively) is situated somewhere between the

Eastern (0.990; 0.027 and 9,132) and Central (0.977; 0.022 and 7.694) Africa; the populations from Eastern Africa having the highest diversity parameters. The indexes of molecular diversity decrease from the East to West Africa, the Berber samples being the most homogenous (0.964; 0.016 and 5.386). We have also tested the null hypothesis of populations evolving at constant size in mutation drift equilibrium by employing Tajima's D and Fu's F_S statistics. All analysed samples had significant values for Fu's F_S statistics (data not shown). The significant F_S values provide an indication of past demographic expansion which is effaced today only in some hunter-gatherers, such as the Pygmies or !Kung (Pereira et al., 2001; Excoffier and Schneider, 1999, 2000).

We assume that the similar molecular diversity values of the Chadic samples which were collected sometimes also in close dwellings in a village could be taken as an indirect proof that our sampling strategy is not biased by overestimation of same or very similar mtDNA sequences (kin-related individuals). Only differences which can be observed in the Chadic samples present the higher values of the variance of the mean number of pairwise differences.

If the mismatch distribution is plotted (not shown), then the greatest departure from a normal distribution occurs in the Mafa sample. Nevertheless, the Harpending's raggedness index does not attain statistical significance. Grouping together all four Chadic populations non-significant departure from normal distribution was observed too (Harpending's raggedness index 0,004; p=0,73).

The AMOVA shows that when the Chadic group is taken as an independent group the proportion of variance among the groups, among the populations within the groups and within the populations is 5.04%, 4.67% and 90.29% respectively. Subsequently, we have tried to merge the Chadic group to the others. The proportion of variance among the groups increase only when the Chadic group is merged with the Eastern group (5.15; 4.65 and 90.20% respectively). It means that the Chadic mtDNA sequences can be considered to some extent as a part of Eastern African group. We tried also to determine which of the Chadic populations correspond at the least with this Chadic-Eastern Africa model. In this respect we can range an order Mafa-Hide-Masa-Kotoko showing approximately the west-east gradient.

The F_{ST} distances among the populations reveal some very interesting observations. The only statistically significant difference among Chadic samples can be found between the Mafa and Masa. The only analyzed population similar to each of the Chadic group is the Kanuri which is, however, predictable from its close geographic proximity. The Hide, as the Chadic population with the most numerous mtDNA similarities, is not differentiated from the Eastern African populations such as Somali, Kikuyu and Nilotic and from all Central Africans. More similarities with Central African populations are for the Hide also well explicable in context of its geographical situation as they live on Cameroon/Nigeria boundary. However, the genetic distances of other Chadic populations are not so easily interpretable according to their geographical situation in the Savanna/Sudan belt. While the Kotoko are differentiated only from the Somali, Hausa, Fulbe and Songhay, the Mafa as the population from the most statistically significant differences is not differentiated only from the Kanuri. The Masa as well as the Kotoko, both living on Cameroon/ Chad boundary, reveal also more similarities with the Eastern African populations than with the Central African group.

The neighbour-joining tree based on the F_{ST} distances is shown in Figure 2. By this application, we can see that whereas the Chadic speaking populations from Mandara Mountains (Hide and Mafa) form their own branch, more eastern Chadic populations from Logone and Chari rivers (Kotoko and Masa) share the branch with Eastern African populations such as the Nilotic, Kikuyu and Turkana. Another branch is composed mainly by the Central African populations (Kanuri, Tuareg, Hausa, Songhai, Yoruba, Fulbe and Mandenka) and finally, the longest fourth branch is put together by all Northern African and most Western African populations.

Another representation of the F_{ST} genetic distances among the populations considered in this study, has been provided by the MDS analysis (Figure 3). The relatively low stress factor (0.092) testifies that the configuration shown in the picture reproduces well the original matrix of genetic distances. We can assess not only the distances between the populations living on the opposite sides of the Sahara, but also the specific relationships among the groups within these clusters. It is interesting that the Chadic populations (particularly Kotoko) are situated very close to the Eastern group which is composed by the populations such as the Kikuyu, Turkana, Nilotic and Somali. This observation confirms the AMOVA and neighbour-joining results. We can see also that the configuration of these distances reflects well the geographical extensions of the populations in sub-Saharan Africa.

According to the molecular resolution which we obtained up to now, we could attribute Chadic mtDNA sequences to the haplogroups whose origins had been established by the phylogeographic studies of different authors dealing with the sub-Saharan sequence and RFLP data (Watson et al., 1996, 1997; Torroni et al., 2001; Alves-Silva et al., 2000; Rando et al., 1998; Bandelt et al., 2001; Salas et al., 2002; Pereira et al., 2001). According to the mutations observed in the coding region and in the HVS-I, we were able to divide our Chadic mtDNA sequences into different haplogroups. From 108 haplotypes, we can attribute only one to the haplogroup of European or Euro-Asiatic origin. It is one Hide man from Tourou village who has the identical sequence motif as 40% of Europeans (haplogroup H). All other individuals can be classified to the different L-type sequences of sub-Saharan origin. It should be noted that the haplogroup L3 and its «daughter» L3e whose origins (as well as higher recent molecular diversities) are located in Eastern Africa and Central Africa/Sudan region respectively are best represented in our Chadic sample (56%). If we count up also the Eastern origin of haplogroups L1a, the affiliations of analysed Chadic sequences to Eastern Africa gene pool is even higher (67%). The geographic origin for L1b and L2a is not yet determined (Salas et al., 2002).

After calculation of reduced median analysis of L3 Chadic haplotypes we have obtained the network (Figure 4) where a cluster, which was not published before, can be identified. It can be considered as composed by specific Central African (Chadic) mtDNA haplotypes represented by the Koto 45, Mafa 8, Masa 95, Masa 89 and Masa 96. The origin of that cluster can be estimated by means of the Network software at 12,108 ± 6,990 years BP. The question is, however, if we could interpret this divergence time in light of Chadic expansion which is proposed by the linguistic and archaeological studies (see Discussion).

DISCUSSION

mtDNA case study

A difficulty may be seen in the fact that the type of sample collection we employed in this study cannot exclude the accumulation of individuals who are genetically related, as people often simply forget or do not mention their kinship relationships - especially those more than five generations back in their genealogies. The authors' questionnaires, therefore, were not able to exclude such individuals from the mtDNA analysis. In spite of the risk of obtaining identical sequences from the descendants of a common, already forgotten, maternal ancestor, the authors' results show that all of the parameters of molecular diversity are perfectly comparable to those samples which have been obtained from the hospitals and rural medical clinics frequented by different certainly unrelated individuals from places where the hospital is available or from surrounding villages. Only the variance of the mean number of pairwise differences is higher in all four Chadic samples. For the instant we have no explication for this observation.

On the other hand, it is interesting to see some biases in the mismatch distributions among populations closely related geographically, culturally and economically. Previous works have interpreted differences in mismatch distribution as a consequence of the expansion reproductive pattern, which differs between hunter-gatherer and agricultural populations (Rogers and Harpending, 1992; Watson et al., 1996). However, it can be seen that even some agricultural or pastoral populations can show significant departures from normal mismatch distribution – the Saharawi in this study sample.

As to the HVS-I of mtDNA, the peri-Saharan populations can be divided into two different groups. The first comprises of the populations of Northern Africa and some populations from Western Africa such as the Saharawi, Mauritanians, Wolof and Serer. The second group is composed exclusively of the populations of sub-Saharan Africa and a certain correlation between the genetic and geographical distances can be identified. The mtDNA differentiation of the Western populations (Serer, Wolof, Mauritanians and Saharawi) and their affinity with the North African populations can be attributed to their geographical separation behind the Middle Delta of Niger. This part of Africa could constitute in Early Holocene period starting about 12,000 years ago hardly penetrable swampland environment which can be considered as barrier of gene flow. Another explication concerns the Saharan or Berber influences during the establishment of Maghreb state polities from 11th century onwards.

The multivariate and phylogenetic analyses of mtDNA sequences obtained from Chadic speaking populations of Northern Cameroon, testifies about their relationships with the Eastern Africans. According to our opinion, it is surprising if we consider the present-day geographical distance (at about 2,000 km) separating these two groups. It is important to note in this respect that according to the linguistic reconstruction of Afro-Asiatic linguistic family the common ancestors of Chadic and Cushitic people inhabited the area of Middle Nile at about 6,000 years ago (Blench, 1993, 1999). Subsequently, two migrations proceeded from this area – the first directed southward contributed to the diversification of Cushitic languages in Eastern Africa and the second directed westward contributed the diversification of the Chadic languages in Chad basin (Blench, 1999). The archaeological remains of the second Chadic migration are visible along the Wadi Howar in Sudan as the «*Leiterband*» pottery (Kuper, 1981; Keding, 1993); unfortunately the area of Chad was not still archaeologically prospected. It is estimated that the Chadic migration could reach the shores of Lake Chad at about 4,000 BP. The recent linguistic study of the Cushitic and Chadic languages would be particularly interesting in this respect. Unfortunately no modern synthetic study is available at the moment (Tourneux, Jungraithmayr, Leger, personal communications).

If the migration or colonization of Chadic peoples really took place from the Middle Nile we should find significantly higher genetic diversity in the Eastern Chadic populations living in Chad compared to Western Chadic populations living mainly in Nigeria. The genetic diversity of populations living in this space is a likely candidate for evidence of the past migration of Chadic peoples from the confluence of the Blue and White Nile through Wadi Howar and Wadi Hawach to the South Chad Basin. Unfortunately, there are no mtDNA sequences available from the Chadic speaking populations actually living in the vast territory east and west of Lake Chad in Chad and Nigeria respectively. The migration route can be seen also in the archaeological record as so-called «*leiterband*» pottery in Wadi Howar, which shows strong links with the Khartoum Neolithic (Kuper, 1981; Keding, 1993). Furthermore, it may also be that the close genetic relationship of the east Sudanese Beja with the Saharan Tuareg (Cavalli-Sforza et al., 1994), otherwise difficult to explain, could also be an ancient relict of such a connection.

It is difficult to say whether the present similarities in the mtDNA sequences of the Chadic and Eastern Sudanese groups are a consequence of ancient movement of «*leiterband*» peoples or of gene flow associated with more recent cultural and political development in the area. It should be noted that most of the data published to date have been obtained from hospitals and rural medical clinics and not from the peoples at defined geographical locations. Individuals of different geographic origins may be present in these samples and the results of more focused regional mtDNA analyses can thus be difficult to carry on. To identify the haplogroups involved in such possible movement we would need not only the samples to be from precise geographic locations and selected Chadic speakers but also to have higher molecular resolution of the data.

Dating of mtDNA diversification by network analysis is commonly based on the phylogenetic estimations of mutation rate. It issues from the differences between the human and chimpanzee mtDNA HVS-I sequences and from the palaeo-anthropological records dating the separation of these two species. Another estimation of mutation rate is based on the genealogical data and reveals that the mutation events of HVS-I are in fact much more frequent (Heyer et al., 2001; Sigurgardottir et al., 2000; Howell et al., 2003). These rates are however not acceptable for the evolutionary biologists since they consider that many new mutations, which were in the past demographically very small, disappear very quickly from the main evolutionary lines. It is certainly true but a question remains if this phylogenetic reasoning can be applied also for much more recent micro-evolutionary scenarios appearing long after the diversification of anatomically modern humans. If we would base our molecular dating on some «calibrated» mutation rates we should obtain dates which could correspond better with linguistically based dating or archaeological evidences. On the other hand we have to admit that the divergence times may also be underestimated because of the influence of recurrent mutations. It is important to remind that the evolution of the genes is fundamentally different from that of cultural or linguistic traits (see nature versus nurture discourse in anthropology).

Genetic sampling method: ethnic or geographic principle?

Since recent discussion on the ethnicity of people and the biological relationships between them (MacEachern 2000, 2001; Spedini et al., 2001) is directly linked to the object (and more-or-less also with the subjects) of this research, the authors feel a need to note some relevant points here. Spedini et al. (1999) suppose the relatively high ethnic stability of Afro-Asiatic populations in their sample, as they expect that recent ethnic groups originated from the first agriculturists of the so called «Savanna complex». This claim is hard to accept given that MacEachern's (2001) work on archaeological assemblages indicates frequent ethnic changes in the area. On the other hand, it should also be noted that for biological anthropologists such social and/or cultural features as the ethnic identity or linguistic affiliation are, unfortunately, often the only ways of attributing a grouping variable to their biological data. Human cultures (including genes and words) are mixed amalgams of elements of different origins and histories, and the ethnonyms should be taken as simple labels in such analyses. The extent of genetic diversity of culturally or linguistically determined groups which have passed through different demographically significant events in their history is, however, interesting. It is the authors' opinion, that it is hard to believe that such ethnic labels could represent anything more than the genetic variability of a limited geographical area in which the people in question more frequently mate. Analyses of the phylogeographic relationships of genetic data do not use the ethnonyms at all - but in a study of the geographical distribution of genetic polymorphisms, such as that of Spedini et al. (1999) or this one, there is little chance of avoiding it.

Another study (Langlois, 2001), dealing with the contemporary distribution of ceramic traditions, and geographically covering a much wider area, has recorded the phenomenon of the distribution of different types of ceramic production among 60 ethnic groups of the Southern Chad Basin. This can also serve as another grouping variable whose genetic diversity can be tested. Since ceramic production in the area is purely an affair of women, it can be supposed that the mtDNA sequences, which are also inherited throw the female line, can be transmitted together. In spite of the promising value of this type of data analysis it is difficult to expect that the mating pattern could be stopped on these cultural borders for a relatively long time, in biological terms. Young girls might pass the borders of ceramic traditions and in a relatively short time adopt the ways of their mothers-in-law. Nevertheless, these «ceramic's type boundaries» could perhaps yield more accurate information in the future. Much as the authors would want to test this correlation, the mtDNA sequences from that area currently cover only a small part of the aforementioned ethnic groups.

The extent of mutual independence and differences of certain ethnic groups in comparison with others is more obvious at the edges than in the centers of their geographical range (Diallo and Schlee, 2000). Expressions of ethnicity are found rather where people meet others speaking a different language, with a substantially different social organization, and holding to different cultural traditions and values. Generally a group which through migration has left its original territory must, in the new social context of its diaspora, re-define a range of its spiritual and material values. The stability of ethnic or national groups can thus be best assessed at its borders, the shape of which may change remarkably over time. For this further reason the authors consider the geographic aspect (complemented secondarily by archaeological, linguistic and ethnographic observations) as the main criterion of sample formation for an archaeogenetic microregional survey.

ACKNOWLEDGEMENTS

Anthropological investigation in the area was authorized by a research permit granted by the Cameroon's authorities and obtained through the aid of local assistants. The authors wish to express their gratitude to the volunteers for their confidence and their helpful participation in the study. We are particularly indebted to our assistants Isa Kawalde, Pierre Ndoumai, Pongo Loumnagué and Moumoun Malloum Mey. The authors are also very grateful Pastor Hans and Gertrude Eichenbergers for their understanding of the biological research and the invaluable help that they provided in Cameroon. The project was supported by the Grant Agency of the Czech Republic (under grant no. 404/03/0318), the CNRS (Unit 5809) and the Mellon Fellowship program (CAORC).

References

ALVES-SILVA, J., da Silva Santos, M., Guimaraes, P. E., Ferreira, A. C., Bandelt, H.-J., Pena, S. D., Prado, V. F., 2000, *The ancestry of Brazilian mtDNA lineages. American Journal of Human Genetics*, 67, 444-461.

ANDERSON S., BANKIER A. T., BARRELL B. G., BRUIJN M. H. L., COULSON A. R., DROUIN J., EPERON I. C., NIERLICH D. P., ROE B. A., SANGER F., SCHREIER P. H., SMITH A. J. H., STADEN R., YOUNG I. G., 1981, Sequence and organization of the human mitochondrial genome, *Nature*, 290, 457-465.

BANDELT, H.-J., FORSTER, P., RÖHL, A., 1999, Median-joining networks for inferring intraspecific phylogenies, *Molecular Biology and Evolution*, 16, 37-48.

BANDELT, H.-J., FORSTER, P., SYKES, B. C., RICHARDS, M. B., 1995, Mitochondrial portraits of human populations using median networks, *Genetics*, 141, 743-753.

BANDELT, H.-J., ALVES-SILVA, J., GUIMARAES, P. E., SANTOS, M. S., BREHM, A., PEREIRA, L., COPPA, A., LARRUGA, J. M., RENGO, C., SCOZZARI, R., TORRONI, A., PRATA, M. J., AMORIM, A., PRADO, V. F., PENA, S. D., 2001, Phylogeography of the human mitochondrial haplogroup L3e: a snapshot of African prehistory and Atlantic slave trade, *Annals of Human Genetics*, 65, 549-563.

BARRETEAU D., DIEU M., 2000, Linguistique, *Atlas de la province Extreme-Nord Cameroun,* Seignobos C., Iyébi-Mandjek O. (Editors), Paris, Editions IRD, p. 64-70.

BARRETEAU D., JUNGRAITHMAYR, H., 1993, Calculs lexicostatistiques et glottochronologiques sur les langues tchadiques, *Datations et chronologie dans le bassin du lac Tchad.* Barreteau D., von Graffenried Ch. (Editors), Paris, Editions ORSTOM, p. 103-140.

BLENCH R., 1993, Recent developments in African language classification and their implications for prehistory, *The Archaeology of Africa: Food, Metals and Towns,* Shaw T., Sinclair P., Andah B., Okpoko A. (Editors), London and New York, Routledge, p. 126-138.

BLENCH R., 1999, The westward wandering of Cushitic pastoralists. Explorations in the prehistory of Central Africa, *L'Homme et l'animal dans le bassin du lac Tchad.* Baroin C., Boutrais J., (Editors), Paris, Editions IRD, p. 39-80.

BRAKEZ, Z., BOSCH, E., IZAABEL, H., AKHAYAT, O, COMAS, D., BERTRANPETIT, J., CALAFELL, F., 2001, Human mitochondrial DNA sequence variation in the Moroccan population of the Souss area, *Annals of Human Biology*, 28, 295-307.

BREUNIG P. A., 1995, *The Dufuna dugout: Africa's oldest boat,* Abstracts: 10th congress of the Pan African Association for Prehistory and Related Studies, p. 16. Harare.

BREUNIG P. A., 1996, The 8000-year-old dugout canoe from Dufuna (NE Nigeria), *Aspects of African Archaeology*, Papers from the 10th Congress of the PanAfrican Association for Prehistory and Related Studies, G. Pwiti and R. Soper (Editors), Harare, University of Zimbabwe Publications, pp. 461-468.

CALAFELL F., COMAS D., PÉREZ-LEZAUN A., BerTranpetit J., 2000, Genetics and population history of Central Asia, *Archaeogenetics: DNA and the population prehistory of Europe,* Renfrew C., Boyle K., (Editors), Cambridge, McDonald Institute for Archaeological Research, p. 259-266.

CANN R., STONEKING M., WILSON A., 1987, Mitochondrial DNA and human evolution, *Nature*, 325, 31-36.

CAVALLI-SFORZA L. L., MENOZZI P., PIAZZA A., 1994, *The history and geography of human genes,* Princeton, Princeton University Press.

CONNAH G., 1981, *Three thousand years in Africa. Man and his environment in Lake Chad region of Nigeria,* Cambridge, Cambridge University Press.

CÔRTE-REAL, H. B., MACAULAY, V. A., RICHARDS, M. B., HARITI, G., ISSAD, M. S., CAMBON-THOMSEN, A., PAPIHA, S., BERTRANPETIT, J. and SYKES, B.C., 1996, Genetic diversity in the Iberian Peninsula determined from mitochondrial sequence analysis, *Annals of Human Genetics*, 60, 331-350.

DAVID N., MACEACHERN S., 1988, The Mandara Archaeological Project: preliminary results of the 1984 season, *Le millieu et les hommes, recherches comparatives et historiques dans le bassin du Lac Tchad. 2éme colloque Méga-Tchad, octobre 1985*, Barreteau D., Tourneux H. (Editors), Paris, ORSTOM, p. 51-80.

DAVID N., STERNER S., 1987, *The Mandara archaeological project, 1984-87,* Nyame Akuma, 29, 2-8.

DAVID N., STERNER S., 1989, *The Mandara archaeological project, 1988-89,* Nyame Akuma, 32, 5-9.

DE GARINE I., 1964, *Les Massa du Cameroun. Vie économique et sociale*, Paris, Etudes Ethnographiques.

DELNEUF M., 1998, Les recherches archéologiques menées par l'Orstom au Cameroun septentrional, *Paléo-anthropologie en Afrique centrale: un bilan de l'archéologie au Cameroun,* Delneuf M, Essomba J-M and Froment A. (ed), Paris, L'Harmattan. P. 91-124.

DIALLO Y., SCHLEE G., 2000, *L'ethnicité peule dans des contextes nouveaux*, Paris, Karthala.

EHRET C., 1995, Reconstructing Proto-Afroasiatic (Proto-Afrasian): Vowels, Tone, Consonants, and Vocabulary, *University of California Publications in Linguistics*, Vol. 126, Berkeley and Los Angeles, University of California Press.

EXCOFFIER L., PELLEGRINI B., SANCHEZ-MAZAS A., SIMON Ch., Langaney A., 1987, Genetics and history of sub-Saharan Africa, *Yearbook of Physical Anthropology*, 30, 151-194.

EXCOFFIER L., SCHNEIDER S., 1999, Why hunter-gatherer populations do not show signs of Pleistocene demographic espansions, *Proceedings of the National Academy of Sciences of the United States of America*, 96, 10597-10602.

EXCOFFIER L., SCHNEIDER S., 2000, The demography of human populations inferred from patterns of mitochondrial DNA diversity, *Archaeogenetics: DNA and the population prehistory of Europe,* Renfrew C., Boyle K., (Editors), Cambridge, McDonald Institute for Archaeological Research, p. 101-108.

FORSTER L., FORSTER P., LUTZ-BONENGEL S., WILLKOMM H., BRINKMANN B., 2002, Natural radioactivity and human mitochondrial DNA mutations, *Proceedings of the National Academy of Sciences of the United States of America*, 99, 13950-13954.

GRAVEN L., PASSARINO G., SEMINO O., BOURSOT P., SANTACHIARA-BENERECETTI S., LANGANEY A., EXCOFFIER L., 1995, Evolutionary correlation between control region sequence and restriction polymorphisms in the mitochondrial genome of large Senegalese Mandenka sample, *Molecular Biology and Evolution*, 12, 334-345.

GRIAULE M., 1943, *Les Sao legendaires*, Paris, Gallimard.

GRONENBORN D., 1996, Beyond Daima: recent excavations in the Kala-Balge region of Borno state, *Nigerian Heritage*, 5, 34-46.

GRONENBORN D., 1998, Archaeological and ethnohistorical investigations along the southern fringes of Lake Chad, 1993-1996, *African Archaeological Review*, 15, 225-259.

GRONENBORN D., MAGNAVITA C., 2000, Imperial expansion, ethnic change, and ceramic traditions in the Southern Chad Basin: a terminal nineteenth-century pottery assemblage from Dikwa, Borno state, Nigeria, *International Journal of Historical Archaeology* 4, 35-70.

HAESELER A., SAJANTILA A., PÄÄBO S., 1996, The genetical archaeology of the human genome, *Nature Genetics*, 14, 135-140.

HALL, T.A., 1999, BioEdit: a user-friendly biological sequence alignment editor and analysis program for Windows 95/98/NT, *Nucleic Acids Symposium Series*, 41, 95-98.

HALLAIRE A., 1991, *Paysans montagnards du Nord-Cameroun. Les monts Mandara,* Paris, Editions ORSTOM.

HARPENDING H. C., SHERRY S. T., ROGERS A. R., Stoneking M., 1993, The genetic structure of ancient human populations, *Current Anthropology*, 34, 483-496.

HARPENDING R.C., 1994, Signature of ancient population growth in a low-resolution mitochondrial DNA mismatch distribution, *Human Biology*, 66, 591-600.

HEYER E., ZIETKIEWICZ E., ROCHOWSKI A., YOTOVA V., PUYMIRAT J., LABUDA D., 2001, Phylogenetic and familial estimates of mitochondrial substitution rates: study of control region mutations in deep-rooting pedigrees, *American Journal of Human Genetics*, 69, 1113-1126.

HOLL, A. F. C., 2002, The land of Houlouf. Genesis of a Chadic polity, 1900 B.C.-A.D. 1800, *Museum of Anthropology*, University of Michigan, Number 35, Ann Arbor, Michigan.

HOWELL N., SMEJKAL C. B., MACKEY D. A., CHINNERY P. F., TURNBULL D. M., HERRNSTADT C., 2003, The pedigree rate of sequence divergence in the human mitochondrial genome: there is a difference between phylogenetic and pedigree rates, *American Journal of Human Genetics*, 72, 659-670.

JANSEN G., GAUTHIER J. G., 1983, Ancient art of the Northern Cameroons: Sao and Fali. Oosterhout, *Anthropological publications.*

KEDING B., 1993, Leiterband sites in the Wadi Howar, North Sudan, *Environmental change and human culture in the Nile Basin and Northern Africa until the Second millennium B.C.*, Krzyzaniak L., Kobusiewicz L., Alexander J, (Editors), Poznan Archaeological Museum, p. 371-380.

KRINGS M., SALEM A. H., BAUER K., GEISERT H., MALEK A. K., CHAIX L., SIMON Ch., WELSBY D., DI RIENZO A., UTERMANN G., SAJANTILA A., PÄÄBO S., STONEKING M., 1999, mtDNA analysis of Nile river valley populations: a genetic corridor or a barrier to migration?, *American Journal of Human Genetics*, 64, 1166-1176.

KUPER R., 1981, Untersuchungen zur Besiedlunsgeschiche der östlichen Sahara. Vorbericht über die Expedition 1980, *Beitrage zur Allgemeinen und Vergleichenden Archäologie*, 3, 215-275.

LANGLOIS O., 2001, La distribution des techniques de façonnage de la poterie au sud du bassin tchadien: un outil pour la recherche historique régionale, *Journal des Africanistes*, 71, 225-256.

LEBEUF J-P., 1969, *Carte archéologique des abords du Lac Tchad Cameroun, Nigeria, Tchad.* Paris, Editions C.N.R.S.

LEBEUF J.-P., LEBEUF A.M.D., 1977, *Les arts des Sao*, Paris, Editions Chêne.

MACEACHERN S., 2000, Genes, Tribes, and African History, *Current Anthropology*, 41, 357-384.

MACEACHERN S., 2001, Montagnard ethnicity and genetic relations in Northern Cameroon: comment on «the peopling of sub-Saharan Africa: the case study of Cameroon,» by G. Spedini et al., *American Journal of Physical Anthropology*, 114, 357-360.

MALEY J., 1981, *Etudes palynologiques dans le bassin du Tchad et paléoclimatologie de l'Afrique nord-tropicale de 30.000 ans a l'epoque actuelle,* Paris, Editions ORSTOM.

MANNI F., BARRAI I., 2000, Patterns of genetics and linguistic variation in Italy: a case study, *Archaeogenetics: DNA and the population prehistory of Europe,* Renfrew C., Boyle K., (Editors), Cambridge, McDonald Institute for Archaeological Research, p. 333-338.

MARLIAC A., LANGLOIS O., DELNEUF M., 2000, Archéologie de la région Mandara-Diamaré. In: Seignobos C, Iyébi-Mandjek O. (Editors), *Atlas de la province Extreme-Nord Cameroun,* Paris, Editions IRD, p. 71-76.

MARTIN J-Y., 1970, *Les Matakam du Cameroun: essai sur la dynamique d'une société pré-industrielle*, Paris, Mémoire ORSTOM, Sciences Humaines 41.

MATEU E., Comas D., Calafell F., Perez-Lezaun A., Abade A., Bertranpetit J., 1997, A tale of two islands: population history and mitochondrial DNA sequence variation of Bioko and Sao Tome, Gulf of Guinea, *Annals of Human Genetics*, 61, 507-518.

NEI M., 1987, *Molecular evolutionary genetics*, New York, Columbia University Press.

NEWMAN J.L., 1995, *The peopling of Africa: a geographic interpretation*, New Haven, Yale University Press.

PEREIRA L., MACAULAY V., TORRONI A., SCOZZARI R., PRATA M. J., AMORIM A., 2001, Prehistoric and historic traces in the mtDNA of Mozambique: insights into the Bantu expansions and the slave trade, *Annals of Human Genetics*, 65, 439-458.

RANDO J.C., PINTO F., GONZALEZ A. M., HERNANDEZ M., LARRUGA J. M., CABRERA V. M., BANDELT H. J., 1998, Mitochondrial DNA analysis of northwest African populations reveals genetic exchanges with European, near-eastern, and sub-Saharan populations, *Annals of Human Genetics*, 62, 531-550.

RAPP J., 1984, *Quelques aspects des civilisations Néolithiques et post-Néolithiques de l'extreme Nord-Cameroun. Etude des décors céramiques et essai de chronologie,* Tome I/II. [PhD dissertation]. Université Bordeaux I.

RELETHFORD J. H., 1998a, Mitochondrial DNA and ancient population growth, *American Journal of Physical Anthropology*, 105, 1-7.

RELETHFORD J. H., 1998b, Genetics of modern human origins and diversity, *Annual Review of Anthropology*, 27, 1-23.

RICKARDS O., MARTÍNEZ-LABARGA C., CASALOTTI R., CASTELLANA G., TUNZI SISTO A.M., MALLEGNI F., 2000, MtDNA variability in extinct and extant populations of Sicily and Southern Italy, *Archaeogenetics: DNA and the population prehistory of Europe*, Renfrew C., Boyle K., (Editors), Cambridge, McDonald Institute for Archaeological Research, p. 175-183.

ROGERS A. R., HARPENDING H., 1992, Population growth makes waves in the distribution of pairwise genetic differences, *Molecular Biology and Evolution*, 9, 552-569.

RUHLEN M., 1987, *A guide to the world's languages,* Volume 1: Classification. Stanford, Stanford University Press.

SALAS A., RICHARDS M., DE LA FE T., LAREU M. V., SOBRINO B., SANCHEZ-DIZ P., MACAULAY V., CARRACEDO A., 2002, The making of the African mtDNA landscape, *American Journal of Human Genetics*, 71, 1082-1111.

SEIGNOBOS Ch., 2000, Mise en place du peuplement et répartition ethnique, *Atlas de la province Extreme-Nord Cameroun,* Seignobos C., Iyébi-Mandjek O. (Editors), Paris, Editions IRD, p. 44-51.

SCHNEIDER S., ROESSLI D., EXCOFFIER L., 2000, *Arlequin ver. 2.000: A software for population genetics data analysis,* Genetics and Biometry Laboratory, University of Geneva, Switzerland.

SIGURGARDOTTIR S., HELGASON A., GULCHER J. R., STEFANSSON K., DONNELLY P., 2000, The mutation rate in the human mtDNA control region, *American Journal of Human Genetics*, 66, 1599-1609.

SPEDINI G., DESTRO-BISOL G., MONDOVI S., KAPTUE L., TAGLIOLI L., PAOLI G., 1999, The peopling of sub-Saharan Africa: the case study of Cameroon, *American Journal of Physical Anthropology*, 110, 143-162.

SPEDINI G., MONDOVI S., PAOLI G., DESTRO-BISOL G., 2001, Biological and cultural contradictions? A replay to MacEachern, *American Journal of Physical Anthropology*, 114, 361-364.

TAJIMA F., 1983, Evolutionary relationship of DNA sequences in finite populations, *Genetics*, 105, 437-460.

TAJIMA F., 1993, Measurement of DNA polymorphism, *Mechanisms of Molecular Evolution. Introduction to Molecular Paleopopulation Biology,* Takahata N., Clark A.G. (Editors), Tokyo, Sunderland: Scientific Societies Press, Sinauer Associates, Inc., p. 37-59.

TEMPLETON A.R., 1993a, The «Eve» hypothesis: a genetic critique and reanalysis, *American Anthropologist*, 95, 51-72.

TEMPLETON A.R., 1993b, «Eve»: hypothesis compatibility versus hypothesis testing, *American Anthropologist*, 96, 141-147.

TISHKOFF S. A., DIETZSCH E., SPEED W., PAKSTIS A. J., KIDD J. R., CHEUNG K., BONNE-TAMIR B., SANTACHIARA-BENERECETTI A. S., MORAL P., KRINGS M., 1996, Global patterns of linkage disequilibrium at the CD4 locus and modern human origins, *Science*, 271, 1380-1387.

TORRONI, A., CHIARA, R., GUIDA, V., CRUCIANI, F., SELLITTO, D., COPPA, A., CALDERON, F. L., SIMIONATI, B., VALLE, G., RICHARDS, M., MACAULAY, V., SCOZZARI, R., 2001, Do the four clades of the mtDNA haplogroup L2 evolve at different rates?, *American Journal of Human Genetics*, 69, 1348-1356.

VIGILANT L., STONEKING M., HARPENDING H., HAWKES K., WILLSON A.C., 1991, African human populations and the evolution of human mitochondrial DNA, *Science*, 253, 1503-1507.

WATSON E., BAUER K., AMAN R., WEISS G., VON HAESELER A., PÄÄBO S., 1996, mtDNA sequence diversity in Africa, *American Journal of Human Genetics*, 59, 437-444.

WATSON E., FOSTER P., RICHARDS M., BANDELT H-J., 1997, Mitochondrial footprints of human expansions in Africa, *American Journal of Human Genetics*, 61, 691-704.

WEIR B.S., COCKERHAM C.C., 1984, Estimating F-statistics for the analysis of population structure, *Evolution*, 38, 1358-1370.

TABLE 1. Diversity indices for hvs-i
in 26 African populations.

Population	**Reference**	**LF**	**n**	**k**	**S**	**TTR**	**h_s**	**$V(h_s)$**
Hide	this study	AA	25	23	47	41/8	0,993	0,013
Kotoko	this study	AA	16	11	39	32/4	0,942	0,041
Mafa	this study	AA	32	23	55	43/14	0,980	0,012
Masa	this study	AA	31	28	42	36/4	0,991	0,012
Turkana	Watson et al. 1997	NS	37	35	65	59/3	0,996	0,008
Somali	Watson et al. 1997	AA	27	24	48	39/4	0,992	0,013
Kikuyu	Watson et al. 1997	NC	25	23	50	44/4	0,993	0,013
Nubian	Krings et al. 1999	NS	78	51	74	67/7	0,973	0,010
Nilotic	Krings et al. 1999	NS	72	61	78	71/7	0,995	0,004
Hausa	Watson et al. 1997	AA	20	19	35	30/1	0,995	0,018
Kanuri	Watson et al. 1997	NS	14	13	36	32/1	0,938	0,031
Fulbe	Watson et al. 1997	NC	61	39	48	44/2	0,973	0,010
Songhai	Watson et al. 1997	NS	10	9	32	29/1	0,978	0,054
Tuareg	Watson et al. 1997	AA	26	21	42	38/2	0,985	0,014
Yoruba	Watson et al. 1997	NC	33	31	48	43/4	0,996	0,009
Serer	Watson et al. 1997	NC	23	20	37	28/7	0,988	0,016
Wolof	Watson et al. 1997	NC	48	40	75	57/13	0,992	0,006
Mandenka	Graven et al. 1995	NC	79	29	44	43/3	0,947	0,011
Saharawi	Rando et al. 1998	AA	25	20	32	32/0	0,973	0,022
Mauritanian	Rando et al. 1998	AA	30	23	40	37/3	0,975	0,017
Egyptian Lower	Krings et al. 1999	AA	59	53	68	64/6	0,994	0,005
Egyptian Upper	Krings et al. 1999	AA	35	32	59	47/5	0,995	0,008
Moroccan Berber	Rando et al. 1998	AA	60	38	53	50/3	0,963	0,015
Moroccan Arabs	Rando et al. 1998	AA	32	29	44	44/1	0,988	0,014
Berber Souss	Brakez et al. 2001	AA	50	34	38	38/1	0,961	0,018
Mozabite	Côrte-Real et al. 1996	AA	85	30	37	37/0	0,943	0,010

(continued on next page)

(TABLE 1 continued)

Population	**π**	**V(π)**	**D_{ii}**	**V(D_{ii})**	**HRI**	**pHRI**
Hide	0,026	0,014	8,863	18,680	0,012	0,610
Kotoko	0,024	0,013	8,175	19,961	0,024	0,724
Mafa	0,024	0,013	8,260	23,643	0,019	0,108
Masa	0,024	0,013	8,092	15,537	0,007	0,734
Turkana	0,032	0,016	10,887	13,742	0,007	0,558
Somali	0,024	0,013	8,399	10,795	0,008	0,852
Kikuyu	0,026	0,014	8,890	11,904	0,009	0,898
Nubian	0,025	0,013	8,721	14,785	0,005	0,876
Nilotic	0,026	0,013	8,765	11,924	0,004	0,808
Hausa	0,019	0,010	6,447	6,799	0,010	0,938
Kanuri	0,022	0,012	7,593	10,733	0,018	0,750
Fulbe	0,021	0,011	7,282	11,216	0,009	0,557
Songhai	0,028	0,016	9,600	13,382	0,041	0,559
Tuareg	0,022	0,012	7,375	10,822	0,012	0,598
Yoruba	0,023	0,012	7,864	9,606	0,009	0,716
Serer	0,015	0,009	5,233	7,053	0,047	0,093
Wolof	0,020	0,011	7,033	11,128	0,013	0,355
Mandenka	0,019	0,010	6,361	12,741	0,011	0,650
Saharawi	0,013	0,008	4,547	4,924	0,075	0,020
Mauritanian	0,015	0,008	4,949	4,878	0,032	0,136
Egyptian Lower	0,022	0,012	7,628	11,905	0,008	0,671
Egyptian Upper	0,024	0,013	8,247	11,759	0,004	0,976
Moroccan Berber	0,016	0,009	5,434	7,091	0,011	0,737
Moroccan Arabs	0,020	0,011	6,683	7,029	0,018	0,272
Berber Souss	0,014	0,007	4,604	7,702	0,010	0,863
Mozabite	0,016	0,009	4,822	5,469	0,018	0,298

Note: LF - language family (NC: Niger-Congo, AA: Afro-Asiatic, NS: Nilo-Saharan); n - sample size (some sample sizes are not equal to those of the original publications because of the higher number of missing nucleotides in their sequences or because of uncertainties in their geographic location); k - number of different sequences; S - number of polymorphic sites; TTR - transition / transversion rate; h_s - gene (sequence) diversity; V(h_s) - variance of gene diversity; π - nucleotide diversity; V(π) - variance of nucleotide diversity; D_{ii} - mean number of pairwise differences (mismatch observed mean); V(D_{ii}) - mismatch observed variance; HRI - Harpending Raggedness index; pHRI - probability of Harpending Raggedness index.

FIGURE 1. Geographic situation of the Chadic populations from North Cameroon (the Hide from Tourou, the Mafa from Soulede, the Kotoko from Houlouf, Kala Kafra and Maltam and the Masa from Kalak, Marao, Zebe and Hinimdou).

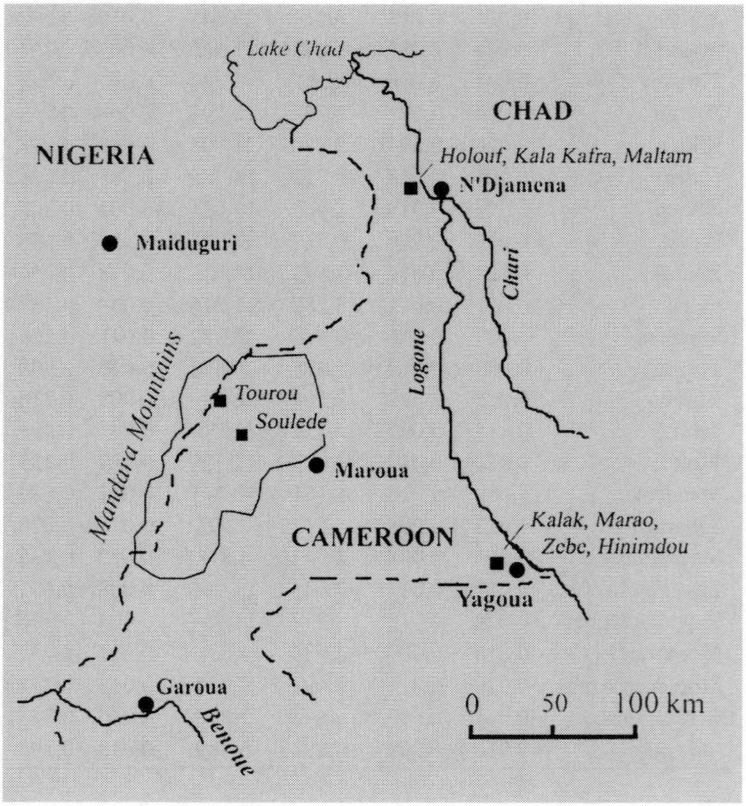

FIGURE 2. The neighbour-joining tree
of the 26 African POPULATIONS based on the fst distances.

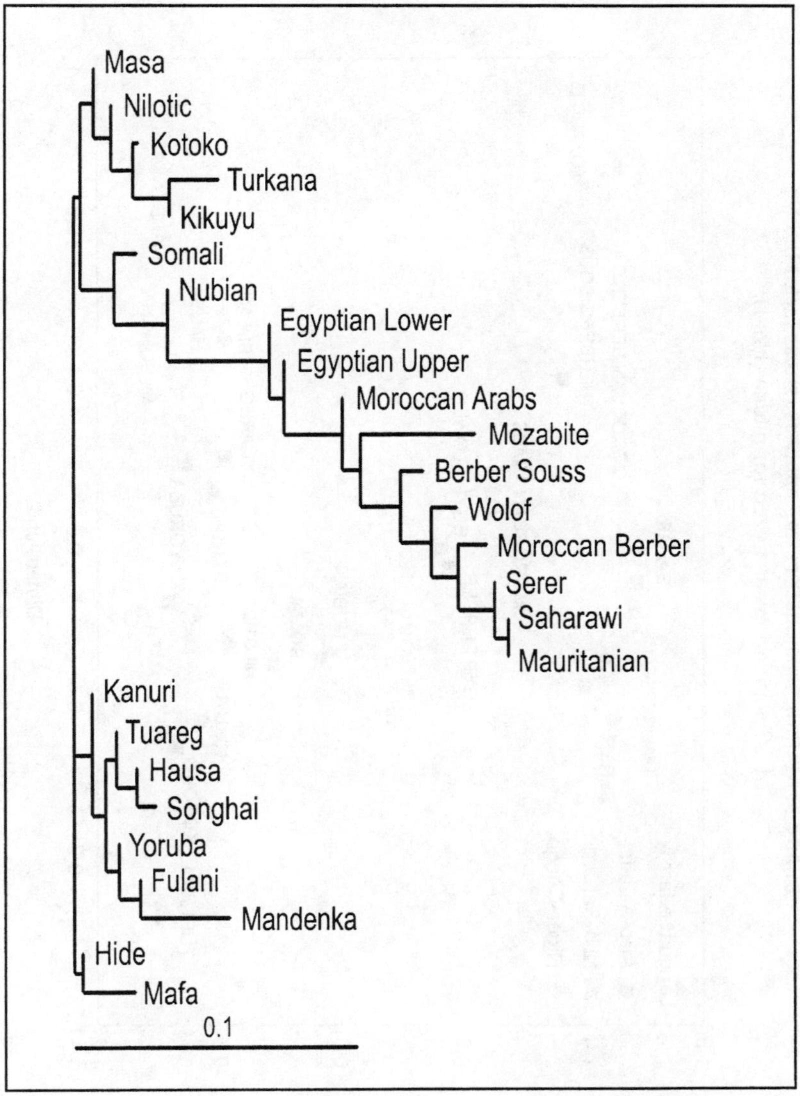

Figure 3. Multidimensional scaling analysis (stress factor 0.092) of 26 populations analyzed for mtdna (hvs-i).

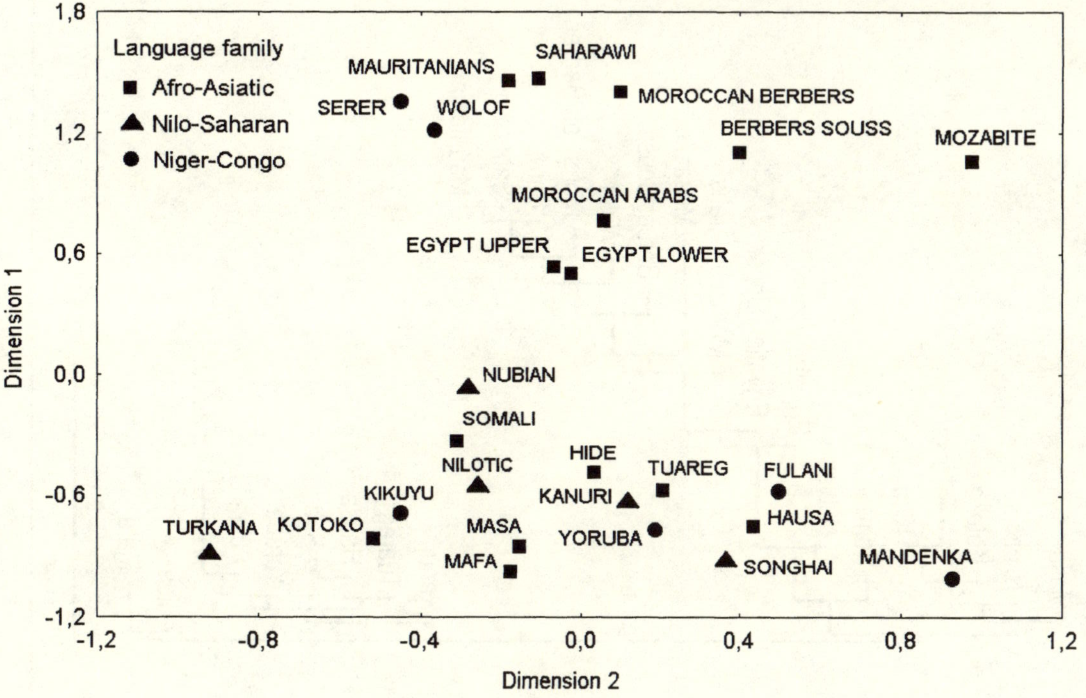

FIGURE 4. Network of l3 haplotypes of Chadic speaking populations from Northern Cameroon and the cluster with its time depth estimation.

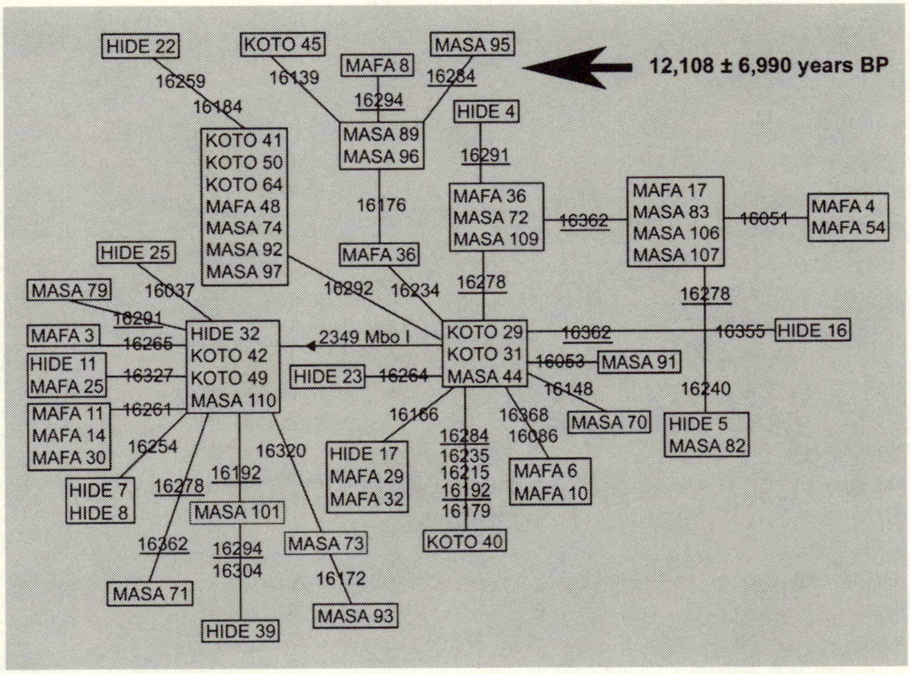

South-Bauchi West Pronominal and TAM Systems

Bernard CARON

LLACAN* caron@vjf.cnrs.fr

Abstract

This study of the SBW pronominal and TAM system is based on personal data collected in Nigeria on 8 languages : Zaranda, Langas, Dir, Danche, Baraza, Dott, Sigidi and Zaar. In their pronominal system, these languages have lost the gender, inclusive/exclusive and dual marks characteristic of AfroAsiatic (AA) languages. They have in common a system that has eroded and realigned to the point that (i) the exponents of persons are the same in the plural and the singular ; (ii) number is expressed by specific elements: a change of tone, a –N suffixed to the pronoun or addition of a suffix to the verb. It should be noted that the AA feminine mark *t- has become the general common mark for the 3s pronouns. As far as TAM systems are concerned, Zaar stands out as oddly original : it has three tone levels, when the others have two; it has ten TAM paradigms that can combine, when the others only have between three and five that don't ; it marks aspect, tense and mood, whereas the others don't express time in their verbal system, the future being a clear case of mood subcategorization. These differences have sociolinguistic origins: whereas all the other SBW languages are spoken in no more than one village and its wards, Zaar is spoken in over sixty, close to eighty if we add Sigidi. The Zaars have come to their present situation by incorporating exogeneous populations which are still identified by the clan system : Angas, Boi, Pyem, Jaar, etc. It has resulted in a complexification of the language which goes against the general assumption that when absorbing a large quantity of foreign population, a language goes through a process of pidginization.

Résumé

Cette étude des systèmes de pronoms et de marques de conjugaison des langues SBW repose sur des matériaux originaux récoltés au Nigeria sur 8 langues : zaranda, langas, dir, danche, baraza, dott, sigidi et zaar. Dans leurs systèmes pronominaux, ces langues ont perdu les marques de genre, ainsi que le duel et l'opposition inclusif/exclusif caractérisiques des langues Afroasiatiques (AA). Ils ont en commun un système qui s'est érodé et recomposé au point que (i) les exposants de la personne sont les mêmes au singulier et au pluriel; (ii) le nombre est exposé par des éléments spécifiques: un changement tonal, un –N suffixé au pronom ou au verbe. On notera que la marque *t- du féminin est devenue la marque neutre pour les pronoms 3s. Pour les systèmes de conjugaison, le zaar frappe par son originalité: il a trois niveaux tonals, les autres langues deux; il a dix paradigmes de conjugaison qui peuvent se combiner, alors que les autres en ont entre trois et cinq qui ne se combinent pas; il marque l'aspect, le temps et le mode, alors que les

* Langage, Langues et Cultures d'Afrique Noire (UMR 8135: CNRS, Inalco, Paris 7)

autres ne marquent pas le temps dans leur système verbal, le futur étant un exemple clair de sous-catégorisation modale. Ces différences ont une origine sociolinguistique: alors que les autres langues SBW sont généralement parlées dans un seul village, le zaar en couvre soixante, près de quatre-vingt si l'on y inclut le sigidi. Les Zaar ont acquis leur statut actuel en incorporant des populations exogènes qui sont identifiées par le système des clans: Angas, Boi, Pyem, Jaar, etc. Il en résulte une complexification de la langue qui contredit l'opinion générale selon laquelle, par absorbtion d'une grande quantité de population exogène, une langue subit un processus de pidginisation.

List of abbreviations

1, 1st person; 2, 2nd person; 3, 3rd person ; AA, AfroAsiatic; AOR, Aorist; COMP, Complementizer ; COMPL, Completive ; COND, Conditional; CONT, Continuous; COUNT, Counterfactual; DAT, Dative ; DO, Direct Object; FUT, Future; GEN, genitive ; GL, Genitive Link; H, Hi tone; HAB, Habitual; ICOMPL, Incompletive ; ICP, Intransitive Copy Pronoun ; IMM, Immediate; INDEP, independent ; INFL, Inflection ; L, Lo tone; TAM, Tense-Aspect-Mood; P, plural ; PCW, Proto-Chadic West ; PST, Past; PUNCT, Punctual; REC, Recent; REM, Remote; S, singular ; SBW, South-Bauchi West ; SUBJ, Subjunctive ; TAM, Tense-Aspect-Mood.; VN, Verbal Noun.

INTRODUCTION

The 27 or so lects grouped into the SBW sub-group of Chadic languages are spoken in the South of the Bauchi State (Nigeria) stretching from Bauchi to the south of the state over less than 100 kms. Among them, only *Zaar* is relatively less unknown (Caron 2002a, 2002b ; Schneeberg 1971, 1974) and is often used to characterise the whole SBW group.

These languages or dialects are obviously closely related when their basic vocabulary is compared. However, various elements tend to set *Zaar* (Saya) and *Gùùs* (Sigidi) apart:

- From a socio-linguistic and historical point of view: the name *ɓarawa* used by Shimizu to name the group is not acknowledged by the *Zaar* (Sayawa) and *Gùùs* (Sigidi) people. If all the *ɓarawa* agree to be closely related and all originate from the same area, viz. the Buli and Zaranda hills near Bauchi, the Zaars say they came from Bornu through Zaria; they say they settled in the hills South of Tafawa Balewa after some cohabitation with the Angas, Pyem and Jarawa.
- *Zaar* and *Gùùs* have three tone levels, the others only two.[1]
- *Zaar* and *Gùùs* have a very elaborate and profusive TAM system when compared to the other languages.

[1] Hi is marked with an acute accent; Lo with a grave; Mid is left unmarked.

All these elements single out the SBW group of languages for what Petr Zima has called a laboratory for the study of language evolution. This gives us an opportunity to first describe the extraordinary variation among languages that are so small in terms of number of speakers, and so close in terms of geographical and genetic proximity, and then to try and account for this variation.

In order to do so, we have picked one language from the Geji, Polci and Zeem clusters (resp. *Bùù*, *Nyámzàk* and *Cààrí*) and two from the Dass and Saya clusters: *Bərááz*ə (Baraza) and *Zòɗî* (Dott) for Dass; *Gùùs* (Sigidi) and *Zaar* for Saya.

SBW CLASSIFICATION[2]

Language clusters	Languages	(Dialects)
Sub-group North		
Geji	Migang	(Booluu)
	Pelu	
	Gyannzi	(Gèèjì)
	Buu	(Zàràndaa)
Polci	Zùl	
	Barang	(Baram)
	Dìir	(Baram Dutse)
	Bili	(Bùlì)
	Nyámzax	(Laŋas)
	Lundur	
	Posi	(Polcì)
Sub-group South		
Zeem	Zeem	
	Tule	(Tulai)
	Chaari	
	Dokshì	(Lushi)
Dass	Dikshi	(Bàraza)
	Bandas	(Dùr)
	Bòodli	(Zumbul)
	Wangdày	(Wanɗì)
	Zòdì	(Dwàt)
Saya	Zàksì	(Zàkshì)
	Bòòt	(Boto)
	Zaarə	(Zari)
	Sigidi	
	Zaar of Kàl	
	Zaar of Gàmbar Lèère	
	Zaar of Lùsa	

[2] After Shimizu 1978, p. 13

SYNTACTIC FUNCTIONS

Syntactic functions in Chadic are originally marked by word order, sometimes reinforced by particles. As a consequence, personal marks in Chadic and SBW in particular show few syntactic variants. The existence of a specific paradigm will be the criteria of the pertinence of a syntactic function for personal marks.

Independent pronouns

They appear as topic, and as one of the two terms in an identification relation. See an example of identification in Zaar:

nə myáání[3].
be 1S.INDEP
It's me.

and an example of topic in Zoɗi:

ərì à wóm-tì wát.
3S.INDEP 3S.ICOMPL feel-VN hunger
He feels hungry.

Subject pronouns

Non-verbal predicates

Non-verbal predicates are used to attribute a quality, locate, express possession, etc. Pronominal subjects of such predicates belong to a specific paradigm. See the expression of possession in Zaar:

mì tə́ mààʃìn.
1P with motorbike
We have a motorbike.

Verbal predicates

Pronominal subjects of verbal predicates are fused with TAM markers into an inflection. The INFL can be either a clitic or a word preceding the verb. In SBW, at least one paradigm of these subject+TAM, called the Aorist, has a zero TAM morpheme, leaving only the bare subject pronoun. See an example in Guus.

mà mbwaa yààɮí.
1P.AOR shoot bird
We shot a bird.

In the comparison, we will use the Ø TAM (Aorist or Completive, depending on the language) to exemplify subject pronouns.

[3] Zaar and Gùùs (Sigidi) have 3 tone levels; the other languages have 2. Hi is marked with an acute accent; Lo with a grave; Mid is left unmarked.

Intransitive Copy Pronouns

They are personal pronouns cliticised to intransitive verbs, marking the agreement with the subject of the verb. They are not common in SBW. See an example in Luri:

à	**yát**	**mə̀**	**mə̀**	**rígà = mì.**
3S.AOR	want	COMP	1P.AOR	leave=1P.ICP

He wants us to leave.

Direct Object pronouns

Direct object pronouns are clitics, as can be seen from Zaar phonological processes: 2s /**k**/ > [ɣ] /V_V; the L tone of the verb spreads on to the direct object:

á	**və̀r = kə.**	**[və̀r = ɣə̀]**
3S.AOR	give=2S.DO	

He gave (it) to you.

Dative pronouns

Contrary to Hausa, there is no specific paradigm for Dative in SBW. Direct object pronouns are used with a dative particle at the end of the sentence. Ex: Zaar **mə́n**:

tə̀	**mán**	**fi-mí**	**zùkn**	**mə́n.**
3S.SUBJ	come	do.1p	medicine	DAT

[...] in order for him to come and do magic for us.

Genitive pronouns

Genitive pronouns have two forms in SBW, corresponding to two structures of the nominal genitive construction: the 'heavy' structure <N Genitive link N> and the 'light' structure <N N>. In Zaar for example, the light structure keeps the trace of the Genitive link (**kə/gə**) in the form of a floating tone that attaches to the preceding noun:

heavy			light	
kot	**kə́**	**nóóno**	**kǒt**	**nóóno**
calabash	GL	milk	calabash.GL	milk
calabash of milk			*id.*	

The corresponding genitive pronouns are:

heavy		light
bə̀ndə̀	**g–wàà**	**bə̀ndə̀ = wàà**
pot	GL–2S	pot=2S.GEN
your pot		*id.*

The heavy structure (Genitive link–Pro) forms the independent genitive pronoun: **gwàà** *yours*.

TAM SYSTEMS

All SBW's TAM systems conform to the same structure: conjugation is expressed in a pre-verbal morpheme which includes a person mark. The verb itself is not touched by TAM, with two exceptions: floating tones (or tone progagation) and the use of Verbal Nouns for the Continuous. When the subject is nominal, the personal mark is dropped and a variant of the TAM marker appears alone.

What can be noted though is the common existence of a 'zero' TAM (H. Jungraithmayr's '*Grundaspekt*'), where only the bare Pro is used to conjugate the verb. We have chosen to name this TAM Aorist when it is opposed to the couple Completive + Incompletive, and Completive when it is opposed to an Incompletive only. We have named Continuous the TAM with a locative structure involving Pro's having the form of subjects of non-verbal predicates, and a Verbal Noun.

Bùù **(ZARANDA)**

	AOR	COMPL	CONT	FUT	SUBJ
1S	**à**	**àá**	**ámíí VN**	**àm**	**tà**
2S	**kə̀**	**ká**	**kíí VN**	**kə̀m**	**kə̀**
3S	**tə̀**	**tá**	**tíí VN**	**tə̀m**	**tə̀**
1P	**mə̀**	**màá**	**mìí VN**	**mòm**	**tə̀n Vb(-ní)**
2P	**kə̀ Vb-ní**	**kàá Vb-ní**	**kìí VN-ní**	**kìm VN-ni**	**kə̀ Vb-ní**
3P	**sə̀**	**sàá**	**sìí VN**	**sə̀m**	**sə̀ Vb(-ní)**

The Bùù TAM system is characterised by the use of the plural marker **-ní** suffixed to the Verb and Verbal Noun in the 2p. In the subjunctive, **-ní** can be used for the 1p and 3p as well.

- *Aorist*. The inflection follows the pattern « Pro + **Ø** ».
- *Completive*. The inflection follows the pattern « Pro + **á** ». With a noun subject, the marker is **ap**. Achievement of the process (perfect) is expressed by the addition of **ʔì** at the end of the Verb Phrase. The Negative Completive is formed with the negative marker **wèè** at the end of the sentence. **ʔì** and **wèè** are in complementary distribution.
- *Continuous*. The inflection follows the pattern « Pro + **íí** », followed by a Verbal Noun. With a noun subject, the marker is **ɗə́**. The Negative Incompletive is formed with the discontinuous marker **ɗáá** … **wèè**. Ex: **kíí ɗáá** VN … **wèè** (2S), etc.
- *Future*. The inflection follows the pattern « Pro + **m** », followed by a Verbal Noun. With a noun subject, the marker is **nə́m**. The Negative Future has two variants: one is expressed through the Negative Incompletive; the other uses a discontinuous marker **kə́m ... wèè**: **kí kə́m** VN … **wèè** (2S), etc.

- *Subjunctive.* The form with a noun subject is **tə**. The paradigm ot the Subjunctive is very similar to that of the Aorist. The only difference appears in 1S and 1P. This can be explained by the incorporation of **tə**. Its position indicates that it may be a complementizer. The Negative Subjunctive has two forms. With a noun subject they are (1) S **ɓáá** Vb and (2) S **bə** Vb … **wèè**. With pronominal subjects, **ɓàà** and **bə** form new paradigms:

	NEG SBJ (1)	NEG SBJ (2)
1S	**ɓâ**	**bàà ... wèè**
2S	**ɓì**	**bìì ... wèè**
3S	**ɓə̀**	**bə̀ ... wèè**
1P	**ɓân Vb-ní**	**bə̀n ... wèè**
2P	**ɓì Vb-ní**	**bìì Vb-ní ... wèè**
3P	**ɓə̀ Vb-ní**	**bə̀s ... wèè**

Dìr

	COMPL	ICOMPL	CONT	FUT
1S	**à H**	**á**	**ám dàn**	**âr kə̀**
2S	**kə̀ H**	**kə́**	**kə́ dàn**	**kə́r kə̀**
3S	**yàà H**	**yáá (bə́)**	**yàx dàn**	**yààr kə́** **yaa bár kə̀**
1P	**mù L**	**mú –R**	**mì dàn**	**mûr kə̀**
2P	**kə̀ L- -nə̀**	**kə́ –R**	**kə̀n dàn**	**kə̂r kə̀**
3P	**wù H**	**wú**	**wú dàn**	**wûr kə̀**

Negation is expressed with **yáŋ hǹ** at the end of the sentence.

- *Completive.* The inflection follows the pattern « Pro + **Ø** ». It is followed by a floating L tone in 1p and 2p and H elsewhere. The plural **-nə̀** is suffixed to the verb in 2P. (NB: contrary to Bùù, **-nə̀** appears in this context only). Achievement of the process is expressed by the addition of **wi** at the end of the Verb Phrase.
- *Incompletive.* It is restricted to the expression of habits and future events. The inflection follows the pattern « Pro + **Ø** » and bears a H tone. With noun subjects, the form is **bə̀/bà**. A **bə́** variant appears between the subject pronoun and the verb in the 3S.
- *Continuous.* The inflection follows the pattern of a locative construction « Pro + **dàn** + VN » using the pronominal paradigm of non-verbal predicate subjects.
- *Future.* The inflection follows the pattern « Pro + **rə́ kə̀** ». With a noun subject, the future marker is **bàr**.

Nyámzàk (LANGAS)

	COMPL	ICOMPL	CONT	FUT I	FUT II
1s	**à**	**á**	**àm pə́**	**nàà**	**à rə́gə̀**
2s	**kə̀**	**káá**	**kə̀ pə́**	**kàà**	**kàà rə́gə̀**
3s	**yáá**	**yáá**	**yáx pə́**	**yáà / yáá də̀**	**yáá rə̀gə̀**
1p	**mə̀ H-**	**máá**	**mì pə́**	**màà**	**màà rə́gə̀**
2p	**gə̀ H-**	**gáá**	**gə̀n pə́**	**gàà**	**gàà rə́gə̀**
3p	**wù**	**wáá**	**wùr pə́**	**wàà**	**wàà rə́gə̀**

The negation is formed with **ràŋ** at the end of the sentence.

- *Completive.* The inflection follows the pattern « Pro + **Ø** ». Its functional values are those of general past, subjunctive, and default TAM for state verbs (e.g. *love*). Perfect is expressed by the addition of **wì** at the end of the Verb Phrase.
- *Incompletive.* The inflection follows the pattern « Pro + **aa** », except for 1S where the vowel is short. With a noun subject, its form is **də́**.
- *Continuous.* The inflection follows the pattern of a locative construction « Pro + **pə́** + VN » using the pronominal paradigm of non-verbal predicate subjects.
- *Future I* is derived from the Incompletive through apotony: H > L. With a noun subject, its form is **də̀**. The 1S /**n**/ in **nàà** is probably etymological.
- *Future II* is a more recent derivation from the Incompletive through the insertion of the **rə́gə̀** morpheme, as can be seen from the 1s **à rə́gə̀**. With a noun subject, its form is **rə̀gə̀**.

Cààrí (DANCHE)

Cààrí is the only surviving language of the Zeem subgroup, the other three (Zeem, Tule and Dokshi) being extinct.

	COMPL	ICOMPL	SUBJ	CONT	FUT
1s	**áá**	**mə́**	**mə́**	**á káá**	**mîr**
2s	**káá**	**kə́**	**kə́**	**ká káá**	**kîr**
3s	**táá**	**tə́**	**tə́**	**tá káá**	**tîr**
1p	**màá**	**mìí**	**mə̀**	**mù káá**	**myèérì**
2p	**kàá**	**kìí**	**kə̀**	**kà káá**	**kyèérì**
3p	**tàá**	**tìí**	**tə̀**	**tà káá**	**tyèérì**

The negation is formed with **bà** at the end of the sentence.

- *Completive.* With a noun subject, its form is **á**, and with a pronominal subject the inflection follows the pattern « Pro + **á** ». Its functional value is that of perfect.
- *Incompletive.* The inflection follows the pattern « Pro + **Ø** ». Its functional values are those of general present, future, and default TAM for state verbs (e.g. *love*). With a noun subject, its form is **Ø**.

- *Subjunctive* is the same as ICOMPL except for the plural where the pattern is « Pro + **-íí** ».
- *Continuous*. The inflection follows the pattern « Pro + **káá** + VN », using the pronominal paradigm of non-verbal predicate subjects. With a noun subject, its form is **káá**.
- *Future* is a more recent derivation through the addition of the **-îr** (s) / **-érì** (p) morpheme to the Incompletive TAM.

Bə̀rá́ázə̀ **(BARAZA)**

	COMPL	ICOMPL	HAB	SUBJ
1s	**á**	**ámáá**	**ám tə́**	**nàà H-**
2s	**kə́**	**káá**	**kə́ tə́**	**nə́kə̀ H-**
3s	**yèè**	**yàá/yàà H-**	**yèè tə́**	**nə́yèè H-**
1p	**mù**	**màá/màà H-**	**mù tə́**	**nə́mə̀ H-**
2p	**kù**	**kwàá/kwàà H-**	**kù tə́**	**nə́kù H-**
3p	**kì**	**kyàá/kyàà H-**	**kì tə́**	**nə́kì H-**

- *Completive*. The inflection follows the pattern « Pro + Ø ». The Perfect is expressed by the addition of **ɓá** at the end of the Verb Phrase. It is in complementary distribution with the negation **ɗáá ... bà**. Iteration is expressed by the addition of the combination **róó ɓá** at the end of the Verb Phrase.
- *Incompletive*. The inflection follows the pattern « Pro + **aa** ». In the Continuous, the same inflection is followed by a Verbal Noun instead: **ɬàù**, *slaughter* > **ɬàù-tə̀**, *slaughter-ing*.
- *Habitual*. The inflection follows the pattern « Pro + **tə́** ».
- *Subjunctive*. The inflection follows the pattern « **nə́** + Pro ». It takes a Lo tone and is followed by a floating Hi tone. The Subjunctive is substituted for the Completive in [+Foc] contexts.

Negation is expressed with **ɗáá** … **bà**, both for the Completive and the Incompletive. The TAM markers being the same, the difference is in the predicate: a verb for the Negative Completive, and a VN for the Negative Incompletive.

	NEG COMPL & ICOMPL
1s	**ám ɗáá ... bà**
2s	**kə́ ɗáá ... bà**
3s	**yèè ɗáá ... bà**
1p	**mə̀**[4] **ɗáá ... bà**
2p	**kù ɗáá ... bà**
3p	**kì ɗáá ... bà**

[4] The variation *u/ə* for the vowel of the 1P inflection is a phonological phenomenon quite common in SBW languages. *i/ə* is a weak vowel that replaces the others in conditions that need to be further studied.

Zòɗì **(DOTT)**

	COMPL	ICOMPL	FUT
1S	**a**	**ám**	**máá**
2S	**ú**	**kyáà**	**kíí**
3S	**Ø**	**tyáà**	**Ø**
1P	**mà**	**màà**	**màn**
2P	**kò**	**kwàà**	**kòn**
3P	**tì**	**tàà**	**tìn**

- *Completive*. The inflection follows the pattern « Pro + **Ø** ». The Perfect is a combination of the Completive + **CaK** at the end of the Verb Phrase. The habitual is marked by **ɗa** inserted between the Completive subject pronouns and the verb.
- *Incompletive*. Except for 1S, the inflection follows the pattern « Pro + **àà** ». It is followed by a VN. With a noun subject, the Incompletive mark is **à**.
- *Future*. The inflection follows the pattern « Pro + VV » in the singular and « Pro + **n** » in the plural. With a noun subject, the Future mark is **níí**.

Gùùs **(SIGIDI)**

Aspect

	AOR	COMPL	ICOMPL	HAB
1S	**ma**	**map**	**məkap + H**	**məka / mak + H**
2S	**ka**	**kap**	**kəkap + H**	**kəka / kak + H**
3S	**ʧa**	**ʧap**	**ʧikap + H**	**ʧika / ʧak + H**
1P	**mà**	**màp**	**məkàp + H**	**məkà / màk + H**
2P	**kà**	**kàp**	**kəkàp + H**	**kəkà / kàk + H**
3P	**ʧà**	**ʧàp**	**ʧikàp + H**	**ʧikà / ʧàk + H**

- *Aorist*. The inflection uses the pattern « Pro + **a** ». With a noun subject, the marker is **a**.
- *Completive*. The inflection uses the pattern « Pro + **ap** ». With a noun subject, the marker is **ap**.
- *Incompletive*. The inflection uses the pattern « Pro + **kap** » followed by a floating Hi tone. With a noun subject, the marker is **kap**.
- *Habitual*. The inflection uses the pattern « Pro + **ka/ak** » followed by a floating Hi tone. With a noun subject, the marker is **ak**.

Tense

	IMM.PST	REC.PST	REM.PST	FUT
1S	**maa**	**mam +H**	**mə́sə̂n**	**mə +H**
2S	**kaa**	**kam +H**	**kə́sə̂n**	**kə +H**
3S	**ʧaa**	**ʧam +H**	**ʧísə̂n**	**ʧi +H**
1P	**màà**	**màm +H**	**mə̀sə̂n**	**mə̀ +H**
2P	**kàà**	**kàm +H**	**kə̀sə̂n**	**kə̀ +H**
3P	**ʧàà**	**ʧàm +H**	**ʧìsə̂n**	**ʧì +H**

- *Immediate Past*. The inflection follows the pattern « Pro + **aa** ». With a noun subject, the marker is **aa**.
- *Recent Past*. The inflection follows the pattern « Pro + **am** », followed by a floating Hi tone. With a noun subject, the marker is **am**.
- *Remote Past*. The inflection follows the pattern « Pro + **sə̂n** ». With a noun subject, the marker is **âsə́n**.
- *Future*. The inflection follows the pattern « Pro + **Ø** », followed by a floating Hi tone which differenciates it from the Subjunctive. With a noun subject, the marker is **və**.

Mood

	SUBJ	COUNT
1S	**mə**	**mə̂s**
2S	**kə**	**kə̂s**
3S	**ʧi**	**ʧîs**
1P	**mə̀**	**mə̀s**
2P	**kə̀**	**kə̀s**
3P	**ʧì**	**ʧìs**

- *Subjunctive*. The inflection follows the pattern « Pro + **Ø** ». With a noun subject, the markers are **gu** for the singular and **gi** for the plural.
- *Counterfactual*. The inflection follows the pattern « Pro + **s** ». With a noun subject, the marker is **âs**. The mark appears both in the conditional and in the main clauses, and it functions like the Hausa **dàà**...**dàà**.

Zaar (SAYA)

Verb classes

Zaar has 2 verb classes: Middle (M) and Hi (H), which can be observed in the Completive. The M class includes both 1– and 2–syllable verbs. A variant appears with some TAM (sp. the plural Incompletive) and depends on the [+/–V] nature of the initial consonant of the verb: [+V] = nonimplosive voiced obstruent. For short, we call the Completive form 'simple' (= lexical), and the other one 'complex' (= modified). This is probably a complex case of tone propagation from the TAM markers to the verb.

Verb class	H	M; +V	M; 2syl; +V	M; –V	M; 2syl; –V
Simple	**súú**	**bwaa**	**daambár**	**taar**	**tuurá**
Complex	**sùú (R)**	**bwàà (L)**	**dààmbár (LH)**	**táàr (F)**	**túùrá (FH)**
	love	*choose*	*disturb*	*clear*	*push*

Aspect

	AOR	COMPL	ICOMPL	PUNCT	CONC	CONT
1S	**mə**	**máá**	**myáá**	**miyii/myii**	**myáánaa**	**miɣá / myaá**
2S	**kə**	**káá**	**kyáá**	**kiyii/kyii**	**kyáánaa**	**kiɣá / kyaá**
3S	**á**	**àà**	**ʧáá**	**yii**	**ʧáánaa**	**ʧiɣá / ʧaá**
1P	**mə́**	**màà**	**myàá**	**mààyi**	**myàánaa**	**mìɣá / myàá**
2P	**kə́**	**kàà**	**kyàá**	**kààyi**	**kyàánaa**	**kìɣá / kyàá**
3P	**tə́**	**tàà**	**ʧàá**	**tààyi**	**ʧàánaa**	**ʧìɣá / ʧàá**

- *Aorist*. The inflection follows the pattern « Pro + **Ø** ». It has a narrative functional value. The verbs appear with a high tone on their first syllable in the 1st and 2nd persons of the singular. In the 3rd person singular and in the plural, they appear in the complex form.
- *Completive*. The inflection follows the pattern « Pro + **áá** ». The form of the verb is the simple form.
- *Incompletive*. The inflection follows the pattern « Pro + **yáá** ». The verb appears in the simple form in the singular, and in the complex form in the plural.
- *Punctiliar*. The meaning is both punctiliar and iterative. The closest equivalent is the periphrastic Hausa *yi ta*. The inflection follows the pattern « Pro + **yii** ». The verb appears in the simple form.
- *Concomitant*. The inflection follows the pattern « Pro + **yáá** + **naa** ». The verb keeps the simple form.
- *Continuous*. The inflection follows the pattern « Pro + **yi** + **ká** + VN ». **yi**+**ká** is realised [yiɣá]. In the monosyllabic variant, the opposition singular vs plural is marked by a tone contrast between a rising Mid-Hi tone in the singular and a rising Lo-Hi in the plural. It is the only place in the language where this contrast is observed. However, it seems to be unstable and is sometimes replaced by a contrast between Mid in the singular and Rising in the plural.

Tense

	IMM.PST	REC.PST	REM.PST	FUT
1S	**míí**	**mənáá**	**mətá**	**ma**
2S	**kíí**	**kənáá**	**kətá**	**ka**
3S	**áyí**	**ánáa**	**áta**	**wò**
1P	**mìì**	**mənàà**	**mə̀tà**	**má**
2P	**kìì**	**kə̀nàà**	**kə̀tà**	**ká**
3P	**ʧìì**	**tənàa**	**tətà**	**tá**

- *Immediate past.* The Immediate Past refers to events which occurred earlier the same day. The inflection follows the pattern « Pro + **yi** ». The first syllable of the verb receives a low tone.
- *Recent Past.* The Recent Past refers to events which occurred on the previous day. The inflection follows the pattern « Pro + **náá** ». The verb keeps the simple form.
- *Remote Past.* The Remote Past refers to events which occurred more than two days ago. The inflection follows the pattern « Pro + **ta** ». The verb keeps the simple form.
- *Future.* The inflection follows the pattern « Pro + **a** ». The verb appears in the simple form in the singular, and the complex form in the plural.

Mood

	SUBJ	COND	COUNT
1S	**mə**	**myáá**	**mí/míyí**
2S	**àà**	**kyáá**	**kí/kíyí**
3S	**tə̀**	**yáá**	**ʧí/yí/ʧíyí/tíyí**
1P	**mə + L**	**myàá**	**mì/mìyì**
2P	**àà + L**	**kyàá**	**kì/kìyì**
3P	**tə̀ + L**	**yàá/ʧàá**	**ʧì/ʧìyì/tìyì**

- *Subjunctive.* The inflection follows the pattern « Pro + low tone ». In the plural, a low tone is added to the 1st syllable of the verb.
- *Conditional.* The inflection follows the pattern « pronoun + **yáá** ». In the 1st and 2nd persons singular, the verb takes a high tone on the 1st syllable. In the other persons, the verb appears in the complex form. The only difference with ICOMPL is in 3s.
- *Counterfactual.* The inflection follows the pattern « pronoun + **yí** ». The verb appears in the complex form. The Counterfactual is introduced by **yáàn**, *if* and used in contexts that would be translated in Hausa by a *dàà ... dàà* construction.

Composition

Compound aspects

The three basic aspects (Completive, Incompletive, Aorist) cannot be combined.

	COMPL.PUNCT	ICOMPL.PUNCT	ICOMPL.CONT	COMPL.CONT
1S	**máàyi**	**myááyi**	**myááyiɣá**	**miyiiyiɣá**
2S	**kááyi**	**kyááyi**	**kyááyiɣá**	**kiyiiyiɣá**
3S	**ààyi**	**ʧááyi**	**ʧááyiɣá**	**yiiyiɣá**
1P	**mààyi**	**myàáyi**	**myàáyiɣá**	**míyiiyiɣá**
2P	**kààyi**	**kyàáyi**	**kyàáyiɣá**	**kíyiiyiɣá**
3P	**tààyi**	**ʧàáyi**	**ʧàáyiɣá**	**tíyiiyiɣá**

- *Completive Punctiliar*. The inflection has the structure: « Pro + **áá** + **yi** ». All verbs following the **yi** punctiliar morpheme have a simple form. This is true for all combinations.
- *Incompletive Punctiliar*. The inflection has the structure: « Pro + **yàá** + **yi** ».
- *Incompletive Continuous*. The structure of the inflection is « Pro + **yàá** + **yi** + **ká** ». **yi** + **ká** is realised [yiɣá]. The verb appears in the form of a Verbal Noun.
- *Punctiliar Continuous*. The structure of the inflection is « Pro + **yii** + **yi** + **ká** ». **yi** + **ká** is realised [yiɣá]. The verb appears in the form of a Verbal Noun. This combination is not common and Zaar speakers perfer to use the Imperfect continuous instead.

Tense and aspect

	FUT.PUNCT	FUT.CONT	REM.PST COMPL	REM.PST ICOMPL
1S	**mayi**	**mayiɣá**	**máátá**	**mətáyáá**
2S	**kayi**	**kayiɣá**	**káátá**	**kətáyáá**
3S	**wòyi**	**wòyiɣá**	**ààtá**	**átayáá**
1P	**máyi**	**máyiɣá**	**mààtá**	**mə̀tàyáá**
2P	**káyi**	**káyiɣá**	**kààtá**	**kə̀tàyáá**
3P	**táyi**	**táyiɣá**	**tààtá**	**tə̀tàyáá**

	REM.PST PUNCT	REM.PST CONT	REC.PST COMPL	REC.PST COMPL	REC.PST ICOMPL
1S	**mətáyi**	**mətáyiɣá**	**máánáá**	**máánáá**	**mənááyáá**
2S	**kətáyi**	**kətáyiɣá**	**káánáá**	**káánáá**	**kənááyáá**
3S	**átáyi**	**átáyiɣá**	**àànáá**	**àànáá**	**ánáayáá**
1P	**mə̀tàyi**	**mə̀tàyiɣá**	**màànáá**	**màànáá**	**mə̀nààyáá**
2P	**kə̀tàyi**	**kə̀tàyiɣá**	**kàànáá**	**kàànáá**	**kə̀nààyáá**
3P	**tə̀tàyi**	**tə̀tàyiɣá**	**tàànáá**	**tàànáá**	**tə̀nààyáá**

	REC.PST PUNCT	REC.PST CONT	IMM.PST ICOMPL	IMM.PST CONT
1S	**mənááyi**	**mənááyiɣá**	**mááyí**	**mííyìɣá**
2S	**kənááyi**	**kənááyiɣá**	**kááyí**	**kííyìɣá**
3S	**ánááyi**	**ánááyiɣá**	**ààyí**	**áyyìɣá**
1P	**mə̀nààyi**	**mə̀nààyiɣá**	**mààyí**	**mììyìɣá**
2P	**kə̀nààyi**	**kə̀nààyiɣá**	**kààyí**	**kììyìɣá**
3P	**tə̀nààyi**	**tə̀nààyiɣá**	**tààyí**	**ʧììyìɣá**

- *Future Punctiliar*. The inflection has the structure: « Pro + **a** + **yi** ». The verb keeps the simple form.

- *Future Continuous*. The inflection has the structure: « Pro + **a** + **yi** + **ká** ». The verb is in the form of a Verbal Noun.
- *Remote Past Perfect*. The inflection has the structure: « Pro + **áá** + **tá** ». The verb is in the complex form.
- *Remote Past Imperfect*. The inflection has the structure: « Pro + **ta** + **yáá** ». The verb appears in the simple form in the singular, and in the complex form in the plural. (cf. Imperfect).
- *Remote past Punctiliar*. The inflection has the structure: « Pro + **ta** + **yi** ». The verb keeps the simple form. Lusa speakers associate this combination to the **ɓógoró** / **ŋgòɓíyà** dialect. They prefer to use the Recent Past Imperfect.
- *Remote Past Continuous*. The inflection has the structure: « Pro + **ta** + **yi** + **ká** ». The verb is in the form of a Verbal Noun.
- *Recent Past Perfect*. The inflection follows the pattern « Pro +**áá** + **náá** ». The verb appears in the complex form.
- *Recent Past Imperfect*. The inflection follows the pattern « Pro + **náá** + **yáá** ». The verb appears in the simple form in the singular, and in the complex form in the plural. (cf. Imperfect).
- *Recent past Punctiliar*. The inflection follows the pattern « Pro + **náá** + **yi** ». The verbs keep the simple form (cf. Imperfect). This combination is associated to the **ɓógoró** / **ŋgòɓíyà** dialect by the Lusa speakers. They prefer to use the Recent Past Imperfect.
- *Recent past Continuous*. The inflection follows the pattern « Pro + **náá** + **yi** + **ká** ». The verb is in the form of a verbal noun.
- *Immediate Past Perfect*. The inflection follows the pattern « Pro + **áá** + **yi** ». The first syllable of the verb receives a low tone.
- *Immediate Past Imperfect*. The inflection follows the pattern « Pro + **yii** + **yáá** ». The verb appears in the simple form in the singular, and in the complex form in the plural. (cf. Imperfect).
- *Immediate Past Continuous*. The inflection follows the pattern « Pro + **yi** + **yi** + **ká** ». The verb appears in the form of a verbal noun.

Mood and aspect

	REC.PST.COUNT	REM.PST.COUNT
1S	**mínaa**	**míta**
2S	**kínaa**	**kíta**
3S	**tínaa**	**títa**
	ʧínaa	**ʧíta**
1P	**mìnàà**	**mìtà**
2P	**kìnàà**	**kìtà**
3P	**tìnàà**	**tìtà**
	ʧìnàà	**ʧìtà**

Comments

Just looking at the number of paradigms, the situation varies from 3 different paradigms (Zoɗi) to 13 (Zaar) or more if combinations are included. Zaar and Guus are the only languages with three past tenses (when the other SBW languages only have a future tense), counterfactual and conditional moods. From now on, all that will be said concerning Zaar holds for Guus as well.

The diversity can be explained by the development from a basic opposition between a Ø TAM, and an Incompletive. The Incompletive is generally formed with –**aa**, although in Dir, the contrast between Compl and Incompl is tonal. At this stage, the functional value of the opposition is not differenciated from the point of view of tense, aspect and mood. Each morpheme is a mixture of functional values. The Ø TAM combines narrative, past, perfect and subjunctive functions (cf. Nyámzàk Completive). The Incompletive is basically non-past (present and future), progressive and habitual. Depending on the language, either can be used as the default TAM to conjugate state verbs.

Then, new TAM's appear to convey a specification that is absent in the original system. The Continuous is formed through a locative construction. Other TAM's are made through the integration of particles that are prefixed (Subj: Bùù, Bəráázə̀) or more generally suffixed (Zaar pasts; Bùù and Dìr future) to the existing TAM's. These restrict the functional value of the original TAM's. The Completive for example can be reduced to the expression of the subjunctive (Zaar), or the narrative and conjugation of state verbs such as *want/like* (Bùù). The Incompletive can be reduced to the expression of the habitual, although the negative Incompletive is generally still used to negate the Future, and sometimes alternates with a specific Negative Future TAM.

PRONOUN SYSTEMS

SBW languages have lost the gender, inclusive/exclusive and dual marks characteristic of Afro-Asiatic (AA) languages. Except for the genitive pronouns, it is the feminine mark ***t** which has survived as the neutral 3rd person singular.

Bùù **(Zaranda)**

	INDEP	SUBJ (AOR)	SUBJ (NOM)	ICP	DO	GEN
1s	**ámìì**	**à**	**ámí**	**-nə̀**	**-ə́ŋ**	**yíí(ní)**
2s	**kíí**	**kə̀**	**kí**	**-k**	**kí**	**wáà/wáágì**
3s	**tíí**	**tə̀**	**tí**	**-t**	**tí**	**wáàs/wáásì**
1p	**míí**	**mə̀**	**mì**	**-mə̀**	**mí**	**yììnə́ŋ**
2p	**kìníí**	**kə̀ Vb-ní**	**kì**	**-nə́ŋkìn**	**kíŋ**	**wààkə́ŋ**
3p	**síí**	**sə̀**	**sì**	**-sə̀**	**sí**	**wààsə́ŋ**

Dìr

	INDEP	SUBJ (COMPL)	SUBJ (NOM)	DO	GEN
1S	**ám**	**à H**	**ám**	**-ə́m**	**-(y)ènı́**
2S	**kə́**	**kə̀ H**	**kə́**	**-(úú)Ø**	**-ə̀**
3S	**yàx**	**yàà H**	**yàx**	**tə́**	**-ə̀s**
1P	**mì**	**mù L**	**mì**	**mə́**	**-gèèmí**
2P	**kə̀n**	**kə̀ L- -nə̀**	**kə̀n**	**-(úú)n**	**-ə̀ní**
3P	**wúrí**	**wù H**	**wúr**	**-úúr**	**-ə̀zə́ni**

***Nyámzàk* (LANGAS)**

	INDEP	SUBJ (COMPL)	SUBJ (NOM)	DO	GEN
1S	**ám**	**à**	**àm**	**-ə̀n/-ììm**	**-gè**
2S	**kə́ŋ**	**kə̀**	**kə̀**	**kə̀/gə̀**	**-gə̀ŋ**
3S	**yáx**	**yáá**	**yáx**	**tə̀/də̀**	**-gə̀s**
1P	**mìì**	**mə̀ H-**	**mì**	**mìì**	**-gèmí**
2P	**gə̀n**	**gə̀ H-**	**gə̀n**	**gə̀n**	**-gə̀n**
3P	**wúr**	**wù**	**wùr**	**wùr**	**-gə̀zə́n**

***Cààrí* (DANCHE)**

	INDEP	SUBJ (AOR)	SUBJ (NOM*)	DO**	GEN
1S	**âm**	**mə́**	**á**	**mə**	**-yíní**
2S	**kî**	**kə́**	**ká**	**kə**	**-wáágə̀**
3S	**tʃî**	**tə́**	**tá**	**tə**	**-wáásə̀**
1P	**mè**	**mə̀**	**mù**	**mee**	**-yékə̂ŋ**
2P	**kè**	**kə̀**	**kà**	**kee**	**-wókə̂ŋ**
3P	**tʃè**	**tə̀**	**tà**	**ʃee**	**-wósə̂n**

* Cf. Continuous.

** The tone of DO pronouns is opposed to that of the preceding syllable.

The dative pronouns are formed with **–ì** suffixed to DO pronouns.

***Bə̀ráázə̀* (BARAZA)**

	INDEP	SUBJ (COMPL)	SUBJ (NOM)	DO	GEN
1S	**ám**	**á**	**ám**	**-ə́m**	**-kíní**
2S	**kə́**	**kə́**	**kə́**	**kə́**	**-gə̀**
3S	**yèè**	**yèè**	**yèè**	**yèè**	**-kííyè**
1P	**mə̀**	**mù**	**mə̀**	**mə̀**	**-gə̀m**
2P	**kò**	**kù**	**kò**	**kò**	**-gə̀n**
3P	**kèè**	**kì**	**kì**	**kéé**	**-kèè**

***Zòɗî* (DOTT)**

	INDEP	SUBJ (COMPL)	SUBJ (NOM)	ICP	DO	GEN
1S	**ám**	**à**	**ám**	**H**	**-(ә́)m**	**gìn**
2S	**kí**	**ú**	**kí**	**-kí**	**kí**	**gèè**
3S	**ərì**	**Ø**	**ərì**	**-tí**	**ərì**	**gə̀s**
1P	**mà**	**mà**	**mà**	**-mà**	**mà**	**gə̀m**
2P	**kò**	**kò**	**kò**	**-kò**	**kò**	**gə̀ŋ**
3P	**sə́ŋ**	**tì**	**sə́ŋ**	**-sə́ŋ**	**sə́ŋ**	**gə̀sə́ŋ**

Three kinship terms (**baa**, *husband*; **kon**, *son*; **ʧénsi**, *mother's brother*) have a special genitive paradigm:

	Genitive	uncle	husband
1S	**-níí**	**ʧènií**	**bààníí**
2S	**-níŋgee**	**ʧèníŋgèè**	**bààníŋgèè**
3S	**-nə́s**	**ʧènə́s**	**bàànə́s**
1P	**-nə́ma**	**ʧènə́mà**	**bàànə́mà**
2P	**-nə́ŋgən**	**ʧènə́ŋgə̀ŋ**	**bàànə́ŋgəŋ**
3P	**-nə́sə́ŋ**	**ʧènə́sə́ŋ**	**bàànə́sə́ŋ**

ICP's are cliticised to the verb, with frequent consonant assimilation. The 1st person singular is marked by a Hi tone on the last syllable of the verb.

NB: In the 3rd person singular, out of the AA forms ***si** for the masculine and ***ta** for the feminine, it is the feminine form ***ta** that has survived in the ICP, **-tí** and the Continuous **tyàá.** Elsewhere, the 3rd person mark is replaced by the word **ərì**, which is to be compared to the word **ərə́m**, *thing*.

***Gùùs* (SIGIDI)**

	INDEP	SUBJ (AOR)	DO	GEN
1S	**ɲááni**	**ma**	**-(ə)m**	**gùgé / -gè**
2S	**kyááni**	**ka**	**kə**	**gwààgí / -ààgə̀**
3S	**ʧááni**	**ʧa**	**tə**	**gwààʃí / -ààs**
1P	**ɲààné**	**mà**	**mé**	**gwàámmí / -ààgmè**
2P	**kyààné**	**kà**	**kə́n**	**gwààgə́ni / -ààgə̀n**
3P	**ʧààné**	**ʧà**	**ʧán**	**gwààgə́san / -ààgə̀sàn**

The singular DO pronouns have a Mid tone which assimilates to any preceding Lo tone.

Zaar (SAYA)

	INDEP	SUBJ (AOR)	SUBJ (NOM)	DO	GEN
1S	**myááni**	**mə**	**mi**	**-əm**	**-(g)ə̀dn**
2S	**kyááni**	**kə**	**ki**	**-kə**	**-(g)wàà**
3S	**yááni**	**á**	**ʧi**	**-tə**	**-(g)wòs**
1P	**myàànı́**	**mə́**	**mì**	**-mí**	**-(g)wòbm**
2P	**kyàànı́**	**kə́**	**kì**	**-kí**	**-(g)wààn**
3P	**yààʃí**	**tə́**	**ʧì**	**-ʃí**	**-(g)wààsən**

Comments

In this work, my assumption, following Shimizu 78, has been that SBW languages derive from a common original language that was spoken around the lake Chad some 400 years ago. However, it is now interesting to examine the result of synchronic mechanism as a cause of diachronic changes through analogy.

The weakening of the pronominal vowels (generally to the central vowel *i/ə*) has built a system that has eroded and realigned to the point that (i) the segmental exponents of persons are the same in the plural and the singular; (ii) the exponent of number is expressed by specific elements: a change of tone, a change of vowel, a –N suffixed to the pronoun or to the verb in case of subject pronouns.

If we sum up these processes by building a common SBW pronominal system, and compare it to Proto-West-Chadic pronouns (PCW) as reconstructed in (Newman & Schuh 1974), the main feature to be observed is that SBW pronouns do away with the plural dimension:

	PCW		SBW
1S	***ni**	1	***n/m**
2S	***ka** (m), ***ki** (f)	2	***k**
3S	***si** (m), ***ta** (f)	3	***t/*s**
1P	***mu**		
2P	***ku**		
3P	***su**		

Zaar and Guus independent pronouns are characterized by extensive suffixes: **-ani** (s); **-aane/-aashi** (pl).

The AA feminine mark ***t** has become the general common mark for the 3s. ***s** is only observed for 3s in the genitive. 3s **yaa/yee** (Dir, Langas, Baraza) could be either an innovation (cf. Dir **əri** < **ərəm**, *thing*) or a retention of AA 3sm ***y**, opposed to 3sf ***t**.

CONCLUSION

In conclusion, I would like to go back on Zaar. The morphological and functional status of Zaar TAM's as compared to the others look very odd. The basic process at work in the evolution of the Baraawaa languages has been pushed a step futher in its case: proliferation of TAM's; possibility of multiple combinations; development of past tenses. As was mentioned in the introduction, this goes with the appearance of a third tone level (may be an infra-low tone linked to +V consonants). This can be explained by the history of the Zaars. Their population far exceeds that of the other languages: over 125,000 for Zaar; less than 600 for those that are still well spoken (i.e. B'oto, Zoɗi, Zaranda, Dir, Baraza), a handful for those that are dying (Luri, Zeem, Zumbul, Tulai, Lushi). They have mixed with and incorporated alien populations (Angas, Pyem, Jarawa, Boi, etc.), whose existence is still acknowledged in the indentity of clans. But what is remarkable is that, far from becoming a communication language characterized by its morphological pidgin-like simplification, this has lead to a process of phonological, morphological and functional complexification.

References

CARON, B., 2002a, Gùùs, aka Sigidi (Chadic, West-B, South-Bauchi): Grammatical notes and vocabulary, *Afrika und Übersee* 84.

— 2002b, Review of 'Barawa Lexicon: a wordlist of eight South Bauchi (West Chadic) languages: Boghom, Buli, Dott, Geji, Sayanci and Zul' by Ronald Cosper, Munich, LINCOM EUROPA, 1999. *Chadic Newsletter* 1 (23), 46-80.

— 2002, Dott, aka Zod'i (Chadic, West-B, South-Bauchi): Grammatical notes, vocabulary and text, *Afrika und Übersee* 85:161-248.

NEWMAN, P. & R. G. SCHUH, 1974, The Hausa aspect system, *Afroasiatic Linguistics* 1, 1-39.

SCHNEEBERG, N., 1971, Sayanci verb tonology, Special Chadic Issue, (ed) P. Newman, *Journal of African Languages*.

— 1974, *Sayanci Phonology*, Ph.D.: Indiana University.

SHIMIZU, K., 1978, The Southern Bauchi Group of Chadic Languages. A survey report, *Africana Marburgensia* 2 (Special Issue), 50.

Perceptions of time and their conceptualisation in Saharan languages

Norbert CYFFER Norbert.Cyffer@univie.ac.at

Abstract

The Saharan languages (Kanuri, Teda-Daza and Beria) operate a basic aspectual system distinguishing between Perfective and Imperfective aspects. Within this basic distinction sub-categories were established, which differ in number and usage in the individual languages. Kanuri uses more TAMs than the other languages. Here we can observe that there has not only been an increase of categories, but also a change of meaning and function of TAM categories in course of time. For example, S.W. Koelle's Kanuri grammar (1854) evidently does not contain all present TAM categories. Furthermore the meaning and function differs from present usage in Kanuri. We observe internal changes within the past 200 years. We also observe some vicinity to TAM uses between Kanuri, Hausa and Fulfulde. As these similarities go in line with other similar grammatical patterns (e.g. clause subordination), we may propose that areal contact features had an impact on the Kanuri grammar. In this context the question of linguistic alliances or even 'Sprachbund' comes up.

Résumé

Les langues sahariennes (*kanuri*, *teda-daza* et *beria*) utilisent un système aspectuel de base fondé sur la distinction Perfectif – Imperfectif. A l'intérieur de cette distinction fondamentale, des sous-catégories ont été établies, qui diffèrent en nombre et valeur dans les différentes langues. Le *kanuri* utilise plus de TAM que les autres langues. Dans ce cas particulier, on observe qu'il y a eu non seulement augmentation du nombre de catégories, mais également changement au cours du temps, du sens et de la fonction des catégories marquées par les TAM. Par exemple, il est évident que la grammaire *kanuri* de Koelle (1854) ne comporte pas toutes les catégories de TAM actuelles. De plus, leur sens et leur fonction diffèrent de l'usage actuel en *kanuri*. On observe des changements internes depuis les 200 dernières années. On observe également des similitudes dans l'utilisation des TAM entre le *kanuri*, le *hausa* et le *fulfulde*. Comme ces similitudes correspondent à d'autres régularités grammaticales (par ex. dans la subordination), nous pouvons avancer l'hypothèse d'une influence de traits aréaux de contact sur la grammaire *kanuri*. Dans ce contexte, la question se pose de l'existence d'alliances linguistiques ou même d'un 'Sprachbund'.

0. Introductory remarks

It is commonly accepted that concepts of time may differ from language to language. Therefore we apply terms like 'tense', 'mood' or 'aspect' in order to define exact time perception in a specific language. We also know that the awareness of time may change within a language in course of time. In German, for example, the Present and Future tenses as well as Past and Perfect tend to become neutralized in their meaning. In the Saharan language family, a branch of Nilo-Saharan, we also observe processes of changing attitudes towards time in the verbal complex. Different developments contributed to the present shape of T(ense)-A(spect)-M(ood) systems in the individual languages Kanuri, Teda-Daza and Beria (Zaghawa). Though the TAM[1] structure in all Saharan languages are based on a less complex bipartite aspect system, which is still visible in Beria, they have further developed their own individual system. As we assume that time categories in grammar are closely linked with time conceptions in a speech community, new grammatical categories resulted from new reflections about time in a given society.

As the language density in Africa exceeds that of most parts in the world, it is not surprising that linguistic contact situations are much more frequent than elsewhere (with the exception of the South Pacific). In many parts of Africa, societies of different cultural, religious and social backgrounds live in a close neighbourhood. Such situations may lead to changes in the individual language structures. For example, the contact between Kanuri and Beria, both speaking a Saharan language, is today almost insignificant. Both societies have existed in different political and social settings over the past time, and evidently became further alienated. On the other hand, new language alliances, independent of genetic affiliations, evolved.

These developments had, and still have, an impact on the language structure that is well visible in the TAM system of the two languages. Kanuri has adopted new categories, which resemble those in other languages of different genetic affiliation, e.g. Hausa and Fulfulde.

With regard to Kanuri we are in a fortunate position to study the development of the TAM system from the mid 19th century until the present. Thanks to S.W. Koelle's works on Kanuri grammar (1854a) and oral literature (1854b) we can compare the concepts of time and their conceptualisation in the past 150 years. On the one hand we notice a stability in expressing time within the aspectual system, completed versus incompleted, and on the other hand a remarkable semantic and grammatical change of TAM categories within the aspectual system. As Koelle's analyses should be taken as serious scholarly works, we should rely upon them in most cases.

[1] Abbreviations : DER– derivative marker ; MC– meaning carrier ; SJ– subject marker ; TAM– tense-aspect-mood ; VB– verb base ; VEP– verb emphasis past ; ps.– person ; sg.– singular.

In the following we will take a look at the basic Saharan aspectual system and the TAM categories which evolved from them. In our considerations, this is of special interest for Kanuri. Our studies so far revealed that certain TAM patterns were adopted by Kanuri through contact with languages in the west over the past millennium. This resulted in a new contact situation and the development of areal linguistic features. We should note here, that the area west of Lake Chad (present eastern Niger and northeastern Nigeria) was inhabited by Kanuri speakers from the 10th century. The further expansion of the language was also a result of a 'Kanurization' process throughout the subsequent centuries. There is evidence that these processes were still going on in the recent past (Cyffer et al. 1997).

When we compare texts from Koelle's anthology of oral literature (1854b) with texts of the same genre in present Kanuri,[2] we observe considerable changes in the application of perfective TAMs. The following table illustrates that a functional shift of a neutral general perfective to a more specific verb emphatic TAM category has taken place. As it will be later demonstrated, this shift also led to other implications in the Kanuri TAM system.

Table A: TAM distribution (1854 - 1978)

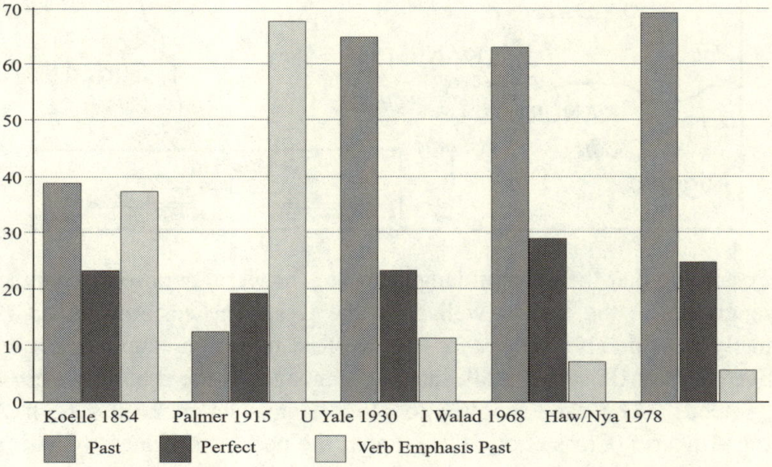

1. Saharan languages

The Saharan languages consist of a small group of languages, which show on the one hand a close structural relationship, e.g. almost identical verb structure, and on the other hand a remarkable lexical distance between the individual languages, e.g.

[2] Under 'present Kanuri' we refer to text materials from about 1930. The date was chosen, because during this time the publication of Kanuri text materials and the linguiustic research on the language became more intensified.

the lexicon in Kanuri and Beria/Zaghawa (Cyffer 1996). In earlier studies I looked at some of these conflicting phenomena. The causes for these developments are not easy to track down, however, we know for certain that contact with other language communities and alienation within the Saharan languages are some of the factors that have led to the present linguistic conditions. For example, there are a number of morphological and syntactic features, which allow the hypothesis that the Lake Chad area makes up an eastern boundary of some common west African linguistic features and, probably also a borderline for features which penetrated from the east to the west (Cyffer 2000).

Table B: Geographical distribution of Saharan languages

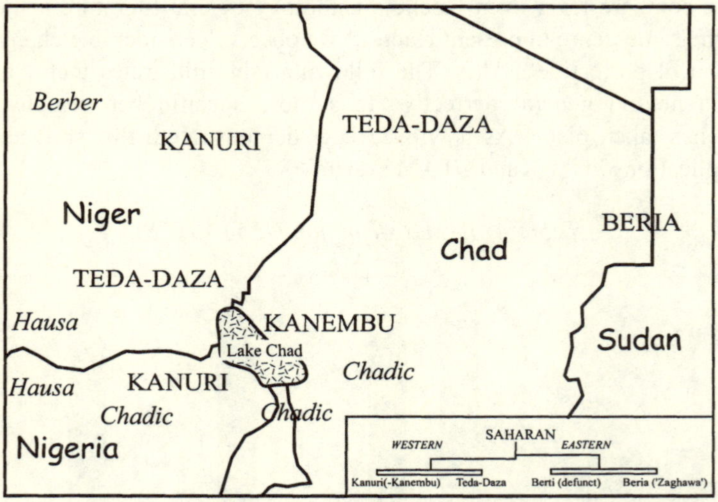

We may assume that the Saharan languages are (or were) exposed to contact with other languages in the east as well as in the west. The eastern contact zone is presumably considerably older than the western one. For example, the general formative of class III verbs in all Saharan languages is the auxiliary verb **n** 'say (think, intend)'. The same applies to other languages in northeastern Africa, including Amharic (Crass et al. 2001). Later, the people of Kanem (Chad) spread to the west of Lake Chad, the present Borno in Nigeria and Niger. The political and economical strength of the Kanem-Borno empire grew, and the exposure to languages in West Africa began to play an increasing role. Here, we may not only expect a linguistic import into Kanuri from outside languages, but also export of Kanuri lexemes and grammatical forms.[3]

[3] Though more studies are needed to support this hypothesis, there are good arguments for this assertion. See also Newman, Paul (2000) *The Hausa Language: An Encyclopedic Reference Grammar.* New Haven & London: Yale University Press, p. 315.

2. The basic Saharan TAM system

The basic Saharan verb structure is almost identical (e.g. three morphologically identical verb classes, affixation of subject markers). However, the TAM system in the individual languages, though based on the same principle, has developed differently (Cyffer 1978, 1998a).

Table C: TAM marking in the verbal complex

Class	MC	TAM: [secondary]	VB	TAM: primary
II		[+]	+	+
III	+	[+]	+	+

The secondary TAM can only be applied in connection with the primary marker. In Kanuri it applies to the Past ant the Potential, in Teda-Daza only to the Potential. The TAM prefixes are related to auxiliary verbs 'go' and 'be' (Schubert 1971-73, Cyffer 1978, Jarrett 1981).

Table D: Ordering of primary and secondary TAM

	TAM	DER	VB	SJ	TAM		
Noun Emphasis Past		**t**	**kór**	**k**	**o**	**kórəko**	I was asked
Past	**ka**	**t**	**kór**	**k**	**o**	**kátə́wórəko**	I was asked
Potential	**ta**	**t**	**kór**	**k**	**o**	**tátə́wórəko**	I may be asked

Before coming back to our initial example and the implications involving TAM, I would rather like to begin with the basic model of aspectual distinction in Saharan. As I have already mentioned, the basic pattern is Perfective versus Imperfective[4]:

Table E: Basic Saharan TAM system

SAHARAN	
perfective	imperfective
r(i)	Locative / instrumental

Example 1

	Loc./Instr		Imperf.	
Kanuri	**Bagân**	in Baga	**Músa Bagáro lejin**	Musa is going to Baga
	jánan	with a knife		
Beria	**Tinari**	in Tina	**nɔ́gi**	I see
Teda-Daza	**nta ke**	with you	**wanərge**	I refuse

[4] We cannot rule out that the basic marking of the Perfective aspect was originally Ø. But in that case we should note that the marking of (r)i became already prevailing at a an early stage, when Saharan languages formed a closer unity, similar to the conceptualization of the Imperfective.

We observe that although individual formatives differ in each language, the basic formation pattern is identical. While the use and formation of the Imperfective TAM is rather homogenous in all Saharan languages, there has been a more complex development in the Perfective. While Beria still keeps the old bipartite system, Teda-Daza expanded to three, and Kanuri four perfective TAM categories, though the basic Saharan formative (**r**)**i** is still retained in all Saharan languages, however, with different functions.

The TAM negation makes clear in all Saharan languages that the distinction between Imperfective and Perfective is the only possible distinction. Again here, too, the formation patterns are identical. The Perfective applies a negative suffix which is attached to a basic TAM marker. The Negative Imperfect, however, is more complex, because it assumes an original syntactic negation strategy by applying a negative verboid meaning 'there is/are not'.

The Negative Potential follows a similar negation principle of the Perfective. This leads us to some hypotheses of the negative in the Saharan family and the contact languages (see Cyffer forthcoming). The following table shows the inventory of TAM categories in the three Saharan languages[5].

	BERIA	TEDA-DAZA	KANURI
Perfective	Completive	i-Form Aorist Perfect	Verb Emphasis Past Noun Emphasis Past Perfect Past
	Negative Completive	Negative Aorist	Negative Perfect
Imperfective	Incompletive	Progressive Future	Imperfect Potential
	Negative Imperfect	Negative Progressive	Negative Imperfect

Note : The terminology for Beria is adapted from Crass & Jakobi (ms), for Teda-Daza from Lukas (1953). Non-aspectual forms (e.g. Imperative) and derivations from the basic TAM categories (e.g. temporal subordination) are not considered here. Negation in Beria is not treated in greater detail. Therefore the mention in this table can only be tentative.

From the table one may conclude an increase of TAM categories from east to west. As some of these TAM categories also occur in other languages of the contact areas, we propose that contact phenomena played a role in the enrichment of the system.

There is convincing evidence that the Potential entered Kanuri and Teda-Daza as a result of contact with other languages, which are spoken in the west of the two languages, e.g. Fulfulde and Hausa.

[5] Command moods are not considered here.

The same may be assumed for the Noun Emphasis Past in Kanuri. This TAM applies when the subject or direct object is focused or topicalised, e.g.

Example 2

Kanuri			
a) Non-focus:	**Músa Kánoro**	***lewóno***	Musa went to Kano
b) Focus:	**Músa Kánoro**	***lezô***	[it was] Musa [who] went to Kano
	ndú Kánoro	***lezô ?***	who went to Kano?
Hausa			
a) Non-focus:	**Músa**	***yáa tafí* Káno**	Musa went to Kano
b) Focus:	**Músa née**	***yá tafí* Káno**	[it was] Musa [who] went to Kano
	waa	***yá tafí* Káno?**	who went to Kano?

We should note that the Noun Emphasis Past in Kanuri is not a basic Saharan TAM category, on the other hand its morphological set-up is more primary than the set-up of the Past. In fact the Past and the Potential are further extensions of the form which now acts a Noun Emphasis Past. This leads us to the assumption, that some TAM categories underwent functional and semantic shifts in the course of their development. K. Jarrett believes that this form was originally aspectless just denoting a punctiliar action (Jarrett 1981).

3. Word formation and TAM use

Kanuri allows abundant word formation processes. One of them is the nominalization of a clause as illustrated in table G (next page). Here the constructions are made up of a clause containing a finite verb form, and a facultative direct object or subject.

What is surprising is the fact that all the verbs of this nominalization process carry a TAM which is today rather peripheric because of its particular meaning. In present Kanuri it denotes a special emphasis on the verbal action. Therefore Lukas (1937) refers to it as 'Predicative'. Later it was named 'Verb Emphasis Past' (Cyffer 1998b).

In our context we observe that all examples apply a TAM ending in **-í**. This form is called in present grammatical descriptions Verb Emphasis Past (VEP), because it denotes the emphasis of the verbal action. However, we have also to note that this TAM is in present Kanuri the most peripheric of the perfective categories. We should also mention that similar word formation strategies don't allow, with the exception of the Imperative, any other TAM categories.

We come now to the question, why does only the VEP, and not the other perfective TAMs (i.e. Past, Noun Emphasis Past, Perfect) occur in such constructions? We may arrive at a plausible answer, when we take a look at the development of the Kanuri TAM system.

Table G: Noun formation involving finite verb forms

form / meaning	noun	3.ps.	verb base	3.ps.	TAM	lit. translation
təmají			**təma(n)**	**j < s**	**í**	*'s/he hoped'*
fiancé(e)			*expect*			
kamcejí	**kam**	**c < s**	**yes**		**í**	*'s/he killed a person'*
killer	*person*		*kill*			
kórórópcí	**kóro**		**láb(n)**	**c < s**	**í**	*'s/he loaded a donkey (with*
cloth (var.)	*donkey*		*load*			*cloth imported from Kano)'*
maimbáují	**mai**		**mbáu(n)**	**j < s**	**í**	*'the king became lower'*
vassal (of ruler)	*king*		*lack*			
nâkójí	**ná**		**kó(n)**	**j < s**	**í**	*'it passed the place'*
excess	*place*		*pass*			
sharawújí	**shara**		**wú(n)**	**j < s**	**í**	*'s/he looked at the court'*
legal	*law*		*look at*			
ílmu mbáují	**ílmu**		**mbáu(n)**	**j < s**	**í**	*'knowledge became less'*
unqualified	*knowledge*		*lack*			

As Kanuri is the best documented among the Saharan languages, and as reliable grammatical descriptions and text documentations date back to the mid 19th century (Koelle 1854a, 1854b), we are in the fortunate position to have access to earlier stages of the grammatical structure of Kanuri. This may not be a long period for detecting possible grammatical changes in a language, yet we can observe some interesting features with regard to different perceptions of time in Kanuri over the past 150 or more years.

The second important pillar to study the development of the TAM system is the examination from a Saharan perspective. All Saharan languages are documented well enough in order to provide a reliable picture of the TAM system in the family. The relatively small language family, only consisting of three languages (or language clusters), operates a similar basic TAM system. The basic distinction is aspectual, it differentiates between Perfective and Imperfective aspects. The Imperfective applies as its formative throughout a locative marker, the Perfective a formative (**r**)**i**. While in Beria this basic formation pattern is still applied, the other languages – Teda-Daza and Kanuri – have elaborated their system and created further differentiations, especially within the Perfective aspect.

In the following, I will throw some light on the development of the Kanuri system and uncover some of the intricacies which evolved in the process of time. Some of the innovative conteptualisations have evolved within the language, others seem to have developed through contact with other languages of the area.

Before coming to the linguistic interpretations, we should consider some historical facts which may have had an influence on the shape of the Kanuri language. The present habitat of the Kanuri speaking people is the area east and west of Lake Chad.

As earlier mentioned, the language began to spread about a 1000 years ago from Kanem in present Chad to the west because of the increasing political and economical influence of the Kanem-Borno empire in central Africa. Consequently, ongoing process of 'Kanurization' took place over the following centuries. This development still goes on in the southeast of the Kanuri speaking area. For example, part of the Malgwa ('Gamergu') people, living in the southeastern neighbourhood, have given up their own Central Chadic language in favour of Kanuri. Even the area around Maiduguri, the actual political, spiritual and cultural centre of the Kanuri, was marked in a map of the mid 19th century as «country of the Gamergu people» (Barth 1862-66). Therefore, we may conclude that a large scale cultural and linguistic shift in the area also left its imprint on the shape of the present structure of the Kanuri language. This may not have necessarily resulted in the adoption of Chadic substrates, but probably led to a take-over of other grammatical concepts. While we can expect that every language is apt to develop new linguistic categories according to new needs of the respective society, the Kanuri language has been even more flexible and adaptable for a long time. This is very overt and evident in the phonology, but may also play a role in its grammatical structure.

Though we cannot go back far into the historical depth, the few sources of the mid 19th century can provide some clues about the earlier structure of the language. In the past years, several studies were carried out to look into different aspects of linguistic contact phenomena. The present Kanuri TAM system has to be seen in this historical setting.[6]

4. S.W. Koelle's TAM description

S.W. Koelle's excellent description of Kanuri from 1854 is a very valuable source to study the linguistic change in the grammar over the past 150 years (Koelle 1854a). The grammar is well supplemented by the comprehensive collection of oral literature (Koelle 1854b). Both publications provide a very good insight into the language of the first half of the 19th century. However, we must keep in mind that the variety of Koelle's language data refers to a northern speech form. The present 'standard' of Maiduguri played a less prominent role.

The TAM categories differ in Koelle to some extent. Apart from using different terms, there also appears to be differences in the semantic and syntactic connotations. Koelle's 'Perfect', is nowadays called Verb Emphasis Past, and 'Aorist' (Past) evidently had a different meaning and function in those days. This is well illustrated by the following quotations.

[6] Our present project 'Linguistic innovation and conceptual change in West Africa' investigates the same process. The project is carried out at the University of Vienna and financed by the Austrian Science Fund (FWF), project nr. 15767.

a) Koelle 1854a, 226:

> «The perfect tense [*Verb Emphasis Past*] indicates past time fully completed. It may be said that the aorist [*Past*] indicates the inceptive, and perfect the completed end of past duration. If, e.g. you say **kádiskō** [*Past*], you convey the idea of your having once started, and then of having been performing the act of coming. If you say **ī′seskī** [*Verb Emphasis Past*] you convey the idea of your having fully completed and actually terminated your act of coming.»

b) Lukas 1937, 35:

> «The Predicative [*Verb Emphasis Past*] generally indicates past action, but differs from the Past in that it gives a predicative emphasis to the verb. But it is also used occasionally to express an action about to occur.»

c) Ellison 1937, 94:

> «The characteristic of this past tense [*Verb Emphasis Past*] is that emphasis is given to the idea contained in the verb itself, not, as in the Past and Relative Past tenses, to other words in the sentence. It emphasizes an achievement and indicates that an action has been accomplished unexpectedly or in spite of difficulty, doubt, initial failure, etc. ...»

He further states :

> «In the northern dialects of Kanuri the Predicative is often used in narrative, instead of Perfect and Past tenses, ...»

c) Hutchison 1981, 125:

> «The characteristic high tone level +**â** ending of the verb emphasis completive seems to corroborate its meaning and use to describe the sudden completion of the action of the verb.»

The so-called Verb Emphasis Past exemplifies well the dynamics of TAM developments in Saharan languages and in Kanuri in specific. This form can be traced in all languages. In Beria, where the distinction between Perfective and Imperfective is still the basic principle of time contrast, we meet the traditional Saharan concept of time relation.[7]

Example 3

Beria: **ɛbɛtɛ́ɪ** ***tɔ́kkɪ́nɪ́*** 'the story *is finished*' (Crass & Jakobi: MS)

Teda-Daza: **gónrī** 'I took' (Lukas 1953: 95, no example sentences given)

Note : Lukas (1953: 95) believes that the TAM is suffixed to the 'Aorist'. This would be a contradiction to our hypothesesis that this TAM is the basic Saharan Imperfective marker. I would therefore propose that the 'Aorist' in Teda-Daza is inherently unmarked and the **i**-form non necessarily suffixed to the Aorist. It should also be noted that Ch. and M. Le Coeur (1956) don't mention this form in their grammar.

[7] A. Jakobi and J. Crass (MS) also mention the existence of a Perfect and a Progressive in Beria. However, it is at present difficult to decide, whether these constructions are part of the Beria TAM system, or whether they are a result of syntactic structuring. In any case, they well illustrate the changing patterns of linguistic change.

Kanuri:	**Músa bâ,** ***lejí*** 'Musa is not [here], *he [just] left*'
but (regular) past:	**Músa bâ,** ***lewóno*** 'Musa is not [here], *he left*'

4.1 The Kanuri TAM system: Koelle's and present analyses

Sigismund Wilhelm Koelle's grammatical description made Kanuri one of the best documented African languages in the middle of the 19th century. Though Koelle lived and worked as a missionary in Sierra Leone[8] – far away from the Kanuri habitat – he produced a scholarly work of accuracy and sensation for the language. Together with the oral literature textbook, the study of West African languages entered into a new phase of linguistic competence and exhaustive description.[9]

It is interesting to note that Koelle treats 'tenses' and 'moods' from a morphological, syntactic and semantic perspective from within the Kanuri language. This at least applies to the general TAM concepts. In so far this is in contrast to many grammars of those times, which apply the categories of Latin, Greek or other European languages.

Table H: Koelle's TAM categories

'Tenses'	*Present Kanuri*
Indefinite I	Imperfect
Indefinite II	Sequential
	Noun Emphasis Past
	Subjunctive
Perfect	Verb Emphasis Past
Aorist	Past
Future	Potential, (Vague) Future
'Moods'	
Imperative	Imperative
Negative	
Negative Indefinite	Negative Completive
Negative Future	Negative Potential, Future
Conjunctional	
Past conjunctional	Dependent Past
Future conjunctional	Dependent Future
Participial	
Present	Perfect
Past	--
Future	(Present Participial)

Note : The terminology follows that of recent publications, e.g. Cyffer 1998.

---

[8] Koelle worked with freed slaves , who were resettled in Freetown.

[9] Koelle's magnificent vocabulary collection of more than 100 mainly West African languages should also be mentioned: S.W. Koelle (1854) *Polyglotta Africana,* Church Missionary Society, London.

Koelle's interpretation differs from the present system in several aspects. Apart from some differing opinions, it is remarkable that some conceptualizations must have changed over the past one or two centuries. However, we have to take into account the fact that there may have already been differences in the TAM system between southern and northern dialects. Koelle's Kanuri belongs to the southern group, probably on the borderline to the north.

a) *Indefinite II.* Here he merges three categories, which today are morphologically and syntactically dealt with separately. Though there is some morphological overlapping of the Sequential, Noun Emphasis Past, and Subjunctive, which may lead to a neutralisation on the surface, the three forms differ in tone (Subjunctive) and their formative (Sequential, Noun Emphasis Past).

b) *Perfect.* This form has evidently undergone semantic and functional changes. In present Kanuri it is rarely used and emphasises the verbal perfective action.

c) *Negative.* Koelle does not note a negative form of the Indefinite I, because he treats negation for this 'tense' as a syntactic construction (see below).

d) *Participial.* Far reaching changes may have taken place here. While the 'Participial Future' still exists in present Kanuri, Koelle's 'Participial Present' has the function of a regular Perfect TAM (see below).

As we possess good Kanuri language data from the mid 19th century onwards, as well as good information about several dialects, we can also make reliable statements about different TAM structures over the time and - possibly - in the different dialects. The following diagram illustrate the frequency and distribution of TAMs in the Perfective aspect.

Table I: TAM distribution in Kanuri

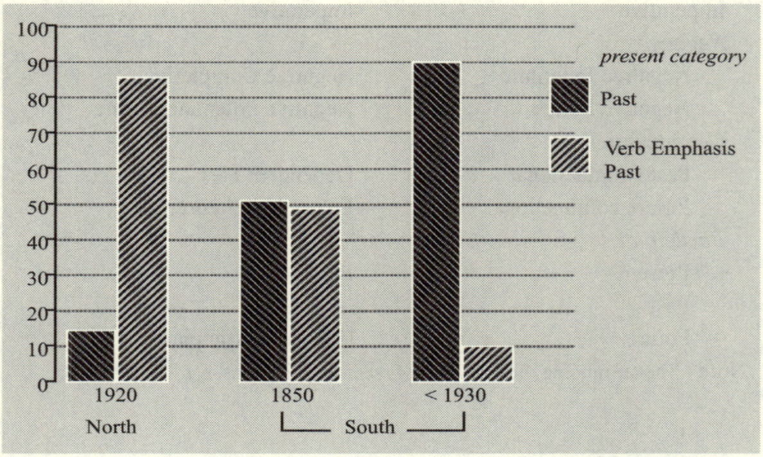

From this table we may draw the following conclusions. If we accept the TAM form ending in **-i**, most likely carrying a high tone, this TAM has been the general

Perfective aspect marker in Saharan languages. Due to functional changes, especially the expansion of the TAM system in Kanuri and Teda-Daza, the general Perfective function was lost. Instead, the role of a more specific mood was adopted in the two languages. In Teda-Daza it may have receded, however, in Kanuri it still exists. It appears to have possessed a more original function at least in the first half of the 19th century, because Koelle (1854a: 226) refers to it as Perfect. It is also remarkable that northern Kanuri dialects used it much more still, most likely as Perfective, in the beginning of the 20th century. This is confirmed by the texts edited by Lukas (1929) and the observations by Ellison (1937).

As mentioned, S.W. Koelle was the first to describe in detail the formation and functions of the Kanuri TAM categories. It is not surprising that Koelle's categories may not always overlap with contemporary interpretations. However, those differences should not at all be seen as misconceptions. In one or the other case there may be misinterpretations because of difficulties in handling tone at that time. In other cases Koelle's description differs, because concepts of time have changed during the past 150 years.

We have also good reasons to believe that in former times the **i**-form had a general perfective function in Kanuri. Several indications support this hypothesis. First, there are several lexicalized forms which can be deducted from former finite verb forms. For example, the adverbial **dají** 'finished, over' is derived from the (still) active verb **da(n)** 'be finished, be over', e.g. **cída dazә́na** 'the work is finished' in the Perfect TAM. Another evidence for the perfective function of the **i**-form in earlier Kanuri is its use when expressing a static meaning of a dynamic verb.

Example 4

no(n)	'get to know'	Present:	**nongә́na**	Koelle:	**nongí**	'I know'
bo(n)	'lay down'		**bongә́na**		**bongí**	'I lie down'

Though the verboid **mbéjí**, pl. **mbézái** 'there is/are' contains a 3rd person subject marker (**j** < **s**, **za** < **sa**), it is generally defective and cannot carry other persons or TAMs, e.g.

Example 5

wú mbéjí	I am / was available
kúngә́na mbéjí	there is / was money
ándí mbéjí / mbézái	we are / were available
tadawá mbéjí / mbézái	there are / were children

In the Manga dialect, however, we can still find a full verb **mbé(n)** 'be available', e.g.

mbézána	they have been available (3rd ps. sg., Perfect)
mbéngin	I will be available (1st ps., sg., Imperfect)

Another evidence for a broader use of the **i**-form comes from a derived TAM which is referred to as *Dependent Future* (Lukas 1937). The form is used in subordinate temporal clauses. It is made up of the (present) Verb Emphasis Past and extended by a suffix **-Ca**, e.g.

Example 6

fandəkí + Ca > fandəkíya 'when I get (*when I will have got*)'

kúngə̂na ***fandəkíya*** **Kánoro lengîn** '*when I get* money, I will travel to Kano («*when I will have got...*»)'

In a strict sense the term 'Dependent Future' is not appropriate, because here, too, we have got a Perfective TAM. Perfective is to be understood with reference to a point of time in the future when a given action will be completed. Therefore a more adequate translation would be «when I will have got the money ...».

We notice that most derived forms carry the suffix **-í** as their original TAM. Therefore I follow Koelle's interpretation (Koelle 1854a) and agree with him that this form was the original and general Perfective marker. Over the time it obtained a more specific function.

The basic difference between Koelle's and the present TAM description shows in table H.

We observe a significant functional and semantic change of the **i**-form in different periods of time. Koelle's Kanuri assistant reflects the language of the 1820s (when Ali Aisami was taken as a slave and deported from Borno). Unfortunately there are no texts documenting the period between that time and ca. 1900. But it appears, that changes of the TAM categories took place during that time. While some northern dialects did not perform the changes at the same time, the 'central' varieties, to which the standard variety belongs, replaced the i-form throughout by the Past. The **i**-form obtained an emphatic function and became less frequently used.

Conclusions

The present Kanuri TAM system is based on several factors:

1. It follows the general Saharan aspectual concept, i.e. the distinction between Perfective and Imperfective.
2. It has undergone internal developments in the enlargement of TAM categories. To these belongs the original Perfective marker **-i**, which has become an verb emphatic TAM.
3. It has taken over TAM concepts from other languages due to linguistic contact. These are in specific the Potential and the focus form ('Noun Emphasis Past'). The following table illustrates the development.

Table J: Development of the Kanuri TAM

ORIGIN	SAHARAN	INTERNAL	EXTERNAL
Imperfective			
Continuative	Imperfect		
Potential			Potential
Perfective			
Past		Past	
NP-Focus			Noun Emphatic Past
Emphatic	[Perfective]	Verb Emphatic Past	
Perfect		Perfect	
Temp. subord.			
Temp./condit. subord.			
Non-aspectual			
Command	Imperative		
Command		Optative	
Temp. sequence		Sequential	

Here, the question of Sprachbund comes up. In this case we come across similarities in the TAM system of Kanuri with languages in the west, e.g. Hausa or Fulfulde. This applies especially to the TAM categories Noun Emphasis Past and Potential. Both are found in a greater number of languages in West Africa. Consequently, Kanuri adopted these concepts from languages in the west. To talk in this context of a Sprachbund, may be premature, because there is no entire overlapping of the common features (including other than TAM similarities). However, what we can say at this time is that there appears to be a more or less well-defined border of common linguistic features extending from Lake Chad to the south (or southeast). As the borders of different features in the west are less defined, unlike in the east, we may speak of contact zones for different grammatical categories, which expanded from west to east and stopped in the Lake Chad region (meeting another contact zone in the east?)

Kanuri, spoken in the west and east of Lake Chad, may be under the influence of different contact zones (see also Cyffer 1998a, 2000).

References

BARTH, Heinrich, 1862/3, 1866, *Sammlung und Bearbeitung Central-Afrikanischer Vokabularien,* 3 vols., Gotha, J. Peters, Reprint: Frank Cass, London, 2 Bände 1971.

BUKAR, Shettima & John P. HUTCHISON, 1978, *Hawarwa Kanuribe,* Zaria, Northern Nigerian Publishing Company.

BUKAR, Shettima & John P. HUTCHISON, 1978, *Nyariwa Kanuribe,* Zaria, Northern Nigerian Publishing Company.

CRASS, Joachim & Angelika JAKOBI, (manuscript), *Grammaire descriptive du beria. Le dialecte kúbé.*

CRASS, Joachim, Barbara DEHNHARD, Ronny MEYER & Andreas WETTER, 2001, Von 'sagen' zum Verbbildungsmorphem: Die Grammatikalisierung des Verbs 'sagen' einmal anders, *Afrikanistische Arbeitspapiere,* 65: 129-141.

CYFFER, Norbert, 1978, Die Verbalstruktur im Kanuri, *Afrika und Übersee,* 61: 294-311.

CYFFER, Norbert, 1996, *Die saharanischen Sprachen - Innere und äußere Beziehungen.* Axel Fleisch & Dirk Otten (eds) *Sprachkulturelle und Historische Forschungen in Afrika. Beiträge zum 11. Afrikanistentag, Köln, 19.-21. September 1994.* Köln, Rüdiger Köppe, 103-118.

CYFFER, Norbert, 1998a, Basic time relations in the Saharan verbal systems, Petr Zima & Vladimir Tax (eds), *Language and location in space and time,* München, Lincom Europa, 45-53.

CYFFER, Norbert, 1998b, *A sketch of Kanuri,* Köln, Rüdiger Köppe.

CYFFER, Norbert, 2000, Areale Merkmale im TAM-System und in der Syntax der saharanischen Sprachen, R. Voßen, A. Mietzner & A. Meißner (Hgg.), *«Mehr als nur Worte....» Afrikanistische Beiträge zum 65. Geburtstag von Franz Rottland.* Köln, Rüdiger Köppe, 159-182.

CYFFER, Norbert, (forthcoming), *Negation patterns in Kanuri.*

CYFFER, N., D. LÖHR, E. PLATTE & A.I. TIJANI, 1997, Adaptation and delimitation. Some thoughts towards the Kanurization of the Gamergu in Borno, Nigeria, *Berichte des Sonderforschungsbereichs,* 6. Universität Frankfurt, Frankfurt/Main.

ELLISON, R. E., 1937, *English-Kanuri sentence book,* London, Crown Agents for the Colonies.

GAMBORU, Ali [Norbert CYFFER], 1978, *Səmonəm wuro sarusəgənə,* Lagos, Thomas Nelson.

HUTCHISON, John P., 1981, *The Kanuri language. A reference grammar,* Madison, University of Wisconsin, African Studies Program.

JARRETT, Kevin, 1981, The development of the Kanuri aspect system within Western Saharan, Thilo C. Schadeberg & M. Lionel Bender (eds), *Nilo-Saharan. Proceedings of the First Nilo-Saharan Linguistics Colloquium, Leiden, September 8-10, 1980,* 201-215.

KOELLE, Sigismund Wilhelm, 1854a, *Grammar of the Bornu or Kanuri language,* London, Church Missionary House.

KOELLE, Sigismund Wilhelm, 1854b, *African native literature or proverbs, tales, fables & historical fragments in the Kanuri or Bornu language,* London, Church Missionary House.

LE COEUR, Ch. et M., 1956, Grammaire et textes teda-daza, *Mémoires de l'Institut Français d'Afrique Noire* 46, Dakar.

LUKAS, Johannes, 1937 [1967], *A study of the Kanuri language. Grammar and vocabulary,* London, Oxford University Press, [Reprint: Dawson of Pall Mall, London].

LUKAS, Johannes, 1929, Kanuri Texte, *Mitteilungen des Seminars für Orientalische Sprachen zu Berlin,* 32: 41-92.

LUKAS, Johannes, 1953, *Die Sprache der Tubu in der zentralen Sahara,* Berlin, Akademie-Verlag.

NOEL, P., 1923, *Petit manuel français – kanouri,* Paris, Paul Geuthner.

SCHUBERT, Klaus, 1971-73, Zur Bedeutung und Anwendung der Verbalparadigmen im Hausa und Kanuri, *Afrika und Übersee,* 55 (1971/72): 1-49, 208-227, 367-300. 56 (1972/73): 90-118.

YALE, Umar, 1930, *Kitabuwa Kanuribe. Kitabu Kənyaskəmi.* Maiduguri, Bornu Native Administration.

TAM Markers in *Littafen Nahwowin Hausance* : Interpreted as Verbs?

Nikolay DOBRONRAVIN

St.Petersburg State University sokoto95@yandex.ru

Abstract

The article deals with the interpretation of Hausa TAM markers in *Littafen nahwowin hausance*, an Arabic-script work written not later than 1907 somewhere in today's Ghana. An early attempt to define parts of speech in Hausa made by a Hausa speaker is discussed. The anonymous amateur linguist used the Hausa word **suna** for both verbs (without TAM markers) and nouns, apparently treating the formation of plurals, etc., in terms of derivation (« the noun does not change »). Another Hausa word, **aiki**, was used in several sections to denote « work ; job ; action ». The author of *Littafen nahwowin hausance* also referred to **aiki** when he wrote about tense, aspect and mood, so practically about Hausa TAM markers. Only in the latter case was the word **aiki** apparently used as a term for a category opposed to **suna**. Various TAM paradigms in *Littafen nahwowin hausance* are described in the article. The split interpretation of Hausa verbs (verbal "infinitive" as a "noun" and the TAM marker as a "verb") is not entirely unanticipated, if one takes into consideration the peculiarities of the Imperfective forms in Hausa, especially in the North-Western dialect cluster.

Résumé

Cet article traite de l'interprétation des TAM du *hausa* dans *Littafen nahwowin hausance*, texte en alphabet arabe écrit au plus tard en 1907, quelque part dans le Ghana actuel. On y étudie une tentative ancienne faite par un locuteur *hausa*, de définir les parties du discours en *hausa*. Ce linguiste amateur et anonyme utilise le mot *hausa* **suna** à la fois pour les verbes (sans marque de TAM) et les noms, traitant apparemment la formation des pluriels en termes de dérivation (« le nom ne change pas »). Un autre mot *hausa*, **aiki**, est utilisé dans diverses parties pour signifier « travail, action ». L'auteur de *Littafen nahwowin hausance* utilise également le mot **aiki** quand il écrit à propos du temps, de l'aspect et du mode, c'est à dire, pratiquement, à propos des marques de TAM. C'est uniquement dans ce cas que le mot **aiki** est employé pour une catégorie opposée à **suna**. Divers paradigmes de TAM dans *Littafen nahwowin hausance* sont décrits dans l'article. Le clivage dans l'interprétation des verbes *hausa* (l'"infinitif" interprété comme un "nom" et les marques de TAM interprétées comme un "verbe") n'est pas totalement surprenant s'il l'on tient compte des formes de l'Imperfectif en *hausa*, particulièrement dans le continuum dialectal du Nord-Ouest.

The Hausa writings in Arabic script include a few works that represent a development of Islamic/Arabic linguistic thought and may be of interest for the linguists today. Most of these are translations from Arabic, such as a partial Hausa translation of *al-Muqaddima al-Ājurrūmiyya*, Arabic-"Ajami" glossaries and bilingual textbooks of Arabic. Some of them have been published, but were mostly ignored by the Hausaists.

Among these writings, one work seems to deserve special attention. This is *Littafen nahwowin hausance* (*Book of Hausa grammar*[1]). It was produced somewhere in the Northern Territories of the Gold Coast (in today's Ghana), maybe in Gambaga, not later than 1907. The work was brought to Europe by William Bradley Gosset (Gorset) Barne, 1880-1951, who served in the Northern Territories from 1905 to 1907. This and other Hausa manuscripts collected by Barne were eventually acquired by the SOAS Library in London[2].

Littafen nahwowin hausance includes a rich corpus of lexical data from various semantic fields, occasionally with folk etymology (human beings; tools; horses and donkeys; colours; males and females of various animals; locusts; wild animals; plants; hair styles; cotton; personal names; children; feelings; illnesses; age-classes), grammatical notes (possessive affixes and pronouns; verbs; questions and answers) as well as a tale of two rogues, ṣan Kano and ṣan Katsina. The description of the Hausa parts of speech in this work is neither "modern" nor just a translation from an Arabic work. In the following, the interpretation of TAM markers in *Littafen nahwowin hausance* will be discussed.

« SŪNĀ » AND « AIKI » : A SPLIT INTERPRETATION OF VERBS AND TAM MARKERS

The description of verbs in *Littafen nahwowin hausance* begins with a short section on the parts of speech in Hausa :

> **A Hausancī duka abūbuwa daban daban suke. Akoi sūnā. Akoi aiki. Shī kuma aiki ban_ban-ne. Akoi wanda anka-yi anka wanyē. Akoi wanda ake-yi. Akoi wanda za a yi kaman ana-son a yi ammā ba-a yi ba. Akoi wanda anka ce a yi, kaman wani ya-ce ma wani « yi ».**
> **Ammā sūnā shī bā shi jiwuyi. 'In yā rabō namiji kō yā rābō macce duka daya-ne. Haka in yā rābō kadaicī kō yawaicē. Haka nīsa da kusa. Haka kuma in rābe**

[1] Literally, « grammars ». The title could be also translated as « Book of arguments in Hausa », cf. Hausa **kada ka sa nahawu a cikin zancan nan**, « do not make this a matter of quarrelling, argument », in Bargery, who mentioned **nahawu** « **1.** *Grammar*. **2.** *Contradiction*; *disputing* » (1934: 811).

[2] MS 380271, « Hausa Islamic Poems collected by Capt. William B. G. Barne in 1906-1907 ». I am thankful to the SOAS Library, the British Academy, and all other institutions and colleagues in the United Kingdom for the opportunity to study these manuscripts. A special word of gratitude is owted to Graham Furniss.

shi abinda yaw-wuce kō mai-zuwa kō wanda ake ceki kō wanda aka-ce a yi duk daya-ne.[3]

« In Hausa all things are different. There is a noun (**sūnā**). There is a verb (**aiki**)[4]. The verbs are also different. There is what is done and completed. There is what is being done. There is what is about to be done, but it has not been done. There is what was told to be done, as if one told another, « do ».
But the noun does not change. Whether it is linked to a male or to a female, it is the same. Likewise, be it linked to singularity or to plurality. Likewise, be it distant or close. Likewise, whether it is linked to what passed by or to what is coming, or to what one is in the process of doing, or to what was told to be done, it is the same. »

Some nuances of this description, especially in the second part of it, must sound strange to anyone familiar with the Hausa language. As a matter of fact, Hausa has a masculine/feminine gender opposition correlating with the morphonological shape of the nouns and a singular/plural number opposition with many different types of plural formation, even though there is no gender opposition in the plural, and some nouns are singularia tantum or do not have morphologically distinct plurals. What follows makes it clear that the anonymous author of *Littafen nahwowin hausance* wrote about a very different category, in fact about the words that are considered verbs today :

Kotamcin sūnā kaman « tāshi ». « Tāshi » sū_nā ne bā shi jiwuya ga-kōwā. 'Ance ma namiji « kā tāshi », mace « kin tāshi », tārō « kun tāshi », wanda bā-yanan « yā tāshi », wanda bā-tā-nan « tā tāshi », wadanda bā su nan « sun tāshi ». Haka kuma 'a ce ma macce « tāshi » namiji « tāshi », tārō « ku-tāshi », wanda bā shi nan « ya-tāshi », wanda bā ta nan « ta-tāshi », wadanda bā su nan « sutāshi ». To haka sūnayē duka ba-su jiwuya. Kaman « ci » 'ai kā ga bā shi jiwuya sūnā ne. Haka « sha » haka « ji ». Ka-ce « kā ci », « kin-ci », « sun-ci », « kunci », « mun-ci », « nā ci », « yā ci », « tā ci », « 'an-ci », kaman « 'an tāshi ».

« An example of a noun [is] like **tāshi** (« stand up »). **Tāshi** is a noun, it does not change for anybody[5]. One says to a man **kā tāshi** (« you (m.) stood up »), to a woman **kin tāshi** (« you (f.) stood up »), to a crowd **kun tāshi** (« you (pl.) stood up »), to the one (m.) who is not here **yā tāshi** (« he stood up »), to the one (f.) who is not here **tā tāshi** (« she stood up »), to those who are not here **sun tāshi** (« they stood up »). Likewise, one should say to a woman **tāshi** (« stand up ! »), to a man **tāshi** (« stand up ! »), to a crowd **ku-tāshi** (« you (pl.) stand up ! »), to the one (m.) who is not here **ya-tāshi** (« let him stand up »), to the one (f.) who is not here **ta-tāshi** (« let her stand up »), to those who are not here **su-tāshi** (« let them stand up »). Well, likewise all the nouns do not change. Like **ci** (« eat »), you see, it does not change, it is a noun.

[3] The Arabic letters are transliterated in a simplified way. « Long » vowels are always marked, even though they are not necessarily long in any variety of the Hausa language. The choice between **u** and **o**, marked with the same vowel-sign in the manuscript, is made in accordance with modern Nigerian orthography; standard spelling is also given in the examples. The actual pronunciation in the author's « Ghanaian » idiolect of Hausa is often unknown. A graphic word in the manuscript may correspond to more than one word in Roman script, e.g., **bā-ya-nan** « he is not here ». If the contrary occurs, the symbol _ is used, e.g., **ban_bancēwā** « difference ».

[4] Literally, « work ». In modern Hausa linguistics, the cognate word **aikatau** is used to denote the verb.

[5] That is, it does not inflect for gender, number, etc.

Likewise **sha** (« drink ») ; likewise **ji** (« hear »). One should say **kā ci** (« you (m.) ate »), **kin-ci** (« you (f.) ate »), **sun-ci** (« they ate »), **kun-ci** (« you (pl.) ate »), **mun-ci** (« we ate »), **nā ci** (« I ate »), **yā ci** (« he ate »), **tā ci** (« she ate »), **an-ci** (« someone ate »), like **an tāshi** (« people stood up ») ».

It is true that the words referred to as « nouns » in the text are typically unchangeable in Hausa. As stated by Jaggar, « with the exception of the Imperative, the verb as such does not inflect for tense, aspect, and modality, nor for person/number » (2001 : 148). These « verbs as such » have been analyzed as « finite verbs », « verb stems » or, without TAM markers, as « Infinitives » (Wolff 1993; Newman 2000; Jaggar 2001). The author of *Littafen nahwowin hausance* took a different approach. He used the Hausa word **sūnā** for two categories that seem entirely different, that is, verbs (without TAM markers) and nouns, apparently treating the formation of plurals, etc., in terms of derivation rather than inflection (« the noun does not change »)[6].

With such a wide range for the nouns, what could he leave for a category he called **aiki** in Hausa? As a matter of fact, his view of **aiki** was not clearcut. On one hand, **aiki** was used in several sections to denote « work ; job ; action », e.g.:

Sūnan macce mai-sābuwal haifuwā « mai bīƙi ». Kō sūnan aikin-nan « jēgo », macce kuwa « mai-jēgo ». Sūnan abinda jinin ke-yi « kazni », kō « wāri ». Ban_ban-ne akoi « dowoyi », shē-ne dai, akoi « bāshī », akoi « kamshī ». Haka cikin aikinsu akoi « shākawā », akoi kuma « sunsunāwa ».

« The name for a woman who has a new-born baby is **mai bīƙi**. Otherwise, the name for this activity is **jēgo** (« suckling of infant »), and for the woman, **mai-jēgo**. The [effect] produced by the blood is **ƙazni** (« smell of blood, fish, meat, nursing-mother, rancid matter, etc. ») or **wāri** (« stench, bad smell »). It is different; there is **ɗōyi** (« stench », this is one[7]. There is **bāshī** (« bad smell of rotting meat or fish »). There is **ƙamshī** (« fragrant smell »). Likewise, among the actions [connected with] these, there is **shāƙawā** (« smelling, sniffing at something »), also there is **sunsunāwa** (« smelling, sniffing »).

On the other hand, the author of *Littafen nahwowin hausance* referred to **aiki** when he wrote about tense, aspect and mood, so practically about Hausa TAM markers. Only in the latter case was the word **aiki** apparently used as a term for a category opposed to **sūnā.**

This split interpretation of verbs (as we treat them today) as « nouns » and TAM markers as « verbs » may look strange, but it is not entirely unanticipated, if one takes into consideration the peculiarities of the Imperfective forms in Hausa.

---

[6] The exception mentioned in the same chapter of « Littafen nahwowin hausance » concerns what we call « verbal grades » and « verbal extensions », e.g.: **Ammā fa shī sūnā idan an-yi shi an wanyē yakan jiwuya kadan. Akan ƙāra masa nun gudā dayā kuma a sa mata gudā ƙasa a jā ta, dōmin an wanyē duka.** « But the noun, if it is done and completed, changes slightly. One adds to it a « nun », and one adds a dot [to this letter] and pulls it, because everything is completed », with a reference to **ci** « eat » > **canyē** « eat up » and **sha** « drink » > **shanyē** « drink up »).

[7] Or: « this is **ɗ(w)ai** » (Western Hausa).

These features, when a « verbal » form is represented by a combination of a TAM marker and a « verbal noun » (« nominalized verb »)[8], are even more widespread in Western Hausa.

TAM PARADIGMS IN *LITTAFEN NAHWOWIN HAUSANCE*

The account we find in *Littafen nahwowin hausance* is sometimes clumsy. The author selected a few most frequent verbs (« nouns ») and made several lists of possible combinations with TAM markers. Some of the markers were omitted. Nevertheless an overview of the TAM system in a « Ghanaian » Hausa idiolect (in its written representation) may be made on the basis of this description :

		sg.	pl.
Pf1	1	**nā**	**mun**
	2m.	**kā**	**kun**
	2f.	**kin/kē (kē zaka)**	
	3m.	**yā**	**sun**
	3f.	**tā**	
	4		**an**
Pf2	1	**na/niz (zō)**	**muka/munka**
	2m.	**ka/kak(zō), kaC**	**kuka/kunka**
	2f.	**kika/kik (zō)**	
	3m.		**suka/sunka**
	3f.	**ta/tat (zō), taC**	
	4		**aka/anka**
Ipf1	1	**ina**	**muna**
	2m.	**kana**	
	2f.	**kina**	
Ipf2	1	**nake/nika**	**muke/muka**
	2m.	**kake/kaka**	**kuke/kuka**
	2f.	**kike/kika**	
	3m.		**suke/suka**
	3f.	**take/taka**	
	4		**ake/aka**
Fut (a)	1	**nā (?), Neg. bā ni (?)**	**mā (?)**
	2m.		
	2f.		
	3m.	**yā (?)**	**sū/swā (?)**
	3f.	**tā (?)**	
Fut (b)	1	**nā/nī (?)**	**mā/mwā (?)**
	2m.	**kā (?)**	
	2f.	**kī (?)**	
	3m.		**sū /swā (?)**
	3f.	**tā (?)**	
	4		**ā (?)**

[8] As stated by Wolff, « for a Hausa verb to occur in the « progressive » (or: « continuative ») aspect, it must use a nominal form » (1991 : 92).

Subj/ Imperative	1	**in**	
	2m.	**tāshi (m.=f.)**	**ku**
	2f.		
	3m.	**ya**	**su**
	3f.	**ta**	
	4		**a**
Hab	1	**nakan/nikan**	**mukan**
	2m.	**kakan**	**kukan**
	2f.	**kikan**	
	3m.		**sukan**
	3f.	**takan**	
	4		**akan**

The author of *Littafen nahwowin hausance* paid special attention to gender and number distinction in person marking:

> **A hausanci namiji ke da « ya » macci ke-da « ta ». Namiji ke da kaf-lasan da wasali bisa**[9] **macce ke da ka_f-lasan da wasali kasa**[10]**. Amma kaf-lasan mai guda kasa**[11] **jiuye_jiuyensa na-da yawa. Taron da ke-nan ke-da kaf-lasan da rufuDa**[12]**. Taron da ba ya nan ke-da sin kekasashe da rufu'a**[13]**. Taron maza da na-mata duka daya ne haka aka ce tun_tuni.**

> « In Hausa, the masculine has **ya**, the feminine has **ta.**[14] The masculine has **ka**, the feminine has **ki**. As concerns **ke,** it has many varieties. 2pl. (« the crowd that is here ») has **ku**. 3pl. (« the crowd that is not here ») has **su**. The masculine and the feminine plurals (« the crowd of men and women ») are the same, that was said before. »

This description is of interest, as it stresses the stability of person marking with the exception of 2sg.f. The author of *Littafen nahwowin hausance* did not mention the Western Hausa TAM marker **shi** in 3sg.m., although he was certainly familiar with it. The absence of 3sg.m. in several lists may indicate that the writer was familiar with both **ya**- and **shi**-forms, but was not sure which of them would be better for the paradigms. In the text, the **ya**-forms (3sg.m. Ipfl **yana**, Ipf2 **yake**, etc.) are mainly used, but a few « Western » markers are also found.

In the same section of the manuscript, a few more notes are related to Impers. and 1sg.:

> **In an-yi abu ba-ka san wanda yay-yi-ba kō namiji nē kō mace cē, kō tārō ne na-mazā kō na-mātā, kō kuwa garwayē-ni mazā da mātā cē « an-yi ». Abinda bā kēba ba kuma ba-a nufi wani ba nan ne akan-sa alif da wasalī bisa, ta'are**[15] **da nun. Ammā in kā ga alif da wasalī ƙasa ta'are da nun damrarrē kō mai-wasalī bisa na-mai maganan nan-ne, « in kāwō », kō « ina kāwowā ». A nan namiji da macce duka daidai-ne.**

---

[9] That is, **ka**.
[10] That is, **ki**.
[11] That is, **ke**.
[12] That is, **ku**.
[13] That is, **su**.
[14] Literally, « a man has **ya**, a woman has **ta**. »
[15] Read **tāre**.

« If something was done, and you do not know who did it, be it a man, a woman or a crowd of men or women, or a mixture of men and women, say **an-yi** (« someone did », Impers. Pf1). [Speaking about] something that is not set aside[16], and nobody is meant, one usually places an « alif » and a « wasali bisa » together with a « nun»[17]. But if you see an « alif » with a « wasali ƙasa » together with a « bound nun » or [a « nun »] with a « wasali bisa »[18], it is a [reference] to the speaker, **in kāwō** (« (so that) I bring; let me bring », 1sg. Subj.) or **ina kāwowā** (« I am bringing », 1sg. Ipf1). Here a man and a woman are all the same.[19] »

The TAM markers of 1pl. are not described separately in the manuscript, although they are mentioned in the sections where various TAM paradigms are drawn out.

In the text of the manuscript, **na** (Ipf1), **ke** (Ipf2) and **kan** (Hab) are also found without personal affixes, e.g.:

Akoi wani wurī kuma halussa kan sassābā, kaman « jākī » kō « jakkī », « mātuwā », « jākā ».

1	**akwai**	**wani**	**wurī**	**kuma**	**halussa**	**kan**	**sassāɓā**	**kama-n**
	there is/are	Indef.sg.m.	place	Part.	tongues (pl.)	Hab	disagree	like

jākī	**kō**	**jakkī**	**mātuwā**
« donkey »	or	« donkey », Western Hausa	« she-ass », Western Hausa

« There are some places as well, where the words differ, like **jākī** *or* **jakkī** *(« donkey »),* **mātuwā** *[and]* **jākā** *(« she-ass »). »*

The author of *Littafen nahwowin hausance* apparently formed a clear view of Pf1 and Ipf1 and described them together:

Abinda mai maganan nan yay-yi yaw-wanyē in yana-son ya-fadā ma wani sai ya-sa-nun gudā da wasalī bisa ya-jā shi, yac-ci « nā ce », kō « nā shā ». Haka sauran duka. Tārō kuwa abinda suke ciki ba-su wanyē ba in zā su fadē-shi sai su-sa min mai-rufu'a su-sa kuma nun arat mai wasalī bisa su-ce « muna ». In kuwa sun wanyē ne sai su-da_mre nun arat nan su-ce « mun ». In macce kuma zā ta fade abinda take ciki ba-ta wanyē-ba kaman namiji nē ta-ce « 'ina ». Haka tāron mātā su-ce « muna ». In kuwa za'a ka[20] tanbayi namiji abinda yake ciki bai wanyē-ba sai ka-sa kaf-lāsan da wasalī bisa ba-a ja, ka-sa nun gudā kuma da wasalī bisa ba-a ja ka-ce « kana », macce « kina ». Idan kuwa wanda yaw-wanyē-ne sā kaf-lāsan mai-jā da wasalī bisa cē « kā », macce « kin ». Idan kuwa za a ka tanbayi ta'arō[21] abinda suka wanyē sā kaf-lāsan mai-rufu'a da nun gudā damrarrē cī « kun ».

« [As concerns] something that the speaker has done and completed, if he wants to tell [about it] to somebody else, he should put a « nun » with a « wasali bisa » and pull it.[22] He should say **nā ce** (« I said », 1sg. Pf1) or **nā shā** (« I drank »). The same

[16] The marker **a** (Impers.) could be expected here. The supposed elision of **a** after the negative particle **ba** will be discussed below.
[17] That is, **an**.
[18] That is, **in** or **ina**.
[19] That is, there is no gender distinction in the TAM markers.
[20] Read **zā ka**.
[21] Read **tārō**.
[22] That is, « he should say **nā** ».

> with everything else. [As concerns] a crowd, if they are going to speak of something they are doing and have not completed, they should put a « mim » with a « rufu'a », then a « nun », which is similar to a « ra », with a « wasali bisa »[23] and say **muna** (1pl. Ipf1). If they have finished, they should « bind » a « nun », which is like a « ra », and say **mun** (1pl. Pf1). If a woman is going to speak of something she is doing and has not completed, like a man, she should say **ina** (1sg. Ipf1). Likewise a crowd of women should say **muna** (1pl. Ipf1). If you are going to ask a man about something he is doing and has not completed, you should place a « kaf lasan » with a « wasali bisa » and not pull [it], then you should place a « nun » with a « wasali bisa », not pull [it], and say **kana** (2sg.m. Ipf1), [if it is] a woman, **kina** (2sg.f. Ipf1). If [you are going to ask] someone who has finished, place a « kaf lasan » pulling a « wasali bisa »[24] and say **ka** (2sg.m. Pf1), [if it is] a woman, **kin** (2sg.f. Pf1). If you are going to ask a crowd about something they have finished, place a « kaf lasan » with a « rufu'a » and a « bound nun », and say **kun** (2pl. Pf1).

In the same chapter there is another description of the TAM paradigm in Pf1, this time compared with Pf2:

> **Ammā labarin da ya-wuce, lōkacinsa kuma yā wuce, ammā ana-son a fadē-shi yanzu kaman sa'anda anka yi-shi, sai a ce « ba'ara**[25] **da kay-yi-kiranā na-zō », kō « niz-zō ». Haka « ka-zō », kō « kak-zō », « kika zō », « kik-zō », « ta-zō », kō « tat-zō », « suka zō », kō « sunka zō », « muka zō », kō « munka zō », « kuka zō », « kunka zō », « aka zō », kō « anka zō ».**
> **Ammā aikin da aka wanyē, lō_kacinsa bai-wuce ba sai a ce « nā zō », « kā zō », kō « kā zaka » « kin zō », kō « kē zaka », « tā zō », kō « tā zaka », « sun zō », kō « sun zaka », « mun zō », kō « mun zaka », « kun zō », kō « kun zaka », « an zō », kō « an zaka ».**
>
> « As for the matter that has passed, and its time has passed, but one wants to speak of it now, as if it were at the time when it was done, one should say, **bāra da kay-yi kiranā na zō** (« last year when you called me I came »), or **niz zō** (1sg. Pf2). Likewise **ka zō** or **kak zō**[26], (2sg.m. Pf2), **kika zō** [or] **kik zō**[27] (2sg.f. Pf2), **ta zō** or **tat-zō**[28] (3sg.f. Pf2), **suka zō** or **sunka zō** (3pl. Pf2), **muka zō** or **munka zō** (1pl. Pf2), **kuka zō** [or] **kunka zō** (2pl. Pf2), **aka zō** or **anka zō** (Impers.).
> As for the action that was finished, but its time has not passed, one should say **nā zō** (1sg. Pf1), **kā zō** or **kā zaka** (2sg.m. Pf1), **kin zō** or **kē zaka** (2sg.f. Pf1), **tā zō** or **tā zaka** (3sg.f. Pf1), **sun zō** or **sun zaka** (3pl. Pf1), **mun zō** or **mun zaka** (1pl. Pf1), **kun zō** or **kun zaka** (2pl. Pf1), **an zō** or **an zaka** (Impers. Pf1). »

It is thus clear that the author of *Littafen nahwowin hausance* considered both TAM paradigms of PF2 as acceptable. As a matter of fact, they were used indiscriminately in the manuscript. One of these paradigms may be described as Western Hausa, while the other one is common in the dialects of the Eastern/Central complex, in Zima's terms (Zima 2002), and in Standard Hausa.

---

[23] That is, **muna**.
[24] That is, **kā**.
[25] Read **bāra**.
[26] The real pronunciation is unknown, probably **kaz zō**.
[27] Probably pronounced as **kiz zō**.
[28] Probably pronounced as **taz zō**.

Two aspects of this description are worth closer attention. As for Pf2, there is almost no doubt that the the markers **niz (zō)**, **kak (zō)**, **kik (zō)**, and **tat (zō)** should be interpreted as **niC**, **kaC**, **kiC**, and **taC** respectively on the surface level. However, if the author of *Littafen nahwowin hausance* pronounced them in a similar way, as **niz zō**, **kaz zō**, or **taz zō** (as he most probably did), why did he use different letters to mark the assimilated consonant? If we look at the paradigm, it becomes obvious that he saw the initial and final consonants in 2sg. and 3sg.f. as identical, that is, **kVk** and **tVt**. In the text of *Littafen nahwowin hausance*, all such final consonants are marked with a gemination sign, as in **yac ce** « he said », **tac ce** « she said » (3sg.f. Pf2).

As concerns the forms of 2sg.f Pf1 mentioned in this chapter, **kin zō** and **kē zaka** (but neither ***kē zō** nor ***kin zaka**), the actual role of **kē** remains unclear. This marker, similar to the independent pronoun of 2sg.f., is mentioned in Zima (2002 : 269) among the TAM markers of Dogondoutchi Hausa (Arauci, a Northwestern dialect). It is not used anywhere else in the text of *Littafen nahwowin hausance*. It may be assumed that the author of the work was aware of the existence of this TAM marker, but did not use it in his idiolect. The same may be said of the marker reconstructed as **kiC** (2sg.f Pf2), also used in Dogondoutchi Hausa and missing in the text of the manuscript beyond the TAM paradigm.

Before the comparative description of Pf1 and Pf2, one finds a paradigm of Ipf2:

> **Idan kuwa aka ga mutum yana tafiya bai-daina ba aka tanbayē-shi « inā zā ka » ya-ce « gidā nake zuwa », kō « nika zuwa », « kake zuwa », kō « kaka zuwa », « kike zuwa », kō « kuka zuwa »**[29]**, « take zuwa », kō « taka zuwa », « suke zuwa », kō « suka zuwa », « muke zuwa », kō « muka zuwa », « kuke zuwa », kō « kuka zuwa » , « ake zuwa », kō « aka zuwa ».**
>
> « If one saw a person who is walking and does not stop and asked him, **ina za ka** (« where are you going ? »), he would say, « I am going home » (**gidā nake zuwa**, 1sg. Ipf2), or **nika zuwa** ; [this paradigm also includes] **kake zuwa** or **kaka zuwa** (2sg.m. Ipf2), **kike zuwa** (2sg.f. Ipf2) or **kuka** (?) **zuwa**, **take zuwa** or taka zuwa (3sg.f. Ipf2), **suke zuwa** or **suka zuwa** (3pl. Ipf2), **muke zuwa** or **muka zuwa** (1pl. Ipf2), **kuke zuwa** or kuka **zuwa** (2pl. Ipf2), **ake zuwa** or **aka zuwa** (Impers. Ipf2) ».

There was no attempt to describe the meaning of these forms. As in Pf2, two paradigms of the TAM markers are given. It is worth mention that the author of the work did not use any « Western » TAM marker (**nika**, etc.) in his text. As for the marker of 3sg.m. Ipf2, it is found in *Littafen nahwowin hausance* only in its « Eastern » form (**yake**), e.g., next to the TAM marker of 3sg.m. Hab **yakan**:

> **Wadansu kuwa sukan-ce, asalin-miji mai-ja dōmin yakan jā** (3sg.m. Hab) **mātā zuwa inda yake-so** (3sg.nm. Ipf2).
>
> « Some people usually say, [that] the origin of **miji** (« husband ») is [from] **mai-ja** (« dragging »), because he usually drags wives where he wants »

[29] Most probably a wrong vowel-sign, should be **kika zuwa**.

The « Western » variant of 3sg.m. Hab **shikan** is found only once in the manuscript, together with the sole « Western » marker of 3sg.m Subj:

Shē-ne in an-sō shi-yi suka shikan kiya.

2	**shī**	**ne**	**in**	**an**	**so**	**shi**	**yi**	**suka**	**shikan**	**ƙiya**
	Ind. 3sg.m.	Cop.	if	Impers. Pfl	want	3sg.m. Subj	do	galloping	3sg.m. Hab	refuse

« It is [called **tsayayya**, *« stubbornness (of a horse) »], if one wants [the horse] to gallop, and it usually refuses. »*

Both **yakan** and **shikan** are missing in the relevant TAM paradigm:

Abinda kam-maimaitā da yawa, in zā ka fadē-shi yanzu to sā nun gudā da kaf-lāsan da nun arat damrarriyā, cē « bāba kulun kay-yi kirānā ai nakan zō », kō « nikan », « kakan », « kikan », « takan », « sukan », « mukan », « kukan », « akan ».

« [As concerns] something you repeatedly did, if you are going to speak of it now, well, place a « nun », and a « kaf lasan », and a « bound nun », which is similar to « ra ». Say, **bāba kulun kay-yi kirānā ai nakan zō** (« Father, everytime you call me I usually come[30] »), or **nikan** (1sg. Hab); [the paradigm also includes] **kakan** (2sg.m. Hab), **kikan** (2sg.f. Hab), **takan** (3sg.f. Hab), **sukan** (3pl. Hab), **mukan** (1pl. Hab), **kukan** (2pl. Hab), **akan** (Impers. Hab). »

The TAM markers of Fut are described twice in the manuscript. One of the lists includes only the markers (list 1 in the table) :

Idan kuwa an tanbayē-ka abinda za a ka-yi[31] gaba in ka'a yi to amsā da nun gudā da alif damrarrē, cī « na' ». In kuwa ba-ka yi-ba a gaba amsā da bā da alif mai-damri da nun arat cē « ba' ni ». Haka macce. Wanda ba-ya-nan cī « ya' », macce « ta' », tāronku « ma' », tāronsu « su' », kō « suwa'a ». Haka duka aki jijjiuyāwa. Ban_bancēwā ke-nan ta-abinda fadi_nsa yas-sāba halshe yaz-zama biyū kō uku duka kuwa Hausancī ne.

« If one asks you about what you will do in future, if you do, well, answer with « nun » and « bound alif »[32]. Say **na'** (1sg. Fut). If you do not do [it] in future, answer with « ba », and « binding alif », and « nun » which is similar to « ra »[33]; say **ba' ni** (1sg. Neg Fut). The same, [if it is] a woman. [As concerns] one who is not here, say **ya'** (3sg.m. Fut), [if it is] a woman, [say] **ta'** (3sg.f. Fut), [if it is] your crowd[34], **ma'** (1pl. Fut), [if it is] their crowd[35], **su'** or **suwa'a** (3pl. Fut). This is the way everything changes. This is the difference in what disagrees and becomes two or three [variants], and all are Hausa. »

If we compare this incomplete paradigm with that of Standard Hausa, it becomes evident that the author of *Littafen nahwowin hausance* combined two forms of Fut in his idiolect and was aware of it. On one hand, the TAM marker of 1pl. **ma**,

---

[30] The meaning of this sentence, negative and possibly interrogative, is not entirely clear.
[31] Read **zā ka-yi**.
[32] That is, **nā**.
[33] That is, **bā n[i]**.
[34] That is, 1pl.
[35] That is, 3pl.

apparently referred to as « **ma'** »[36] in the manuscript, is also used in the eastern Hausa dialects. The same marker is found in Standard Hausa beside the variant **mwa**, which is common in most Western dialects. The TAM markers **na** (1sg., « **na'** » in the manuscript), **ya** (3sg.m., « **ya'** ») and **ta** (3sg.f., « **ta'** ») are found in both Standard Hausa and most dialects, except a few Hausa varieties in the North-West of the language area (Arewa, Adar, Kurfay). As concerns 3pl., one form of the marker, written as « **suwa'a** » in the manucript (most probably, **swā**), is also used in both Standard Hausa (together with **sa**) and most Hausa dialects. The variant **su** (« **su'** ») is less common and may be compared with **« ba' ni »** (1sg. Neg Fut). The markers **su** and (**ba**) **ni**, are apparently related to the TAM markers of Neg Ipf.

All the markers in the first list are given in an isolated form, without corresponding « nouns ». In the second list, a more complete paradigm is drawn out, together with the « noun » of motion **zō**:

> **Kō yau kuma kay-yi kiranā, « na'a zō », kō « ni'i zō », « ka'a zō », « ki'i zō », « ta'a zō », « su'u zō », kō « suwa'a zo », « ma'a zō », kō « mu'a zō », « 'a'a zō ».**
>
> « If you call me today, I will come (**na'a zō** or **ni'i zō**); [the paradigm includes] **ka'a zō** (2sg.m.), **ki'i zo** (2sg.f.), **ta'a zō** (3sg.f.), **su'u zō** or **suwa'a** (3pl.), **ma'a zō** or **mu'a zō** (1pl.), **a'a zō** (Impers.). »

The presence of two different types of TAM markers is apparent here. The « hamza » (« glottal-stop sign ») in both variants is most probably orthographical, and the pronunciation of the markers may be reconstructed as **nā/nī, kā, kī, yā, tā, mā/mwā, su/swā,** and **ā**. The marker of 2pl. is missing in the lists as well as the other chapters of the work.

As for Subj, the TAM paradigm does not look different from that of Standard Hausa (see Table 1). In the text, other markers are found, **ka** (2sg.m.), **ki** (2sg.f.) and **mu** (1pl.), also with the negative marker **kad** or **kada**. In one case, which has already been mentioned, the « Western » TAM marker **shi** (3sg.m.) was also used in the manuscript.

The author of *Littafen nahwowin hausance* did not place the combinations of personal markers with **zā** among the TAM markers, even though he used **zā ka** (2sg.m., also written as **za-a ka** and **za a ka**), **zai** (3sg.m.), **zā ta** (3sg.f.), **zā mu** (1pl.) and **zā 'a** (Impers.) in his text, e.g.:

Dan Kano yac-ce kaka zā-mu-yi

3	**ɗa-n**	**kano**	**yac**	**ce**	**ƙaƙa**	**zā**	**mu**	**yi**
	son-of	Kano	3sg.m. Pf2	say	how	go	1pl. (Ipf?)	do

« The Kano man said, What are we going to do ? »

[36] This and other markers written with an « alif » and a combination of a « hamza » (corresponding to a glottal stop) and a « sukun » (a « zero-sign », indicating that no vowel is used here) were probab139y pronounced with long vowels: **mā, nā, yā, tā, sū, bā.**

In *Littafen nahwowin hausance* **zā** is found in combinations with two different word classes (in today's terms, with verbs and verbal nouns), as in the section where the linkers, **-n** and **-t/-l**, are described:

> **In zā ka rāba wani abu da wani, dūbi na-fārin in namiji nē sā nūn damrarrē, kada ka-kula da na-biyu. In kuwa na-fari ni nnan macce cē, sā lam damrarrē, kō ka-sa tā damrarriyā, kai-dai-ba' kulā[37] da na-biyu. Idan kuwa yawaicē-ne zā ka rabawā duka sā nūn gudā mazā da mātā.**
>
> « If you are going to link one thing to another, look at the first [word]. If it is masculine, place a « bound nun » [and] do not pay attention to the second one. If the first one is feminine, place a « bound lam » or a « bound ta », [and] do not pay attention to the second one. If it is the entire multitude that you are going to link[38], place a « dotted nun » [for both] men and women[39]. »

Two similar phrases are found here, with **rāɓa**, literally « lean, prop » (against the wall, etc.), usually treated as a verb, and with a cognate word, **raɓawā** (« leaning propping »), commonly described as a verbal noun today.

As the tones are not marked, and the examples of the **zā**-forms are not frequent in the manuscript, it is difficult to compare them with the **za**-markers and with one more **zā**, usually treated as a verb of motion, in various Hausa dialects and Standard Hausa. It is not clear whether the same **zā** was used in the examples quoted above and in the only sentence in the manuscript, where **zā** and a personal marker are followed by the TAM marker of Subj and the corresponding « noun »:

Dan Katsina yac-ce to kai dan Kano zamnā nan zā ni in-nēmo takarkarī yac-ce to ya-tafi.

4	**ɗa-n**	**katsina**	**yac**	**ce**	**to**	**kai**	**ɗa-n**	**kano**	**zamnā**	**nan**	**za**
	son-of	Katsina	3sg.m. Pf2	say	well	2sg.m.Ind.	son-of	Kano	remain	here	go
	ni	**in**	**nēmo**	**takarkarī**	**yac**	**ce**	**to**	**ya**	**tafi**		
	1sg.(Ipf?)	1sg. Subj	seek	pack ox	3sg.m. Pf2	say	well	3sg.m. Pf2	go (away)		

« The Katsina man said, Well, you, Kano man, stay here, I am going to look for a pack ox. The other said, All right. [The Katsina man] went away. »

In any case, the author of *Littafen nahwowin hausance* included both Ipf (with « verbal nouns », as we usually call them now) and Pf (with « finite verbs ») in his description of the TAM system. Therefore, the reason why the **zā**-forms were ignored cannot be related to the peculiarities of the corresponding « nouns ». It is more probable that the author of the manuscript saw **zā** as a « noun » of motion, like **zō**, **zaka**, etc., rather than an element of the TAM marker (in today's terminology).

The author of *Littafen nahwowin hausance* showed very little interest in negative verbal phrases and the corresponding forms of Hausa TAM markers. Only two grammatical references are found in the manuscript. One of them, on the use of

---

[37] The negative particle **ba'** is written with a « hamza » and a « sukun » (most probably pronounced with a long vowel, **bā**). The meaning of the phrase is clear, but it is an unusual equivalent of Subj (a nominal phrase?).

[38] That is, if the first word is plural.

[39] That is, no gender distinction is found here.

« **ba' ni** » (1sg. Neg Fut, probably **bā ni...ba**, if it is different from 1sg. Neg Ipf), has already been mentioned. In the other reference, the complex marker of 1sg. Neg Ipf is described:

In aka tanbayē-ka abinda ba-ka-yi ba tukuna amsā da bā da nun arat damrarriyā cī « ban ».

5	**in**	**aka**	**tambayē**	**ka**	**abin da**	**ba**	**ka**	**yi**	**ba**
	if	Impers. Pf2	ask	d.o. 2sg.m.	« thing-Def.-with »	Neg.	2sg.m. Pf	do	Neg.

tukuna amsa	**da**	**nun arat**	**damrarriya**	**ci**	**« ban »**
(not) yet answer	with	« ra »-like « nun »	bound (f.)	say	**ban** (Neg., 1sg. Pf)

« If one asked you about something you have not done, [answer] with « ba » and a « bound nun », which is similar to a « ra », and say **ban** *(*1sg. Neg Ipf*). »*

Of course, some other combinations of negative particles (**bā/ba** or **bā/ba...ba**) with TAM markers are also found in the text of *Littafen nahwowin hausance*. In Pf, these are **ba ka...ba** (2sg.m.), **bai ...ba** (3sg.m.), **ba ta...ba** (3sg.f.), **ba su...ba** (3pl.), **ba'a ...ba** (Impers.) ; in Ipf, **ba ni** (1sg.), **ba shi/ba ya** (3sg.m.), **ba ta** (3sg.f.), **ba su**[40] (3pl.), **ba'a** (Impers.). No negative sentences with Hab are used in the manuscript. As for Fut, the combinations with TAM markers found in the text, besides **ba ni...**[**ba**], are **ba ka...ba** (2sg.m.) and **ba ya...ba** (3sg.m.), e.g. :

Nā san dai wanda yas-sāmu kāyayyakī haka ba-yā ƙi jākī ba.

6	**nā**	**san**	**dai**	**wanda**	**yas**	**sāmu**	**kāyayyakī**	**haka**	**ba**	**yā**
	1sg.Pf1	know	Part.	Rel.m.	3sg.m. Pf2	get	goods (pl.)	thus	Neg.	3sg.m. Fut

ƙi	**jākī**	**ba**
refuse	donkey	Neg.

« I know, the person who obtained the goods this way will not refuse [to get] the donkey »

While the complexes **ban...ba** and **bai...ba** are well known to the Hausaists, there may be one more combination of the negative particle with a TAM marker in *Littafen nahwowin hausance*. In three or maybe four cases, the combination of **ba** or **ba...ba** with the marker **a** (Impers.) may lead to the elision of the TAM marker, e.g.:

In kuwa bā sa kōmī ciki ba akan-ci « kunbucē ».

7	**in**	**kuwa**	**bā**	**sa**	**kōmī**	**ciki**	**ba**	**akan**	**ce**	**kumbucē**
	If	Part.	Neg.	put	everything	inside	Neg.	Impers. Hab	say	

« If nothing is placed inside [the hair], one usually says **kumbuce** *(a style of woman's hair style). »*

In-kuwa yā yi yawa ammā ba kēwayē-shi da gīni ba sūnansa « alkarya ».

8	**in**	**kuwa**	**yā**	**yi**	**yawa**	**ammā**	**ba**	**kēwayē**	**shi**	**da**	**gīni**
	If	Part.	3sg.m. Pf2	do	abundance	but	Neg.	surround	3sg.m. d.o.	with	rampart

ba	**sūna-n-sa**	**alkarya**
Neg.	« name-his » (Poss.-3sg.m)	(« unwalled town »)

« If [the town] has become crowded, but was not surrounded with a rampart[41]*, it is called* **alkarya**. *»*

---

[40] Also « **ba'a su** »: **Hausāwā ba'a su-son sa** « the Hausa do not like it ».

[41] Literally, « [one] did not surround it (Impers. Pf) with a rampart ».

This elision seems to be optional, although it is not clear whether all the combinations written as **bā/ba a...ba** were really pronounced without elision, cf. the following sentence:

Idan ba-a rage kō kadan ba, wani wurin kuwa bā ƙāra kōmī sai dai a sā gudā ƙasa.

9	**idan**	**ba**	**a**	**rage**	**kō**	**kaɗan**	**ba**	**wani**	**wuri-n**	**kuwa**	**bā**
	If	Neg.	Impers. Pf	reduce	Part.	a little	Neg.	Indef.sg.m.	« place-Def. »	Part.	Neg.

ƙāra	**kōmī**	**sai**	**dai**	**a**	**sā**	**gudā ƙasa**
add	everything	Part.	Part.	Impers. Pf	put	« dot below »

« If nothing was reduced, and nothing was added in another place, one should put a **guda ƙasa** *(that is, the final* **e***). »*

Theoretically, the phrases where **a** is omitted after **ba** may be also interpreted as nominal, but this explanation seems less plausible here.

THE HISTORY OF HAUSA TAM MARKERS OR THE HISTORY OF HAUSA STUDIES?

The split interpretation of what is mostly described as verbs with TAM markers today as a noun and the TAM marker as a verb is not entirely unfounded. The so-called « Hausa verbal system » is in fact an imaginary category corresponding to the verbal system of another language (English, German, Russian, etc.) in translation. The structural integrity of this category is maintained mostly thanks to the presence of TAM markers, and the analysis of at least some of these markers as auxiliary verbs from the historical point of view is plausible. One could argue that there are some fundamental morphological differences between the finite verbs, e.g. in the Perfective, and the nouns. However, the list of these differences would shrink, if we go beyond the standards of « Gaskiyanci » Hausa.

There is one more reason that attracted my attention to the views expressed in *Littafen nahwowin hausance*. In my early unpublished thesis on the syntactical structures of Hausa, I used the terms « verbal complex » and « verbal stem ». The latter was, according to this interpretation, not a verb as such, but a syncretic stem, a « noun in general », that could be used in both nominal and verbal complexes (Dobronravin 1987 : 24-28). To demonstrate the syncretism of such stems, I referred to the use of the premodifiers **ɗan** (diminutive) and **kusan** in the verbal complex, e.g.:

10	**mun**	**ɗa-n**	**dakata**
	1pl Pfl	« son-of »	wait

« We waited a little while. »

11	**mun**	**kusa-n**	**gama**	**wasa**
	1pl Pfl	« nearness-of »	finish	play

« We almost finished playing. »

In my view, the syncretic stems were opposed to the stems that were definitely nominal and not expected to be found in a verbal complex; there seemed to be more syncretic stems in some varieties of diaspora Hausa than in Standard Hausa.

The author of *Littafen nahwowin hausance* took a more radical approach, as he described all « verb stems » merely as nouns. Where I wrote about verbal complexes implying a special role of TAM markers, he seemed to be less cautious, defining them as verbs. Irrespective of what can be said about this early attempt to define parts of speech in Hausa made by an amateur African linguist, it surely deserves attention as an episode in the history of Hausa studies.

Abbreviations

Cop.	Copula	m.	masculine
Def.	Definite	Neg.	Negative
d.o.	Direct object	Part.	Particle
f.	feminine	Pf.	Perfective
Fut	Future	Pl.	Plural
Hab	Habitual	Poss.	Possessive
Impers.	Impersonal	Rel.	Relative
Ind.	Independent	Sg.	Singular
Indef.	Indefinite	Subj.	Subjunctive
Ipf	Imperfective		

Bibliographical references

BARGERY, G.P., 1934, *A Hausa-English Dictionary and English-Hausa Vocabulary,* London, Oxford University Press.

JAGGAR, P.J., 2001, *Hausa,* Amsterdam and Philadelphia, John Benjamins.

NEWMAN, P., 2000, *The Hausa Language. An Encyclopedic Reference Grammar*, New Haven and London, Yale University Press.

WOLFF, E., 1991, Verbo-Nominals in Hausa, *Afrikanistische Arbeitspapiere*, 26, 91-112.

WOLFF, E., 1993, *Referenzgrammatik des Hausa*, Münster and Hamburg, Lit.

ZIMA, P., 2002, Hausa TAM Markers Analyzed in Their Dialectal, Genetic and Areal Context : Interplay of Internal and External Factors, *Corpus*, 1, 265-281.

Elaboration and Simplification in Fula Verbal Morphology

Peter GOTTSCHLIGG

Universität Bayreuth, SFB/FK 560 [1] peter.gottschligg@gmx.at

Abstract

Fula verbal inflectional morphology expresses, inter alia, the category of voice and syntactic markedness of the clause («relative»). In the other Atlantic languages, voice in general but especially middle voice is a derivational not an inflectional category. This article demonstrates that Common Fula middle-voice inflections result from a fusion with a middle derivative, which is still visible in combination with certain other derivatives. In the presence of these, most dialects doubly mark middle voice, both derivationally and flectionally. In the Pular dialect from Guinea, flectional marking of middle voice is absent in the presence of a middle derivative. In the Adamawa dialects (Nigeria/Cameroon), both middle voice and syntactic markedness have largely disappeared as morphological categories of the verb. These processes of elaboration and simplification are attributed to pidginisation in situations where the major contact languages were typologically opposed to the internal developments

Résumé

La morphologie peule flectionnelle exprime entre autres la catégorie de la voix grammaticale et les constructions syntaxiques marquées. Dans les autres langues atlantiques, la voix et surtout la voix moyenne est une catégorie dérivationelle et non flexionnelle. Dans cet article on démontre que les affixes verbaux de la voix moyenne en peul sont le résultat d'une fusion avec un dérivatif moyen, qui apparaît toujours en combinaison avec d'autres dérivatifs. Lorsque ces dérivatifs sont présents, la plupart des dialectes redoublent la marque de la voix moyenne, qui doit apparaître sur le plan dérivationel ainsi que sur le plan flexionnel. Cependant, dans le dialecte poular de Guinée, il n'y a pas de marqueur flexionnel de la voix moyenne en présence d'un marqueur dérivationnel. Dans les dialectes de l'Adamaoua (Nigeria, Cameroun), la voix moyenne ainsi que les constructions syntaxiques marquées ont généralement disparu comme catégories de la morphologie verbale. Ces processus d'élaboration et de simplification

[1] The author wishes to express his gratitude to the German Research Council (DFG) for sponsoring the greater part of this research within the FFB-FK560. His thanks also go to the consultants on whose performances this paper is based: Oumar Bah, M.A. (Vienna), Sileymane Amadou Ba (Arywélé, Senegal), Abdourahmane Diallo (Kolda, Senegal and Kula Mawnde, Guinea), Amadou Anne (Pete, Senegal), Henry Hane (Guede-Chantier, Senegal), Bouraima Diallo (Ouagadougou), Jibilirou Dicko (Ouagadougou), Dr. Bobboi Umar (Maiduguri, Nigeria), Saidou Baba Oumar, M.A. (Maiduguri, Nigeria), Mohammed Goni (Ganye, Nigeria), Ba Buba (Yola, Nigeria), Mohammed Kawu (Gamawa, Nigeria). He is especially grateful to Amanda Delamer for proof-reading in English.

sont attribués à la pidginisation dans des situations où les langues de contact majeures étaient typologiquement opposées à ces développements internes du peul.

FULA

Fula is a Northwest Atlantic language and the only member of its family that has spread eastwards from an area located between Mauritania and Senegal. Today, the Fula dialect continuum extends over 5000 km from Senegal to the Republic of Sudan. For an Atlantic language, Fula is not a very typical member of its family. It has a historically very young system of about 23 or more noun-classes, with initial consonant alternation[2] as well as multifunctional suffixed markers[3] in controllers and targets. Other languages of this same group differ in having prefixing systems with smaller numbers of classes, less concord and eroded markers. Relics from an earlier stage in the development of Fula noun-classes, when class-marked suffixes were determiners[4], are still found – particularly in the Fula Pular dialect of Fuuta Jaloo (J), Guinea[5]. These suffixes otherwise play the role of formatives e.g. in Sereer or Joolaa. In this dialect (J), a group of nominal stems are used without class suffixes for generic reference and with class suffixes as a specific article [1.].

[1.]	**Generic**		**Specific**		
	gerto-ø	«chicken (as a type of meat or a zoological species)»	*gerto-**gal***	«a chicken»	J
	yalage-ø	«cashew nut (as a type of fruit or a botanical species)»	*yalage-**hi***	«an anacardium tree»	J
	boofo-ø	«egg (as a kind of food)»	*woofoo-**nde***	«an egg»	J

VOICE CUMULATIVELY EXPRESSED WITH ASPECT, POLARITY AND SYNTACTIC MARKEDNESS

In the **verbal system**[6], Fula has developed verbal inflections with combined exponence in four different categories[7]: voice, aspect, polarity and syntactic markedness. Following MCINTOSH (1984), I term these inflections «VAP-markers», rather than «tenses», since they basically contrast in the first three

[2] Cf. GOTTSCHLIGG (1995a, 1997a)
[3] Cf. GOTTSCHLIGG (1995a, 1995b, 1999)
[4] Cf. GREENBERG (1977)
[5] Cf. GOTTSCHLIGG (1995b). For a description of this dialect see DIALLO (2000) and ZOUBKO (1996)
[6] Another prominent feature of the Fula verbal inflectional system is initial consonant alternation as a function of number agreement between subject and verb, as well as a trace of inverted subject pronouns. Cf. GOTTSCHLIGG (1995a and forthc.) for a typology and the dialectology of verbal initial consonant alternation. For detailed accounts of Fula verbal derivational morphology cf. DE WOLF (1986, 1987 and 1991), GOTTSCHLIGG (1992a).
[7] Cf. e.g. ARNOTT (1970) and MCINTOSH (1984) for detailed accounts of the Fula verbal inflectional system.

categories. «Tense» otherwise implies «time», a category that is virtually absent from inflectional morphology in Fula.

[2.] Categories cumulatively expressed in Fula inflections

[2.1.] Voice (active, middle or passive)

[2.2.] Aspect (perfective or imperfective)

[2.3.] Polarity (positive or negative) and

[2.4.] «Syntactic markedness». This inflectional category differentiates between the use of verbal morphology in clauses where fronting of a constituent has taken place (often called «relative» aspects or tenses)[8] and clauses without fronting (often called «general» aspects or tenses). There are also other functions of «relative» markers, e.g. for narrative and in durative predicates, which are not discussed in detail.

Non-indicative moods include imperatives and constructions involving markers of Imperfect 1 (often called «subjunctive»), expressing jussive, hortative or desiderative moods. Cf. [40.]. The preterite marker *–no(o)* also marks a hypothetical or counterfactual mood, e.g. [48.3.] and [47.2.]. It is not part of the inflectional verbal morphology but an enclitic that may, in addition, attach to non-verbal forms in some dialects[9]. Only durative constructions[10] involve dialectally variant auxiliaries that are either independent morphemes or affixes to subject pronouns. These «split predicates» still involve inflectional verbal morphology in the main verb. In [29.] *na* is such a durative auxiliary and the main verb is inflected for Imperfect 1 to produce a «progressive» predicate. The same auxiliary in combination with a main verb inflected for the «relative» Perfect produces «stative» predicates. Fula is a SVO-language, in which inversion of certain subject pronouns produces a VSO order and fronting of object NPs produces OSV or OVS (with inversion of subject pronouns) orders[11].

The core verbal inflectional morphology is described in [3.][12]. Details of vowel length in some of these marker are given in [31.] and [54.]. However, in some of these morphemes, certain submorphemes can be identified synchronically, e.g. when the insertion of the preterite marker *-no(o)-*[13] makes their internal boundaries transparent [3.4.]. Diachronically, submorphemes can be reconstructed by dialect comparison, especially in the case of *-o-* as a marker of «middle voice», cf. [3.1.], [3.2.4.] and [3.3.1.].

---

[8] Cf. CARON (2000) and ZIMA (2002) for areal aspects of related syntax and morphology in West African languages.

[9] Cf. GOTTSCHLIGG (1995c).

[10] Cf. GOTTSCHLIGG (1992b) for different types of durative constructions, MIAMOTO (1993) for dialectal variants of these auxiliaries and ENDRESEN (1993) and GOTTSCHLIGG (1999) for the history and dialectology of these auxiliaries in Fula and Atlantic.

[11] Cf. LABATUT (1982) and SYLLA (1993) for detailed descriptions of Fula syntax.

[12] The abbreviations used in this article will be a combination of the Voice and Aspect sigla, e.g. [AI1R-] for *-a* or [MI1R-] for *-oo* in [3.2.1.].

[13] Cf. GOTTSCHLIGG (1995c).

[3.]	Fula VAP morphology	Active [A]	Middle [M]	Passive [P]
[3.1.]	Imperative	*-ø* / *-u*	*-o* (T, J) *-a* (Fulfulde)	
[3.2.1.]	Imperfect1, -relative [I1R-] (citation form for verbs)	*-a*	*-oo*	*-ee*
[3.2.2.]	Imperfect2, -relative [I2R-]	*-at* (T) *-ay* (J) *-an* (Fulfulde)	*-oto*	*-ete*
[3.2.3.]	Imperfect2, +relative [I2R+]	*-ata* *-ay-* (J)	*-otoo*	*-etee*
[3.2.4.]	Imperfect2, negative [I2n]	*-ataa*	*-otaako* (J,T) *-ataako*	*-etaake* (J,T) *-ataake*
[3.3.1.]	Perfect, -relative [PR-]	*-ii*	*-iima* (T) *-ike* (J) *-ake* (Bj, A) *-oke* (Bm)	*-aama*
[3.3.2.]	Perfect, +relative [PR+]	*-i* /*-u-* /*-ø-*	*-ii*	*-aa*
[3.3.3.]	Perfect, negative of stative	*-aa*	–	–
[3.3.4.]	Perfect, negative [Pn]	*-aani* (T) *-aali* (J) *-aay* (Fulfulde)	*-aaki*	*-aaka*
[3.4.1.]	Perfect, -relative + preterite	*-ii-no*	*-i-noo-ma* (T) *-i-no-ke* (J) *-ake-no* (Bj) *-ake-no* (A)	*-a-noo-ma* *-aama-no* (A)
[3.4.2.]	Perfect, negative + preterite		*-a-noo-ki* (J)	*-a-noo-ka* (J)
[3.4.3.]	Imperfect, negative + preterite		*-o-ta-noo-ko* (J)	*-e-ta-noo-ke* (J)

FUSION OF VERBAL DERIVATIONAL MORPHOLOGY WITH INFLECTIONAL MARKERS OF ASPECT AND POLARITY

Considering the form and the typology of voice-marking in closely related Atlantic languages, e.g. Sereer[14], Wolof[15] or Palor[16], where middle voice is always a derivational and not an inflectional category, I feel safe to postulate a historic fusion of derivational middle and inflectional morphology in Fula. Where Fula uses inflectional morphology for marking «middle voice», the other languages of the group use derivational morphology for marking the same category.

[14] Cf. FAYE (1982).
[15] Cf. CHURCH (1981).
[16] Cf. D'ALTON (1987).

[4.]	Fula	Sereer	Wolof	Palor
	-o-	*-u*	*-u*	*-ox*
		-oox	*-ku*	*-u* (neutro-passiv)
			-oo (rec.)	

[5.1.]	*ɓog-ø*	«to wash someone»	Sereer
[5.2.]	*ɓog-**u***	«to wash oneself»	Sereer
[5.3.]	*ɓog-**ox***	«to wash os.»	Sereer
[5.4.]	*ɓog-**oor** < ɓog-**u**-ir saafu*	«to wash os. with soap»	Sereer

[6.1.]	*sang- ø*	«to wash so.»	Wolof
[6.2.]	*sang- **u***	«to wash os.»	Wolof
[6.3.]	*sang- **u** ak saabu*	«to wash os. with soap»	Wolof

[7.1.]	*loot-ir-a saabunnde*	«to wash (so.) with soap»	CF, J
[7.2.]	*loot-**o**-r-a s.*	«to wash os. with soap»	J, T
[7.3.]	*loot-**o**-r-oo s.*	«to wash os. with soap»	CF, J

ALTERNATIVE EXPONENCY OF MIDDLE VOICE IN DERIVATIONAL OR INFLECTIONAL MORPHOLOGY

Though Fula marks middle voice almost exclusively with verbal inflexions, a derivational marker (*-o-*) of middle voice has survived in combination with other derivational suffixes, particularly the associative, the instrumental[17] and the reciprocal extensions [8.]. It is obvious, that the middle derivative *-o-* and some of the morphemes and submorphemes in middle inflectional morphology, e.g. imperative *-o-* [3.1.] or the imperfective middle forms [3.2.] are cognate.

[8.] Derivation	+Inflexion	Derivation -o- (middle)	+Inflexion (CF)	+Inflexion (T, J)
-id (associative)	act., pass.	*-o-d-*	middle	act., middle
-ir- (instr.)	act., pass.	*-o-r-*	middle	act., middle
-indir- (recipr.)	act., pass.	*-o-ndir-*	act. /pass.	act., pass.

In most Fula dialects, derivational marking of middle voice is obligatory in the presence of the associative and instrumental extensions. The combination of the middle voice derivative (in a productive morphological process) with the reciprocal extension seems to be limited to the Pular dialect of Fuuta Jaloo (J). In this dialect, wherever «reciprocal» *-indir-* co-occurs with «middle», «middle» has to be marked derivationally by *-o-* preceding the reciprocal extension and the

[17] «Instrumental» is basically the most common meaning of this extension. Other important meanings include: modal, locative and applicative. For applicative cf. GOTTSCHLIGG (2000).

vowel *-i-* is elided. In this case, middle voice has to be marked derivationally to express coreferentiality of agent and patient roles. The derived middle verb is inflected for active voice [9.1.]. For coreferential patient roles, neither the derivational [9.5.] nor the inflectional [9.4.] form of middle voice morphology is employed.

[9.1.]	_ɓe moft-**o**-ndir-**ii**_ [APR-]	«they have convened (gathered together)»	J
[9.2.]	*_ɓe moft-indir-**ii**_ [APR-]	"	J
[9.3.]	*_ɓe moft-**o**-ndir-**ike**_ [MPR-]	"	J
[9.4.]	_ɓe moft-indir-**ii**_ [APR-] _yimɓe ɓe?_	«they have gathered the people»	J
[9.5.]	*_ɓe moft-**o**-ndir-**ii**_ [APR-] _yimɓe ɓe?_	"	J

In the Pulaar dialect of Fuuta Tooro (T), the form *-ondir-* is used to mark both reciprocal situations [10.]. In other dialects, a single one of the forms *-indir-*, *-undur-* or *-ondur-* is used regardless of the reciprocal situation [11.].

[10.1.]	_ɓe kaɓɓ-**ondir-ii**_ [APR-]	«they have made friends (sexual relationship)»	T
[10.2.]	_ɓe kaɓɓ-**ondir-ii**_ [APR-] _leɗɗe_	«they have tied the pieces of wood together»	T

[11.1.]	_ɓe salm-**o**-ndir-**ii**_ [APR-]	«they greeted each other (in a Muslim way)»	J
[11.2.]	_ɓe hiwr-**o**-ndir-**ii**_ [APR-]	«they greeted each other»	J
[11.3.]	_ɓe njowt-**undur-i**_ [APR-]	"	Bj
[11.4.]	_min koomn-**indir-i**_ [APR-]	«we greeted each other»	A1

In a conservative dialect of Adamawa (A1) as well as in other Nigerian dialects, a reciprocal extension *-ootir-* is used with active inflections. Not found in the Western Fulfulde or Pula(a)r dialects, it expresses coreferentiality of agent and patient roles, cf. [12.1.], [13.1.] and [14.1.], whereas another extension *-indir-* expresses coreferential patient roles, cf. [12.2.], [13.3.] and [14.2.]. The extension *-ootir-* does not express coreferentiality of patient-roles, cf. [12.3.], [13.4.] and [14.3.]. Particularly in the A2 variant, however, *-ootir-* is not productive and *-indir-* is used instead, covering both reciprocal situations, cf. [11.] and [13.2.]. The extension *-ootir-* seems to contain the middle derivative *-o-*. In its typical A1 usage, it corresponds to Fuuta Jaloo *-o-ndir-*.

[12.1.]	_ɓe kaɓɓ-**ootir-i**_ [APR-]	«they have reached an agreement»	A1
[12.2.]	_o haɓɓ-indir-**i**_ [APR-] _leɗɗe_	«he has tied the pieces of wood together»	A1
[12.3.]	*_o haɓɓ-**ootir-i**_ [APR-] _leɗɗe_	"	A1

[13.1.]	*ɓe njill-**ootir-i*** [APR-]	«they are mixing (e.g. men and women)»	A1
[13.2.]	*ɓe njill-indir-**i*** [APR-]	"	A1
[13.3.]	*ɓe njill-indir-**i** kuuje pat* [APR-]	«they have mixed all things»	A1
[13.4.]	**ɓe njill-**ootir-i*** [APR-] *k.p.*	"	A1

[14.1.]	*ɓe sennd-**ootir-i*** [APR-]	«they are different from each other»	A1
[14.2.]	*ɓe sennd-indir-**ii**-ɓe* [APR-]	«they have separated them»	A1
[14.3.]	**ɓe sennd-**ootir-ii**-ɓe* [APR-]	"	A1

Where the derivational marker of middle voice *-o-* occurs simultaneously with the instrumental and associative extensions, the additional exponence of middle voice in inflectional morphology is optional both in the Pular-dialect of Fuuta Jaloo (J) and in the Pulaar-dialect of Fuuta Tooro (T). In [15.1.] and [15.2.], for example, the derivational middle marker *-o-* combines with *-ø-* and *ii,* which are markers of the active +relative perfect [APR+]. Furthermore in [15.3.] and [15.4.], the same derivative combines with *-ii-*, which is a marker of middle perfect +relative [MPR+], and so on. In at least the Pular dialect of Fuuta Jaloo, double exponence of middle voice is considered by its speakers to be «redundant», e.g. in [15.3.], [16.2.], [17.3.], [18.3.] and [19.2.]. The subject pronoun of the 1st person singular *mi* is not inverted in Southern Fuuta Jaloo, e.g. in [15.4.]. See also an example from Northern Fuuta Jaloo [15.3].

[15.1.]	*ko ndee saabunnde loot-**o**-r-**ø**-mi* [APR+]	«it is with this soap I washed myself»	J
[15.2.]	*ko ndee s. mi loot-**o**-r-**i*** [APR+]	"	J
[15.3.]	*ko ndee s. loot-**o**-r-**ii**-mi* [MPR+]	"	J
[15.4.]	*ko ndee s. mi loot-**o**-r-**ii*** [MPR+]	"	J

[16.1.]	*loot-**o**-r-**ø**-ɗo* [APR+] *s.*	«so. who washed himself with soap»	J
[16.2.]	*loot-**o**-r-**ii**-ɗo* [MPR+] *s.*	"	J

[17.1.]	*mi loo-**o**-r-**ay*** [AI2R-] *ndee s.*	«I am going to wash myself with this soap»	J
[17.2.]	*mi loot-**o**-r-**at*** [AI2R-] *ndee ɗo s.*	"	T
[17.3.]	*mi loot-**o**-r-**to*** [MI2R-] *ndee s.*	"	J
[17.4.]	*mi loot-**o**-r-**to*** [MI2R-] *ndee ɗo s.*	"	T

[18.1.]	*s. nde mi loot-**o-r-ta*** [AI2R+] …	«the soap I am washing myself with ...»	J
[18.2.]	*s. nde loot-**o-r-ay**-mi* [AI2R+]…	”	J
[18.3.]	*s. nde loot-**o-r-too-mi*** [AI2R+] ..	”	J
[18.4.]	*s. nde mi loot-**o-r-too*** [MI2R+] ...	”	J

[19.1.]	*loot-**o-r-ay**-ɗo* [AI2R+] *s.*	«so. who washes himself with soap»	J
[19.2.]	*loot-**o-r-too**-ɗo* [MI2R+] *s.*	”	J

While the presence of the middle voice derivative *-o-* in the stem makes the exponence of middle voice in inflectional morphology optional in the Pula(a)r dialects of Fuuta Jaloo and Fuuta Tooro, [20.1.], [20.2.] , it is obligatory to mark it by inflection in the absence of the middle derivative *-o-* [20.3.]. A lexically middle verb without any overt middle marker is ungrammatical [20.4.].

[20.1.]	*leeteraaji ɗi? yott-**o**-d-**aali*** [APn]	«the letters did not arrive at the same time»	J
[20.2.]	*leeteraaji ɗi? yott-**o**-d-**aaki*** [MPn]	”	J
[20.3.]	*leeteraaji ɗi? yott-**aaki*** [MPn]	«the ls. have not arrived»	J
[20.4.]	**leeteraaji ɗi? yott-**aali*** [APn]	”	J

A verbal stem containing the middle derivative *-o-* can, as shown above, combine with either active or middle inflectional morphology, but not with passive inflections [21.]. See furthermore [22.] and [23.] where, in the absence of a derivationally marked middle voice, passive inflections are possible. Cf. also [29.]. Passive morphology expresses agency through an agent that must not be represented by an NP at clause level. Therefore, it is incompatible with middle morphology, which marks either coreferentiality of agent and patient roles present (represented by an NP in the clause) or the absence of agency.

[21.1.]	**mi loot-**o-r-aama*** [PPR-] *ndee s.*	«I have been washed with this soap»	J
[21.2.]	**mi loot-**o-r-aama*** [PPR-] *ndee ɗo s.*	”	T

[22.1.]	*mi loot-**ir-aama** ndee s.* [PPR-]	«I have been washed with this soap»	J
[22.2.]	*mi loot-**ir-aama** ndee ɗo s.* [PPR-]	”	T

[23.1.]	*ko ndee s. loot-**ir-aa**-mi* [PPR+]	«it is with this soap I was washed»	J
[23.1.]	*ko ndee s. mi loot-**ir-aa*** [PPR+]	”	J

Derivational marking of middle voice in combination with the instrumental or locative extension *i(i)r-* also exists in deverbal nouns, cf. [24.2.], [25.2.], [26.2.] and [26.3.]. See [27.2.] for a deverbal noun without a middle voice marker. Cf. also Sereer for derivations that are equivalent in structure and form [28.]. The suffixes -*gal*, *-du*, *-di*, *-de* are Fula noun-class markers[18], *o-* is a Serer noun-class marker.

[24.1.]	*gos-**oo***	«to brush one's teeth»	J
[24.2.]	*gos-**o**-r-gal*	«toothbrush, toothpick»	J

[25.1.]	*ndaar-it-**oo***	«to look at os.»	J
[25.2.]	*ndaar-**o**-r-gal*	«mirror»	J

[26.1.]	*fin-**oo***	«(to) blacken one's eyes (with antimony)»	Bm
[26.2.]	*pin-**o**-r-di*	«powdered antimony, sth. to blacken one's eyes»	Bm
[26.3.]	*fin-**o**-r-du*	«antimony bottle»	A

[27.1.]	*juul-a*	«(to) pray»	CF
[27.2.]	*juul-ir-de*	«mosque»	CF

[28.1.]	*sooc*	«to clean, to brush»	Ser
[28.2.]	*sooc-**u***	«to brush one's teeth»	Ser
[28.3.]	*sooc-**oo**-r* < sooc-**u**-ir	«to brush one's teeth with …»	Ser
[28.4.]	*o-sooc-**oo**-r (ole)*	«(the) toothpick, toothbrush»	Ser

DOUBLE EXPONENCE OF MIDDLE VOICE IN DERIVATIONAL AND IN INFLECTIONAL MORPHOLOGY

In most Fulfulde dialects, e.g. in the Moosiire dialect of Burkina Faso (Bm), an inflectional exponence of middle voice remains obligatory in the presence of a middle derivative. As a consequence, the functional load of the middle voice derivative *-o-* has lessened. With the exception of a few relict forms, «middle voice» has become a category that is obligatorily expressed by inflectional morphology. It has to be noted, that the derivational marking of middle voice in the presence of the derivatives *-id-* and *-ir-* remains obligatory, e.g. in [29.2.].

[29.1.]	*na o loot-**ir-a*** [AI1] *o nde*	«he is washing himself with it»	Bm
[29.2.]	*na o loot-**o**-r-**oo*** [MI1] *k.*	«he is washing himself with soap»	Bm
[29.3.]	*na o loot-**ir-ee*** [MI1] *kaataare*	«he is being washed with soap»	Bm

[18] Fula nouns of instrument carry 3rd grade suffixes, which are pronouns historically, cf. GOTTSCHLIGG (1995a and 1999).

REDUCTION OF MIDDLE MORPHOLOGY IN ADAMAWA

I have demonstrated in the section above, how the functional load of marking the middle voice in Atlantic and in Fula dialects has shifted from derivational to inflectional morphology. In this section of the article, I will demonstrate how middle voice loses morphological exponence, in derivation and in inflection, in an Adamawa dialect of Fula.

We differentiate between three Adamawa[19] dialects spoken in the Nigerian Adamawa and Taraba States, as well as in the three Northern provinces of Cameroon: Extrême-Nord, Nord and Adamaoua. However, the social and geographical distribution of these dialects remains to be clarified. Suffice here to say, that the dialect glossed «A1» is the structurally most conservative of these dialects, on a par with most other Fulfulde-dialects and typically spoken as a L1 by ethnic Fulani in the Cameroonian province of Extrême-Nord (Maroua)[20]. For many A1 speakers, at least in Nigerian Adamawa, A1 and A2 constitute two different registers rather than dialects. The A2 dialect is the typical L1 variant spoken by ethnic Fulani and others in the Cameroonian province of Nord (Garoua) and in the Nigerian Adamawa (Yola) and Taraba (Jalingo) States[21]. The dialect glossed A3 is in many cases a L2 variant, though also the L1 of many ethnic Fulani and of others, particularly in urban areas of the Cameroonian provinces of Adamaoua (Ngaoundéré) and the Nigerian Adamawa and Taraba States[22].

The loss of middle morphology in the A2 and A3 dialects is not an isolated innovation of these dialects, but rather linked to other innovations that have reduced syntactic and morphological complexity in both the nominal and the verbal systems. Furthermore, the loss of middle morphology is also probably conditioned by syntactic changes that have reduced the contexts in which middle and active morphology contrast.

One set of [±relative] markers is employed in syntactically unmarked clauses, the other in clauses with fronted constituents and in the so-called «participles». The latter present a special case of relative clauses. Fronting includes:

---

19 Cf. BOUTRAIS (1993).

20 This dialect is described e.g. in the works of NOYE (1974) and NOYE (1989). On a structural level, TAYLOR (1932), TAYLOR (1953) and KLINGENHEBEN (1963) deal with essentially the same variant, but as spoken in Yola (Nigerian Adamawa), i.e. what these latter authors have dealt with in their works is rather a minority variant in this area.

21 This dialect, though widely spoken and probably the dominant L1 variant in Nigerian Adamawa and in the Cameroonian Nord-province, has received comparatively less attention. Though there are testimonies for the existence of simplified variants from the beginning of the 20th century, LACROIX (1959, 1962, 1967) was the first to describe features of these variants that can plausibly be considered to have originated as a pidgin (at least A3) and to have developed into a Creole language. Recent works on these Adamawa dialects are: GIREI (1999), GOTTSCHLIGG (1998, 1995a, 1995c) and METANGMO-TATOU (2002).

22 See the footnote above for references.

Syntactic Structures involving «Fronting» of Constituents

[30.1.] Relative and adverbial clauses, e.g. in [18.], [36.2.], Participles, e.g. in [16.], [19.], [50.], [51.]
[30.2.] Interrogative clauses, e.g. in [32.4.], [33.2.], [35.2.], [37.]
[30.3.] Clauses with focussed constituents, e.g. in [15.], [23.].

The syntactic conditioning of these alternative uses of verbal morphology is a common feature of all the Fula dialects from Senegal to Central Africa.

AN EMPTY (SKELETAL) SLOT AS A MARKER OF «RELATIVE» ASPECT

In practically all of the Fula dialects, an empty skeletal slot with morphological status participates synchronically in the formation of relative markers.

		Active [A]	**Middle** [M]	**Passive** [P]
[31.1.]	Imp2, -Rel. [I2R-]	*-an* (Fulfulde) *-ay* (Pular + Fulf.)	*-oto*	*-ete*
[31.2]	Imp2, +Rel. [I2R+]	*-ata* *-ay* +Clitic+**V**	*-oto**o*** *-oto* +Clitic +**V**	*-ete**e*** *-ete* +Clitic +**V**
[31.3.]	Perf., -Rel. [P2R-]	*-ii*	*-ake* (A, Bj, etc.) *-ike* (J)	*-aama*
[31.4.]	Perf., +Rel. [P2R+]	*-i*	*-ii* *-i* +Clitic +**V**	*-aa* *-a* +Clitic +**V**

Non-relative markers [31.1.], [31.3.] have fixed final vowel length, invariable before auto-stressed elements [32.1.] or enclitics [32.2.], [32.3.]. The enclitics themselves, when occurring after non-relative markers, are short-vowelled [32.2.], [32.3.], [34.1.], [35.1.], [36.1.]. Relative aspect markers [31.2.], [31.4.] are marked by an empty skeletal slot. If this slot is directly added to the marker, the last vowel of the inflection spreads into it and lengthens [32.4.], [32.5.]. If the inflected verb is followed by certain enclitic elements, especially the preterite marker *-no-* or the object pronoun *ma* (2nd p. sg.), the last vowel of this enclitic is lengthened, cf. *maa* in [32.6.] and *noo* in [34.2.], [36.2.] and [37.2.]. Note, that particularly the final vowels of the anaphoric, class-marked object pronouns, e.g. *mo* [32.5.] or *ki* [33.2.] or the inverted subject pronoun of the 1st p. sg. *mi* [37.2.] do not lengthen.

[32.1.]	*o jaŋ f-**oto*** [MI2R-] *kodo o?*	«he will cheat the stranger»	J
[32.2.]	*o jaŋ f-**oto**-ma* [MI2R-]	«he will cheat you»	J
[32.3.]	*o jaŋ f-**oto**-mo* [MI2R-]	«he will cheat him»	J
[32.4.]	*ko honnde tuma o jaŋf-**otoo*** [MI2R+] *kodo oŋ?*	«when will he cheat the stranger?»	J
[32.5.]	*ko honnde tuma o jaŋf-**otoo**-mo?* [MI2R+]	«when will he cheat him?»	J
[32.6.]	*ko honnde tuma o jaŋf-**oto**-ma**a**?* [MI2R+]	«when will he cheat you?»	J

[33.1.]	*mi wa''-**oto**-ki* [MI2R-] *jonta*	«I am going to climb it (tree) now»	A1
[33.2.]	*ndey o wa''-**otoo**-ki?* [MI2R+]	«when will he climb it?»	A1
[34.1.]	*men rem-**ay-no*** [AI2R-] *duŋe setto*	«we used to farm it during spring»	J
[34.2.]	*ko duŋ men rem-**ay-noo*** [AI2R+] *e setto*	«this is what we used to farm in spring»	J
[35.1.]	*mi hoɗ-**u-no*** [APR-] *doŋ*	«I had lived there»	J
[35.2.]	*ko doŋ mi hoɗ-**u-noo*** [APR+]	«this is where I had lived»	J
[36.1.]	*si o war-**ii-no*** [APR-] *keeŋa, min njah-**an-no*** [AIR-] *luumo*	«if he had come yesterday, we would have gone to the market»	Bm
[36.2.]	*Nde o war-**ø-noo*** [APR+] *keeŋa ndeen, min njehi luumo*	«when he came yesterday, we went to the market»	Bm
[37.1.]	*ki'i lekki mba''**ii**-mi* [MPR+]	«it is this tree that I have climbed»	A1
[37.2.]	*ki'i lekki mba''-**i-noo**-mi* [MPR+]	«it is this tree that I had climbed»	A1

In practically all Fula dialects, this added vowel-slot differentiates not only between [±relative] markers within the active, middle and passive paradigms as demonstrated above (e.g. between *-oto* [MI2R-] and *-otoo* [MI2R+] as shown in [32.]) but also between active [38.1.] and middle [38.2.] voice in the «relative» perfective aspect. See the corresponding non-relative markers in [38.3.] and [38.4.]. Note that there is morphological opposition between the *-ii* [MPR+] and *-ii* [APR-] markers as shown in [38.2.] and [38.3.]. The verbs *ƴeeng-a* (active) and *wa''-oo* (middle) are almost synonymous in these A1 examples.

[38.1.]	*ndey o ƴeeng**i**-ki?* [APR+]	«when did he climb it?»	A1
[38.2.]	*ndey o wa''**ii**-ki?* [MPR+]	"	A1
[38.3.]	*to o ƴeeng**ii**-ki* [APR-], *o do''oto*	«if he climbs it, he will fall»	A1
[38.4.]	*to o wa''**ake**-ki* [MPR-], *o do''oto*	"	A1

NEUTRALISATION OF VOWEL LENGTH IN FINAL POSITION & ITS PROTECTION BY ENCLITIC PRONOUNS

However, in the A2 and A3 dialects and only in these Fula dialects is the opposition between the two sets of syntactically conditioned verbal markers being neutralised. Amalgamated in verbal inflectional morphology, the expression of «middle voice» and of the category [±relative] survived and perished together in a phase of pidginisation and creolisation in the 19th and 20th century Adamawa.

While the length of final vowels is still noticeable in all possible environments in the Pula(a)r-dialects of Senegal (T) and Guinea (J), it tends to be neutralised prepausally and when followed by an item belonging to the following stress-group in many Fulfulde dialects. It is definitely neutralised in these phonetic environments in some Nigerian and Cameroonian dialects, e.g. in [39.1.] and [40.1.], where the underlyingly long markers *-ii* [APR-] and *-oo* [MI1R-] are shortened to *-i* and *-o* respectively when followed by auto-stressed nouns.

Some of the oppositions between relative and non-relative verbal markers, carried by this vowel slot, are neutralised as a result of this phonetical reduction of vowel length. However, many speakers are conscious of the fact that these vowels are underlyingly long. This is perhaps due to the fact that in most Fulfulde dialects, certain enclitic pronouns, the preterit marker as well as the suffixes of participles protect the vowel-length in the verbal inflections they attach to. For example, the enclitic object pronouns *mo* [39.2.] and *ki* [40.2.] protect the underlyingly long marker *-ii* [APR-] from being shortened.

[39.1.]	*to o soodan-**i*** [APR-] *Jebu gude, o soodanay Biigila*	«if he has bought (cloth) wrappers for *Jebu*, he will (also) buy for Biigila»	Nb
[39.2.]	*to o soodan-**ii**-mo* [APR-] *gude, ...*	«if he has bought wrappers for *her...*»	Nb
[40.1.]	*Hiddeeko a tonng-**o*** [MI1R-] *huɗo sekko maa, a fidɗa ko tawon*	«before you bundle the grass for your roof-mats, you first remove the leaves»	A1
[40.2.]	*Hiddeeko a tonng-**oo**-ko* [MI1R-] ...	«before you bundle it ...»	A1

The preservation of vowel length in markers followed by enclitics is becoming an optional rule for most speakers of A2, cf. [41.2.], but not for A1 speakers, cf. [41.1.]. To some A2 speakers, long-vowelled markers as in [41.1.] are a feature of «Mbororo-dialects», «Gombe-dialect» or other Central Nigerian dialects, which correspond in their structures to the A1 variant.

[41.1.]	*to a sorr**ii**-nge* [APR-], *a heɓan riiba*	«if you sell it, you will profit»	A1
[41.2.]	*to a sorr**i**-nge* [APR-], *a heɓan riiba*	"	A2

LOSS OF CONDITIONING ENVIRONMENT (INVERSION, PARTICIPLES) WHERE VOWEL LENGTH IS PROTECTED AND WHERE OPPOSITIONS OF SURFACE FORMS ARE VISIBLE

Fronting in relative clauses, interrogative clauses and in clauses with focus triggers the inversion of 2nd and 1st person subject pronouns. The so-called Fula participles, whose anaphoric suffixes are functionally subject pronouns, are not only similar constructions but also contain the same type of verbal markers. The vowel length of verbal markers is protected by all the anaphoric suffixed subject pronouns in participles as well as by the subject pronoun of the 1st p.sg.[23] with invariable final-vowel length.

In the A2 and A3 dialects, inversion of 1st and 2nd person subject pronouns is no longer existent, e.g. in [42.2.], [43.2.], [44.3.] and [45.4.] the subject pronoun *mi* is preposed instead of inverted as in Common Fula and A1 [42.1.], [43.1.], [44.2.] and [45.3.] The formation of participles has too become largely optional, particularly in A3. Furthermore, many A1 speakers, at least from the Nigerian Adamawa State, tend to use inverted forms only in careful speech. Consequently, there is a considerable reduction in environments, where final vowel length is protected and where oppositions between certain inflectional surface forms like *-ii* and *-i* are visible or remain conscious to the speaker.

[42.1.]	*wakkati ɗaanin-**oo-mi*** [MPR+]	«at the time I had slept, ...»	A1
[42.2.]	*wakkati **mi** ɗaan-in-**o*** [MPR+]	"	A2
[43.1.]	*wakkati njipp-**ii-mi*** [MPR+]	«at the time I got off/down...»	A1
[43.2.]	*wakkati **mi** jipp-**i*** [MPR+]	"	A2
[44.1.]	*mi nast-**i*** [APR-] *luumo*	«I entered the market»	A1,2
[44.2.]	*luumo nast-**u-mi*** [APR+]	«it is the market that I entered»	A1
[44.3.]	*luumo **mi** nast-**i** [*APR+]	"	A2
[45.1.]	*mi wurt-**i*** [MPR-] *luumo*	«I came out of the market»	A1,2
[45.2.]	*mi wurt-**ake*** [MPR-] *luumo*	"	A1
[45.3.]	*luumo ngurt-**ii**-mi* [MPR+]	«it is out of the market that I came»	A1
[45.4.]	*luumo mi wurt-**i***	"	A2

As a consequence, the oppositions between the markers *-i* or *-u-* of [APR+], of [APR-] *-ii* and [MPR+] *-ii* have been neutralised in A2, cf. [44.2.] and [44.3.],

[23] The suffixed subject pronouns of the 2nd person singular as well as the pronouns of the 1st and 2nd persons plural interact in essentially the same (though in a more complicated way) with verbal inflections, as do the object pronoun *ma* and the preterit marker *no*.

[46.] and [47.1.] as well as [44.3.] and [45.4.]. In A1 the same markers still contrast when their final vowel length is protected by enclitics, e.g. by the preterite marker *-no* [47.2.], whereas in A2 the short-vowelled form [47.3.] has been generalised in the same environment, the long-vowelled form [47.2.] being still acceptable.

[46.]	*ndey o war-**i*** [APR+]*?*	«when did he come?»	A1,2
[47.1.]	*to ni o war-**i*** [APR-]*, kuugal ngal woodɗan*	«if he comes, the work will be good»	A1,2
[47.2.]	*to ni o war-**ii-no*** [APR-]*, kuugal ɗo woodɗanno*	«if he had come, the work would have been good»	A1
[47.3.]	*to ni o war-**i-no**, kuugal ngal woodɗanno*	"	A2

In A2, short- [48.2.], [48.5.] or long-vowelled [48.4.] forms of this marker (*-i(i)*) have replaced the [MPR-] marker *-ake* [48.1.]. However, in A2, the length of the marker vowel no longer differentiates either between middle and active voice, or between relative and non-relative aspects.

[48.1.]	*to o ɗaan-**ake*** [MPR-]*, o finan law*	«if he sleeps, he will get up early»	A1
[48.2.]	*to o ɗaan-**i**, o finan law*		A2
[48.3.]	*to o ɗaan-**ake-no*** [MPR-]*, o finilawan*	«if he had slept, he would have got up early»	A1
[48.4.]	*to o ɗaan-**ii-no**, o finilawan*	"	A2
[48.5.]	*to o ɗaan-**i-no**, o finilawan*	"	A2

The short-vowelled [APR+] marker *-i* has the Common Fula variants *-u-* and *-ø-* which are obligatorily used before the preterite element *-noo*, e.g. in [35.], before inverted subject pronouns, e.g. in [44.2.], and in participles, e.g. in [50.2.]. In A2, the sequence *-u-no(o)* has become obsolete or even unacceptable [49.2.], instead, the sequence *-i-no* [49.1.] is used, although without marking middle voice.

[49.1.]	*leggal ngal on, o nyaam-**i-no** les mum*	«it is this tree that he ate under»	A2
[49.2.]	**leggal ngal on, o nyaam-**u-no** les mum*	"	A2

In active participles, e.g. in [50.1.], the long vowelled, Common Fula middle form *-ii-* [MPR+] has replaced the Common Fula active [APR+] form *-u-* [50.2.]. However, *-u-* is still acceptable, though perhaps as an epenthetic vowel. The A2 use of *-ii-* in participles of middle verbs [51.2.] corresponds to Common Fula usage, though without marking middle voice. The use of *-u-* in participles of middle verbs [51.1.] is unacceptable in other dialects, where the verb *nyaam-a* «to eat» is lexically active while the verb *jooɗ-oo* «to sit» is lexically middle.

[50.1.]	*nyaam-**ii**-ɗo*	«so. who has eaten»	A2
[50.2.]	*nyaam-**u**-ɗo* [APR+]	"	CF, A1,2
[51.1.]	*jooɗ-**u**-ɗo*	«so. who is seated»	A2
[51.2.]	*jooɗ-**ii**-ɗo* [MPR+]	"	CF, A1,2

The only relict of imperfect middle voice in A2 and A3 is the negative imperfect -*ataako*. It is also used in A2 and A3 with lexically middle [52.] and active verbs [53.] to Common Fula and has acquired in A2 the function of marking emphatic negation [52.2.], [53.2.].

[52.1.]	*mi waal-**ataa***	«I am not going to lie down»	A2
[52.2.]	*mi waal-**ataako***	«I am (definitely) not going to lie down»	A2
[52.3.]	*mi waal-**otaako*** [MIn]	«I am not going to lie down»	J
[53.1.]	*mi fij-**ataa***	«I am not going to play»	A2
[53.2.]	*mi fij-**ataako***	«I am (definitely) not going to play»	A2
[53.3.]	*mi fij-**ataa*** [AIn]	«I am not going to play»	J

While Common-Fula imperfect middle inflections have in most cases been levelled out in favour of corresponding active morphology, the levelling of perfect middle morphology is conditioned by neutralisations on the level of phonetic realisation. The innovated, 'new' active, perfective A2 paradigm [54.3.] shows reflexes of both active and middle morphology. Note that in the A3 variant, no passive morphology is employed. Passive constructions are replaced by active periphrastic constructions, involving a subject pronoun «they», without an antecedent or referent recoverable from the context. Thus, in A3, the Common Fula system of three *genera verbi* has reduced to one, the «new active».

[54.] Verbal Morphology in Adamawa Fulfulde

		A1	**A1**	**A2**	**A1, A2**
		Active	**Middle**	**Active (new)**	**Passive**
[54.1.]	Imperative	*-u*	*-a*	*-u*	
[54.2.]	Imperfect1	*-a*	*-oo > -o**	*-a*	*-ee > -e**
	Imperfect2	*-an*	*-oto*	*-an*	*-ete*
	Imperfect2 (relative)	*-ata*	*-otoo > -oto**	*-ata*	*-etee > -ete**
	Imperfect negative	*-ataa*	*-ataako*	*-ataa*	*-ataake*
	Imp., neg. emphatic	–	–	*-ataako*	–
[54.3.]	Perfect	*-ii > -i**	*-ake*	*-i, -i-, -ii-*	*-aama*
	Perfect (relative)	*-i (-u-)*	*-ii > -i**	–	*-aa*
	Perfect negative	*-aay*	*-aaki*	*-aay*	*-aaka*

*in A1: VV > V/__#
*in A2 unconditioned

LOSS OF MIDDLE-MARKING IN DERIVATIONAL & INFLECTIONAL MORPHOLOGY

The neutralisation of oppositions between Common-Fula active and middle inflectional morphology in A2 and A3 is accompanied by a loss of derivational marking of middle voice in the same dialects.

[55.1.]	*mi wuyɓ-**o**-r-ike* [MPR-] *(ndiyaŋ) wulɗaŋ*	«I rinsed (my mouth) with hot (water)»	J
[55.2.]	*mi wusɓ-**o**-r-ake* [MPR-] *nguldam*	"	A1
[55.3.]	*mi wusɓ-ir-i nguldam*	"	A2

[56.1.]	*ɓe jipp-**o**-d-ii* [MPR+]	«they disembarked together»	J
[56.2.]	*ɓe njipp-**o**-d-i* [MPR+]	"	A1
[56.3.]	*ɓe jipp-id-i*	"	A2

[57.1.]	*(leggal) jooɗ-**o**-r-gal*	«(a piece of wood) to sit on»	J
[57.2.]	*(leggal) jooɗ-**o**-r-gal*	"	A1
[57.3.]	*(leggal) jooɗ-ir-gal*	"	A2

Otherwise, middle derivatives and inflections tend to survive in fixed expressions like names, sayings and proverbs, e.g. in names being or containing a Common-Fula middle imperative as in [58.] and [59.]. In imperatives formed currently, the middle marker is replaced by the Common-Fula active marker *-u* [58.3.] and [59.3.].

[58.1.]	*Jooɗ-**a*** [Imperative, Middle]	«name of a person»	A1,2
[58.2.]	*jooɗ-**a**!* [Imperative, Middle]	«stay!, sit!»	A1
[58.3.]	*jooɗ-**u**!*	"	A2

[59.1.]	*Jokk-**a** ɗi!* [Imperative, Middle]	«name of a person»	A1,2
[59.2.]	*Jokk-**a** ɗi!* [Imperative, Middle]	«follow them, catch up with them (cows)!»	A1
[59.3.]	*tokk-**u**!, jokk-**u**!*	«follow!, catch up!»	A2

SUMMARY

The shift of exponence of «middle voice» from derivational morphology to inflectional morphology and from there to non-exponency on the morphological level is just one aspect of Fula language change that is visible across dialect and language. On a Common Fula level, the concatenation of derivational and inflectional morphology has lead to an amalgamation of inflectional morphology with some derivatives, notably «middle». In two Adamawa dialects, the levelling out of middle inflectional morphology has been contributed to by phonological processes, particularly the shortening of final vowels and the loss of conditioning environment for the protection of final vowel length, due to syntactic simplifications. A simplification of the verbal morphology of Fulfulde in Adamawa is paralleled by simplifications in syntax (e.g. loss of inversion) and in the nominal domain as well. Pidginisation has similarly reduced initial consonant alternation, concord and interclass derivation considerably.

How does the development of both [±relative] markers and markers of the middle voice relate to language contact as an areal phenomenon, when it can be accounted for at least partially by internal factors such as final vowel shortening?

When Fula developed inflexional marking of the middle voice, it was the only member of its family to do so – and Fula was still very much living at home with its family at that time. My hypothesis is, that language contact was the reason for a collapse of Atlantic morphology in the nominal and the verbal systems of Fula, probably during a phase of pidginisation and creolisation, followed then by revernacularisation and morphological elaboration. This all took place before Fula started to spread over the vast areas it covers today.

When some Adamawa-variants of Fula 4000 km away from the Atlantic area lost a major part of their verbal morphology marking middle and passive voice and [±relative], it was pidginisation and creolisation that were very obviously the reason. Again this occurred in a linguistic environment where its major contemporary contact language Hausa is typologically opposed to these innovations, at least as far as [±relative] is concerned. The opposition between «relative» and «general tenses» is a feature of Hausa, the most important contemporary language of contact with Fula in Nigeria. It is, however, questionable whether Hausa played an equally important role in 19th century Adamawa when Fula was creolised.

The fact alone that pidginisation reduces redundancy and morphological complexity seems to account not only for the neutralisations of oppositions in categories «voice» and [±relative] but also for the reduction of the conditioning environment of the latter. Both innovations occurred in linguistic environments which are typologically opposed to them: one innovation developing an inflexional expression of middle voice, the other neutralising the same oppositions within the category of voice and partially reducing the oppositions between relative and non-relative aspects.

Abbreviations

A	Fulfulde (Fula) dialects of Adamawa
A1	Conservative Fulfulde dialect of Adamawa, spoken in Nigeria and Cameroon
A2	Fulfulde dialect of Adamawa, spoken in Nigeria (Adamawa and Taraba States) and Cameroon (Nord)
A3	Adamawa Fulfulde Pidgin or Creole, spoken by L1 and L2 speakers in Nigeria and Cameroon
Bj	Jelgoore (Fula) dialect, spoken in Northwestern Burkina Faso
Bm	Moosiire (Fula) dialect, spoken on the Mossi-Plateau in Burkina Faso
CF	Common Fula, i.e. forms common to most of the Fula dialects
Ser	Sereer
T	Pulaar (Fula) dialect of Fuuta Tooro, spoken in the Senegal valley in Senegal and Mauretania
J	Pular (Fula) dialect of Fuuta Jaloo (Guinea-Conakry)
Nb	Fulfulde (Fula) dialect of Bauchi (Nigeria)

Bibliography

ARNOTT, D. W., 1970, *The Nominal and Verbal Systems of Fula,* Oxford.

BOUTRAIS, J. (ed), 1993, *Peuples et Cultures de l'Adamaoua. Actes du colloque de Ngaoundéré du 14 au 16 janvier 1992,* Paris.

CARON, B., 2000, Assertion et préconstruit : topicalisation et focalisation dans les langues africaines, *Topicalisation et focalisation dans les langues africaines*, B. Caron (ed), pp. 7-42, Paris.

DE WOLF, P. P., 1986, Verbal extensions in Nongaare Fulani: causative, dative, celerative, distantive and simulative, *Afrika und Übersee* 69(1), pp. 45-60.

DE WOLF P. P., 1987, Further verbal extensions in Nongaare Fulani: reciprocal, iterative, iterative-reciprocal and verbalizing extensions, *Afrika und Übersee* 70, pp. 61-72.

DE WOLF, P. P., 1991, On four more verbal extensions in Nongaare Fulani: associative, comprehensive, modal and locative, *Afrika und Übersee* 74, pp. 49-66.

DIALLO, A., 2000, *Grammaire descriptive du pular du Fuuta Jaloo (Guinée)*, Frankfurt-am-Main.

ENDRESEN, R. T., 1993, The Eastern Fula Auxiliaries don and e and their Historical Relationship to Western Fula Long Subject Pronouns, *Nordic Journal of African Studies* 2(1), pp. 57-78.

FAYE, S., 1982, *Morphologie du verbe sérère*, Dakar.

GIREI, A. U., 1999, *A Comparative Analysis of Morphosyntactic Variation Between Adamawa and Gombe Dialects of Fulfulde,* Unpublished M. A. Thesis, Maiduguri.

GOTTSCHLIGG, P., 1992a, *Verbale Valenz und Kasus im Ful*, Dissertationen der Universität Wien 232, Wien.

GOTTSCHLIGG, P., 1992b, Durative Prädikate und Verbsemantik im Ful, *Komparative Afrikanistik. Sprach-, geschichts- und literaturwissenschaftliche Aufsätze zu Ehren von Hans G. Mukarovsky anläßlich seines 70. Geburtstages*, Ebermann, E., E. R. Sommerauer, K.E. Thomanek (Hrsg.), pp. 151-170. Wien.

GOTTSCHLIGG, P., 1995a, Sprachwandel und Dialektologie des Anlautwechsels im Ful, *Afrika und Übersee* 78, pp. 1-38.

GOTTSCHLIGG, P., 1995b, Determination und Referenz in der Entwicklung der Nominalklassensysteme des Ful und anderer atlantischer Sprachen, *Sprachkulturelle und historische Forschungen in Afrika*, Fleisch A. & D. Otten (Hrsg.), pp. 157-175, Köln.

GOTTSCHLIGG, P., 1995c, Research note on the Fulfulde-Pulaar preterite marker «no» in Adamawa, *Méga-Tchad* 95(1), pp. 17-20.

GOTTSCHLIGG, P., 1997a, Nominale Morphophonologie des Ful von Klingenheben bis Paradis: Keine Rezeptionsgeschichte, *Afrika und Übersee*, 80, pp. 161-187.

GOTTSCHLIGG, P., 1997b, Zur Spezialisierung pronominaler Reliktformen im Ful, *Fulfulde-Studien – Fula Studies. Frankfurter Afrikanistische Blätter* 9, R. Leger (Hrsg.), pp. 103-125.

GOTTSCHLIGG, P., 1998, Nominale Formen im Adamawa Ful, *Afrikanische Sprachen im Brennpunkt der Forschung,* Fiedler, I., C. Griefenow-Mewis & B. Reineke (Hrsg.), pp. 109-133, Köln.

GOTTSCHLIGG, P., 1999, Sénégal-language deixis and its development in Fula dialects, *Frankfurter Afrikanistische Blätter*, 11, pp. 51-82.

GOTTSCHLIGG, P., 2000, Subject Choice of Applicative Verbs in North-Atlantic, *Proceedings of the 2nd World Congress of African Linguistics Leipzig,* Wolff, E.H. & O. Gensler (eds), pp. 543-558, Köln.

GOTTSCHLIGG, P., forthc., Dialectal Variance, Standardisation and the Development of a Written Language: the Case of Fula, *African languages in global society/Les langues africaines à l'heure de la mondialisation*, Th. Bearth et al. (eds).

GREENBERG, J., 1977, Niger-Congo Noun Class Markers: Prefixes, Suffixes, both or neither, *Studies in African Linguistics*, Suppl. 7, pp. 97-112.

KLINGENHEBEN, A., 1963, *Die Sprache der Ful (Dialekt von Adamawa). Grammatik, Texte und Wörterverzeichnis*, Hamburg.

LABATUT, R., 1982, *La phrase peule et ses transformations*, Paris.

LACROIX, P.-F., 1959, Observations sur la «koiné» peule de Ngaoundéré, *Travaux de l'Institut de Linguistique, Faculté des Lettres et Sciences Humaines de l'Université de Paris* IV, pp. 57-101, Paris.

LACROIX, P.-F., 1962, Distribution géographique et sociale des parlers peul du Nord-Cameroun, *L'Homme*, sept.-déc., pp. 75-101, Paris.

LACROIX, P.-F., 1967, Quelques aspects de la désintégration d'un système classificatoire (peul du sud de l'Adamaoua), *La classification nominale dans les langues Négro-Africaines*, pp. 291-311, Paris.

METANGMO-TATOU, L., 2002, La koinè peule de Ngaoundéré: évolution des schèmes d'accord du système nominal et reconstruction morphosyntaxique, *Ngaoundere-Anthropos*, VII, pp. 197-214.

MCINTOSH, M., 1984, *Fulfulde Syntax & Verbal Morphology*, Boston.

MIAMOTO, R., 1993, A Study of Fula Dialects: Examining the Continuous/Stative Constructions, *Senri Ethnological Studies* 35, pp. 215-230.

NOYE, D., 1974, *Cours de foulfouldé (dialecte peul du Diamaré, Nord-Cameroun)*, Maroua.

NOYE, D., 1989, *Dictionnaire foulfouldé-Français*, Paris.

SYLLA, Y., 1982, *Grammaire moderne du pulaar*, Dakar.

SYLLA, Y., 1993, *Syntaxe Peule. Contribution à la recherche sur les universaux du langage*, Dakar.

TAYLOR, F. W., 1932, *A Fulani-English Dictionary*, Oxford.

TAYLOR, F. W., 1953, *A Grammar of the Adamawa Dialect of the Fulani Language (Fulfulde)*, Oxford.

ZIMA, P., 2002, Hausa TAM markers analyzed in their dialectal, genetic and areal context: interplay of internal and external factors, *Lexical and Structural Diffusion. Interplay of Internal and External Factors of Language Development in the West African Sahel*, Nicolai R. & P. Zima (eds).

The verb in Chadic - State of the Art[1]

Herrmann JUNGRAITHMAYR

Johann Wolfgang Goethe-Universität, Frankfurt, Germany

Abstract

After a brief introduction and the presentation of an exemplary text in Mokilko, a short history and an overview of the dominant topics of research on the Chadic verb are forwarded. The description and interpretation of the verbal piece and its characteristic features follow. The sequence of stages in the development of verbal stem types as already outlined by the author in 1978 is being discussed: Strong apophony (ablaut) – Weak apophony – Tonal mutation («apotony») – Stem-external TAM morphology. Verb stem inflection, segmental or tonal, is replaced by verb stem immobility and stem-external TAM productivity. The paper concludes by highlighting the most important issues of Chadic verb morphology as well as by hinting at the most urgent needs of future research in the field.

Résumé

Après une brève introduction et la présentation d'un texte d'exemple en mokilko, on aborde un bref historique et un survol des principaux sujets de recherche sur le verbe tchadique, suivis de la description et de l'interprétation du groupe verbal et de ses caractéristiques. On discute la séquence des étapes dans le développement des types de thème verbal ainsi qu'il a été présenté par l'auteur en 1978: Apophonie forte (*ablaut*) – Apophonie faible – Mutation tonale ("apotonie") – morphologie TAM extérieure au verbe. L'inflexion du thème verbal, segmentale ou tonale, est remplacée par l'immobilité du thème verbal et la productivité des TAM externes au verbe. L'article termine en mettant en évidence des traits saillants de la morphologie verbale tchadique et en signalant les besoins les plus urgents de la recherche future dans le domaine.

---

[1] The author wishes to express his special appreciation for Paul Newman's carefully arranged Hausa and Chadic bibliography (1996), which has served as a major source for the present paper.

1. Introduction: Nominal and verbal spheres

The principal components of a linguistic utterance in any Chadic language are the nominal or pronominal subject (S), the verbal piece, form or complex (V) and the nominal or pronominal object (O). Thus, we have for instance in Hausa:

	S	V	O	
	Yaro	*ya tambayi*	*yarinya*	'The boy asked the girl'
or:	*(Shi)*	*ya tambaye*	*ta*	'He asked her'

As a rule, the word order is SVO, though other sequences also occur.

As a matter of fact, the life of an utterance lies within the verbal piece which may display a high degree of mutability. Indeed, it constitutes the centre of the communication. In general, the nominal pieces (S and O) with their major categories of gender and plural formation are much less mutable and flexible. Typical examples of this type of morphological inequality are to be found among the southern Bole-Tangale languages where special gender and plural forms are practically non-existent with the noun, whereas verbal morphology is rich and abundant.

Languages like Hausa, Ron, Mubi and Migama which possess a copiously differentiated morphology in both realms are rather exceptional.

A particularly prominent example of the prevalence of verbal over nominal mutability is found in Mokilko, a language of the far-eastern branch (cf. Jungraithmayr 1990). In this language, gender is mostly marked by a change of suffix vowels, i.e. *–u* or *–e* for masculine and *–o* and *–a* for feminine; e.g.

mòɗú	'he-goat'	:	*mòɗó*	'goat'
wèdùsú	'male person'	:	*wèdìsó*	'female person'
gédè	'dog'	:	*gádà (<*gédà)*	'bitch'

Similarly, plurals are also mainly formed by suffix change, usually by the morpheme *-àgí* or similar shapes; e.g.

ɓúlè	'slave'	:	*ɓúlàgí*	'slaves'
kùunó	'wound'	:	*kùnɗàyí*	'wounds'

As exceptions from the rule, there are also a few other modes of plural formation including some internal, 'broken' plurals; e.g.

'ìlìlsó	'feather'	:	*'ìlàlí*	'feathers'
bízé	'mouth'	:	*bó''á*	'mouths'

2. The Mokilko verb in action

A few lines of a text with appropriate comments may give an idea of the verbal piece's especially high degree of flexibility in Mokilko phrases (Jungraithmayr, 'La femme et la mort ...', unpubl. manuscript):

(1) *Ùntùsú* ***yàazìkò*** *máalà-ɓ-ɓáadàŋ; máagùtù* ***yídítélé*** *à ùntùsù.*
Death assembled many treasures; her father gave her to Death.

(2) ***Yìttélé*** *ùntùsú màŋ.*
He gave her to Death then.

(3) ***Ánìidé*** *mán dɛ́.*
They went then alright.

(4) ***Ánîisè*** *mòoné máŋ,* ***yíppúukìyò*** *wíik,* ***yíttissó'ó*** *àddí ...*
They started sleeping then, he was breathing IDEO, he was swallowing her into his belly ...

(5) ***Tággìrbà, tà'ìngílè.***
She stood up, she took off.

The nine verb forms contained in this text fragment may be analyzed and interpreted in the following manner (following Jungraithmayr 1990):

(1a) ***yàazìkò***, to be analyzed as ***y-àa-zìk-ò*** 'he assembled' is based on *sìkí* (subjct.) / *sòkìyó* (VN) / *zìkí* (PF) plus *-o* (ventive); the *-aa-* following the SP (*y-*) is a TAM marker in the past tense;

(1b) ***yídítélé*** (= *y-í-dí-t-élé*) 'he gave her to': SP3m-TAM *-i-* infixed OP3f-MV-VS. *(t)élé* or *(t)éelè* (subjct.) / *'élìyó* or *'èelìyó* (VN) / *'élé* or *'éelè* (PF) 'to give', obviously conceived of in Mokilko as middle! *-í-*, fully amalgamated with the preceding SP, is the TAM marker of a simple past;

(2) ***yìttélé*** (= *y-ìt-t-élé*) 'he gave her (= acc.)'; *y-ìt-* is the SP plus *-ít-* as the marker of TAM 11;

(3) ***'ánìidé*** (= *'án-ìidé*) 'they went (on)': SP3p plus VS (PF); *'étté* (subjct.) / *'éttìyó* (VN) / *'ìidé* (PF) 'to go (on)'; *'án-* is the form of the SP3p in TAM 8;

(4a) ***'ánîisè*** (= *'án-íisè*): SP3p plus VS (PF); *(t)éesé* (subjct.) / *'éesìyó* (VN) / *'íisé* (PF) 'to begin';

(4b) ***yíppúukìyó*** (= *y-ít-púukìyó*): *y-ít-* SP3m plus TAM 11; *púukè* (subjct.) / *púukìyó* (VN) / *búukè* (PF) 'to breathe';

(4c) ***yíttissó'ó*** (= *y-ít-tí-s-só'ó*): SP3m plus TAM 11 plus OP3f -?- VS (VN); *sí'è* (subjct.) / *só'ò* (VN) / *'í'è* 'to swallow';

(5a) ***tággìrbà*** (= *tá-g-gìrbà*): SP3f plus TAM 5 plus VS, based on *gòrbá* (subjct.) / *gòrbé* (VN) / *gìrbá* (PF) 'to leave promptly';

(5b) ***tà'ìngílè*** (= *tà-ìngílè*): SP3f plus TAM 2 plus VS, based on *'èngílè* (sbjct.) / *'èngílsò* (VN) / *'ìngílè* (PF) 'to go away'.

It is particularly noteworthy that the verbal piece in Mokilko forms a tightly composed unit in which the three components – subject pronoun, (secondary) TAM morpheme and verb stem – are no longer divisible. This phenomenon is certainly untypical for an East Chadic language.

3. The study of the verbal piece

The term 'verbologist' is unusual but useful. It designates researchers whose contributions have helped to improve our insight into the structure, behaviour and potentialities of the verbal piece and its multiple functions in a given sentential context.

The number of verbologists in the field of Chadic is rather small. Alphabetically ordered the following names deserve to be listed here: Véronique de Colombel, Zygmunt Frajzyngier, Claude Gouffé, Herrmann Jungraithmayr, Paul Newman, F.W. Parsons, Russell Schuh, Henry Tourneux, Ekkehard Wolff. There are of course others whose works have also contributed to the study of the verb in Chadic: Khalil Alio, Daniel Barreteau, Jack Carnochan, Karen Ebert, Carl Ebobissé, Philip Jaggar, Elizabeth Jarvis, August Klingenheben, Rudolf Leger, Johannes Lukas, Joe McIntyre, Victor Porkhomovsky, Nina Pilszczikowa, Laurice Tuller, Werner Vycichl, Petr Zima.

As to the initial stages of 'Chadic verbology' Klingenheben's early articles on *Die Tempora Westafrikas und die semitischen Tempora* (1928/29) and *Die Silbenauslautgesetze des Hausa* (1927/28) mark the outset of this research field. Apart from Johannes Lukas, the founder of Chadic linguistics, to whom we are indebted for basic data on verbs of several Chadic languages (Lukas 1937), special research works on the structure and functions of the verb did not take off before the fifties and sixties of the past century. Thus, real progress in Chadic verbology was made only in the past forty years. On the one hand, careful, deep, descriptive research has been carried out on and in individual languages. On the other hand, comparative studies have initiated fruitful discussions and disputes on theoretical issues like the character of the verbal aspect system, the reconstruction of Proto-Chadic verbal roots, the nature of verbal classes, etc. Outstanding examples of the former type of research are Parsons (1960), Hoffmann (1963), Gouffé (1963-68), de Colombel (1986), Newman (1974), Schuh (1981), Tourneux (1978), Wolff (1983), Frajzyngier (1989) and Jungraithmayr (1970). Important contributions to the comparative-theoretical field came from Newman (1990), Newman and Schuh (1974), Frajzyngier (1977), Wolff (1984) and Jungraithmayr (1978).

4. Dominant topics of research

The main areas of research interest include the following:

- Root/base/stem structure (e.g. mono-, bi-, triradical)
- Verbal extensions, e.g. directional, ventive, allative
- Verb classes
- Verbal plurals/pluractional verbs
- Conjugational systems
- (Binary) aspect systems (perfective versus imperfective)
- TAM morphemes (tense-aspect-mood)
- Voice: middle voice, passivity; transitivity / intransitivity
- Intransitive copy pronoun (ICP)
- Verbo-nominals
- Apophony and apotony
- Apocopation and syncopation (reduction of verbal stem)
- Auxiliary verbs
- Prefix and suffix conjugation
- «Absolute» (independent) and «relative» (dependent) forms
- Reconstruction and history of development of verbs
- Genetic relations with other Hamitosemitic languages

A few of these research topics have already become the object of more general, comparative discussion forums and/or publications; e.g. *Fonctionnement du verbe dans trois langues tchadiques* (1982); *Études tchadiques: Classes et extensions verbales* (1987); *Études tchadiques: Transitivité et diathèse* (1988); *Études tchadiques: Verbes monoradiquaux* ... (1990); «La pluralité dans le syntagme verbal» (XIXème réunion du Groupe d'études tchadiques, Paris 1994); «La dérivation verbale» (XXème reunion du Groupe d'études tchadiques, Paris 1995), «L'organisation du syntagme verbal en tchadique» (XXIème réunion du Groupe d'études tchadique, Paris 1997); P. Newman, *Nominal and Verbal Plurality in Chadic* (1990); E. Wolff, «Grammatical categories of verb stems and the marking of mood, aktionsart and aspect in Chadic» (1979); H. Jungraithmayr, «A tentative four stage model for the development of the Chadic languages» (1978); dto., «On mono- and triradicality in early and present-day Chadic: How reliable are reconstructions?» (1983); P. Newman, «Proto-Chadic verb classes» (1975); dto., «The formation of the imperfective verb stem in Chadic» (1977b); R. Schuh, «West Chadic verb classes» (1977); V. de Colombel, «Mode, temps, aspect en tchadique» (1988). Recently, Uwe Seibert has embarked on a Chadic-wide investigation of verbal extensions.

From the list of major topics of research presented above it becomes clear that most properties of the verbal piece have already received appropriate attention, although some to a greater and others to a lesser extent.

5. The verbal piece and its description

To summarize and illustrate the situation, the following diagram may be of use; it certainly does not take into consideration minor deviations from the rule:

VERBAL PIECE

I	II	III	IV
subject pronoun (SP)	tense-aspect-mood (TAM)	verb stem (VS)	subject pronoun (SP)
		root/base/stem	intr. copy pron. (ICP)
		extensions	suffix conjugation (SC)
		plural	
		class	
		verbo-nominal	

An example of a complete representation of this basic model may be taken from Tangale (Jungraithmayr 1992: 59):

I	II	III	IV
na -	*ṇ*	*wẹẹ -*	*nọ*
I	am	fleeing	I

This ambifixal type of conjugation where a possessive pronoun kind of second subject pronoun is suffixed to the verb stem seems to be restricted to certain West Chadic languages (cf. Leger 2002); it is, however, also attested for Margi (Hoffmann 1963) and Mulwi (Tourneux 1978). In addition, there are the cases of an apparently genuine suffix conjugation found in some East Chadic languages (cf. Alio 1988, Jungraithmayr 1987) where, however, the preposed SP is omitted when the suffixed SP is in place.

In general, the verbal piece consists of SP+TAM+VS only, whereby the question to what extent these three component elements form an indivisible unit deserves special attention; their tight composition in Mokilko has been mentioned above. Compare for instance Mokilko with Hausa:

Mokilko:	*méegutu **yíditélé** á untusú.*
Hausa:	*ubánta **yáa báa ta** ga mútuwaa.*
English:	Her father gave her to Death.

In the sense of Hodge's linguistic cycle this tightly knit verbal complex in Mokilko may well be seen as a neosynthetical form having developed from an earlier analytical form (Hodge 1970, Jungraithmayr 1993).

So far, as it is to be expected, the majority of studies have concentrated on the inflectional and functional nature of the verb stem (VS). For instance:

- There is the question of whether, and if so in which way, verbal classes are dependent on structural features of the root or base of a verb.
- A vast field of research is that on verbal plurality which has already considerably been discussed by P. Newman (1990). The hypothesis according to which a decrease of nominal plurals evokes an increase of verbal plurals should be further examined.
- Much attention has been paid to the complex topic of the formation of the aspect stem – whether the binary opposition between perfective and imperfective is marked only by stem-internal inflection (apophonic or apotonic) or by stem-external modifications (TAM morphemes), leaving the stem itself unchanged (cf. Jungraithmayr 1978). Of course, it has fervently been disputed, whether the apophonic nature of the imperfective stem, e.g. Mubi *măt* (pfv.) versus *mùwáat* (impfv.) 'to die', is due to secondary Chadic-internal morphophonological developments or is rather an archaic feature common to proto-Hamitosemitic (cf. Newman 1977a, Jungraithmayr 1977).
- The crucial issue of reconstructing proto-Chadic verb roots has received much attention culminating e.g. in the challenging question whether for 'to drink', e.g. Ha. *shaa*, Sura *shwaa*, Mubi *sii*, **sa* (Newman 1977c) or **swC$_3$* (Jungraithmayr and Ibriszimow 1994) should be reconstructed.
- An exciting topic that still deserves to be pursued in greater depth is that of dependent (relative) and independent (absolute) verbal forms (cf. Jungraithmayr 1994). In which Chadic languages does this basic morphosyntactic dichotomy play a role? By which morphological means is it represented and expressed?
- Another challenging problem lies in the adequate description and analysis of the verbal form(s) usually termed 'aorist', 'subjunctive', 'narrative' or 'Grundaspekt'. Within the framework of most Chadic verbal systems it occupies the place of a / the third basic form underlying the central dichotomic aspect system.

6. The verbal piece and its interpretation: Some general observations

6.1 In an earlier paper (1978) I schematically proposed the following sequence of verbal stem types as they have probably developed in the history of Chadic languages:

Stem-internal:

I. Strong apophony e.g. in Ron-Daffo	*shōh*	«drink»	*shwāáh*
II. Weak apophony e.g. in Bole	*mòtí*	«die»	*mòtá*
III. Tonal mutation ('apotony') e.g. in Mwaghavul	*shwāā*	«drink»	*shwáá*

Stem-external:

IV. TAM morphemes e.g. in Giziga	*ɗòm*	«hide (o.s.)»	***rá*** *ɗòm*

It is hereby understood that the historical development of the verbal system in Chadic went from verb stem internal flexibity (inflection, segmental or tonal) towards verb internal immobility (inflexibility) and consequently to verb stem external productivity, i.e. to the emergence of more and more auxiliary morphemes which usually precede the verb stem. Thus, a late stage type of a verbal piece would display the following shape:

Subject pronoun + auxiliary morpheme + inflexible verb stem

As to the degree of amalgamation between the three positions different stages can be observed. They go from total independence – as for instance in Angas – to complete amalgamation – as in Mokilko. In general, the auxiliary morpheme – which is, of course, what is well known as the TAM (tense-aspect-mood) marker – approaches the subject pronoun more than the verb stem; the only exception seems to be Mokilko where all three positions form an inseparable compound unit; e.g.

y-áàd-íìmí
he-TAM-eat-PF
«he has eaten of it once more»

Mokilko seems to be the only Chadic language which displays a combined system of stem internal AND external verb morphology, i.e. it abounds in a highly inflectional internal apophonic flexibility but possesses, at the same time, a great number of TAM-marking elements which are inserted between the subject pronoun and the verb stem. As to the processes of ablaut (apophony) marking the binary aspect system, some examples may illustrate the astonishing richness of this language:

	Perfective	Imperfective
«count»	*gízè*	*kázà*
«eat (hard th.)»	*'íìɗîmá*	*'áàɗûmú*
«look for»	*dí'é*	*dé'ú*
«die»	*'ìndá*	*'ûntó*
«eat (soft th.)»	*'íìmí*	*'ômɓó*
«divide»	*dìikìɗá*	*dòokìɗé*

For further information, especially regarding the complex TAM system of Mokilko, see Jungraithmayr 1990: 34ff. and 45f.

A language with a neat subject pronoun + TAM morpheme amalgamation is Hausa. Compare for instance *ná-**á** sháá* «I have drunk» : *ná-**à** sháá* «I shall drink» : *ń-**nàà** sháà* «I am drinking» : ***zá**-ǹ sháa* «I will drink». Note that the latter form (Near Future or Intentional) displays the sequence TAM + subject pronoun + verb stem which is rather uncommon in Chadic.

Tonal or suprasegmental inflection of the verb stem which represents stage III of the stem internal mobility can be found mostly in languages of Chadic-Nigritic border areas, e.g. in Tumak (Caprile 1975), Masa, Muzgu and even in Ron-Fyer; for Hausa, the phenomenon is restricted to the CV(V) verbs. Compare the following examples all denoting «to drink»:

	Perfective	Imperfective
Tumak:	*hě*	*hè*
Masa:	*cī'é*	*cí'è*
Muzgu:	*sà*	*sá*
Ron-Fyer:	*shō*	*shó*
Hausa:	*sháá*	*sháà*

It is probable that the transformation of inflected verb stems originally marked by apophony (ablaut) to tone-marked aspect stems is due to the influence of some substratum to which vocalic inflection in verb stems was/is alien.

6.2 There is no evidence for any kind of influence exercised by different verb stem or verbal piece types on matters of word order. Nominal objects generally follow the verbal piece; pronominal ones, however, may enter the slot between TAM and verb stem, this sequence even being the obligatory and regular one in Mokilko; e.g. *kíi-**ní**-wóllìyó* «you are looking at me» (Jungraithmayr 1990: 37).

6.3 As to the negation of verbal paradigms, both major basic types, i.e. the additive and the suppletive, occur in Chadic, although the fore-mentioned one is by far the most frequent one. In the additive type, negative particles are added to the verbal paradigm – mostly placed behind it, but sometimes accompanied by a morpheme preceding the verbal piece. The position in front of the verbal piece seems to be preferred by the subjunctive mood. Thus, Hausa has ***kádà*** *sù zóo* «they may not come» and Ron-Daffo ***kà****-á hon nîn nì* ... «don't let us ...» (Jungraithmayr 1970: 204). The suppletive type implies that the verbal form to be negated changes when a negative particle is added. The classical Chadic example for this type is Hausa where the perfect tense form is substituted by the aorist-subjunctive form; e.g.

*sún/sú**kà** zóo*	***bà****sù zóo* ***bá***
«they came»	«they did not come»
	(comp. *sù zóo* «that they come»)

In Gude, a Central Chadic language (Hoskison 1983: 90), the situation is similar to that in Hausa. There, the morpheme marking the perfect tense, *kə*, is not compatible with the particle of negation, *pooshi*:

kə *kii Musa faara*	:	***pooshi*** *Musa kii faara*
«Musa threw a stone»		«Musa did not throw a stone»

6.4 As already mentioned above (6.3), at least Hausa and Ron-Daffo place the negative marker in front of a subjunctive, jussive or hortative form. Sura (Mwaghavul) follows the same rule but adds a second morpheme at the end of the phrase; e.g.:

> ***táji̇̀*** *a mandɛr ŋ̀ án* ***kás***
> «don't forget me!»

6.5 A special treatment of non-indicative verbal paradigms seems to be widespread in Chadic. The negative markers tend to be different in indicative forms from those used in non-indicative (subjunctive, etc.) forms. The typical constellation found in Hausa, i.e. *bà ... bá* (negative indicative) versus *kádà ...* (negative subjunctive), appears to occur quite often in Chadic.

6.6 As already demonstrated under 6.1, the contrast between perfective and imperfective or accompli versus inaccompli is perhaps the most basic constituent feature of Chadic verbal systems. The contrast may be marked either by stem-internal or -external vocalic mutation, e.g. Mubi *'éwít : 'úwáat* «to bite», or by tonal mutation, e.g. Ron-Fyer *ngòr : ngór* «to bite». When this binary opposition, either segmental or suprasegmental, is no longer in function, the first step towards externalising the marking of the aspectual opposition is to transfer the tonal mutation from the verb stem (*thème verbal*) to the preceding subject pronoun. This process can be observed e.g. in Mbara (Tourneux et al. 1986: 185f.): ***ì tór*** *wúrìi kée* «ils ont sarclé le champ» versus ***í tìi*** *dùbúìi ná* «ils préparent la nourriture». From here, the last step is taken by introducing various types of segmental TAM morphemes as can be shown in most Chadic languages, especially of the central branch and its neighbouring (mid-)western and -eastern groups, including Hausa. In Tangale, a member of a mid-western group, the TAM morphemes of the Continuous and the Future are *-ṇ* and *waa*, respectively: *na-ṇ saa-ni̥* «I am eating» and *na waa saa-ni̥* «I shall eat».

6.7 A number of Chadic languages distinguish verbal paradigms dependent on their syntactic role, i.e. whether they are absolute or relative, independent or dependent, focalised or non-focalised forms. Thus, Hausa has the dual forms *sún* and *súkà* for the past and *súnàa / súkèe* for the present-continuous. To mark such a distinction, Mubi and Bidiya, for instance, oppose the regular prefix conjugation to special paradigms of a suffix conjugation. For details see Jungraithmayr 1987, 1994 and Alio 1986.

7. Conclusion and prospect

In summarizing and concluding, the following points deserve to be kept in mind including important future research needs.

7.1 Although research of Chadic languages that include studies on the verb have made considerable progress in the past 40 to 50 years, certainly one third of the ca.

150 languages still remain only poorly documented and some not even at all. Apart from recording the full inventory of verbal forms for all Chadic languages, especially thorough studies on the semantics of a verb in morphosyntactic contexts are urgently needed. To this end text collections are a *conditio sine qua non*.

7.2 The degree of amalgamation – from totally analytical to highly synthetisized forms – of the three principal components of a verbal form may be a criterion of the historical 'age' of a given language's verbal system.

7.3 The manner as to how individual Chadic languages classify their verbs is an exciting topic which should continue to be treated intensively. So far, considerable work has already been accomplished, e.g. by Newman 1975, de Colombel 1987a, Frajzyngier 1982a, Leger 2002, Schuh 1977, Tourneux 1982b.

7.4 The question of intransitivity and middle voice ought to be investigated in each individual language. It seems as if only eastern languages mark the transitive: intransitivity dichotomy by vowel change (apophony), e.g. Migama ***zìwwò*** 'to hang': ***zàwwò*** 'to hang oneself' (Jungraithmayr and Adams 1992: 47). Cf. also Newman 1971, Leger 1989, Jungraithmayr 1988a,b, Tuller 1997.

7.5 A research area which has already yielded some important results, e.g. Frajzyngier 1987, Jarvis 1983, Jungraithmayr 2003a, and which deserves to receive further intensive inspection is what is generally referred to as 'verbal directionals', 'ventive' and 'centrifugal'.

7.6 Non-Hamitosemitic features in Chadic stemming from neighbouring, but originally also substratal Niger-Congo and/or Nilo-Saharan languages ought to be identified in the course of trans-genetic comparative studies.

7.7 The formation of the imperfective stem, mostly a verbo-nominal, needs to be studied in each Chadic language: what are the methods of deriving it either from the perfective or the aorist stem or from the common verbal base or root?

7.8 The Grade system of Hausa seems to be unique in the entire Chadic family. Efforts should be made to search for systems in other Chadic languages that may be comparable or related to the Hausa system.

Abbreviations

f.	feminine	pfv.	perfective (aspect)
ICP	intransitive copy pronoun	S	subject
impfv.	imperfective (aspect)	SC	suffix conjugation
m.	masculine	SP	subject pronoun
MV	middle voice/verb	subjct.	subjunctive
O	object	TAM	tense-aspect-mood
OP	object pronoun	V	verb stem
PF	perfect/past tense		

Journals and Collections

AAL	Afroasiatic Linguistics
AAP	Afrikanistische Arbeitspapiere
AM	Africana Marburgensia
AuÜ	Afrika und Übersee
ÉT	Études Tchadiques
FAB	Frankfurter Afrikanistische Beiträge
GLECS	Comptes Rendus du Groupe Linguistique d'Études Chamito-Sémitiques, Paris: Geuthner
ZDMG	Zeitschrift der Deutschen Morgenländischen Gesellschaft

The 4 volumes of ÉT, edited by H. Jungraithmayr and H. Tourneux, are:
— 1987, ÉT: Classes et extensions verbales
— 1988, ÉT: Transitivité et diathèse
— 1990, ÉT: Verbes monoradicaux
— 1991, ÉT: La phrase complexe

Selected bibliography

ALIO, K., 1986, *Essai de la description de la langue bidiya du Guéra (Tchad). Phonologie – Grammaire*, Berlin, Reimer.

— 1987, Les classes verbales en bidiya, *ÉT*, 11-15.

— 1988, Transitivité et conjugaison à suffixes en bidiya, *ÉT*, 21-31.

BARRETEAU, D., 1978, Structure du lexème verbal en mofu-gudur, *Préalables à la reconstruction du proto-tchadique*, J.-P. Caprile and H. Jungraithmayr (eds), Paris, SELAF, 115-42.

— 1987, Du mbara au mofu-gudur: approches comparées des systèmes verbaux, *Langues tchadiques et langues non-tchadiques en contact en Afrique Centrale*, H. Jungraithmayr (ed), Paris, SELAF, 37-60.

— 1988, *Description du mofu-gudur (langue de la familie tchadique parlée au Cameroun): 1. Phonologie, 2. Lexique*, Paris, ORSTOM.

— 1995, Vowel and tonal variations within the consonantal framework of the verbal stem in Central Chadic languages, *Studia Chadica et Hamitosemitica*, D. Ibriszimow and R. Leger (eds), Cologne, Köppe, 197-228.

— and H. JUNGRAITHMAYR, 1982, Le verbe en sibine, *The Chad Languages in the Hamitosemitic-Nigritic Border Area*, H. Jungraithmayr (ed), Berlin, Reimer, 192-229.

— 1990, Les verbes monoradicaux dans les langues tchadiques, *ÉT*, 37-214.

— and Yves LE BLEIS, 1987, Lexèmes et thèmes verbaux en mafa, *Cahiers du LACITO 2*, 31-52.

— 1990, *Lexique mafa (langue de la famille tchadique parlée au Cameroun)*, Paris, Geuthner/ORSTOM.

CAPRILE, Jean-Pierre, 1975, *Lexique tumak-français*, Berlin, Reimer.

CARNOCHAN, Jack, 1970, Categories of the verbal piece in Bachama, *African Language Studies 11*, 81-112

CARON, Bernard, 1980, Aoristique et subjonctif haoussa, *Études sur le subjonctif en tchadique (AM Spec. Issue 4)*, H. Jungraithmayr (ed), Marburg, 13-39.

— 1986, Les accomplis I et II du haoussa et la subordination, *Aspects, modalités: problèmes de catégorisation grammaticale*, Paris, Univ. de Paris VII, 103-120.

— 1989, The verbal system of Ader Hausa, *Current Progress in Chadic Linguistics*, Z. Frajzyngier (ed), Amsterdam, Benjamins, 131-69.

DE COLOMBEL, Véronique, 1986, *Phonologie quantitative et synthématique: propositions méthodologiques et théoriques avec application à l'ouldémé (langue tchadique du Nord-Cameroun)*, Paris, SELAF.

— 1987a, Classes verbales en ouldémé?, *ÉT*, 25-31.

— 1987b, Les extensions verbales productives, mi-figées ou fossilisées en langue ouldémé, *ÉT*, 65-91.

— 1988, Mode, temps, aspect en tchadique, *Temps et aspects*, ed. by N. TERSIS and A. Kihm, Paris, Peeters/SELAF, 103-15.

— 1990, Évolution du système verbal en linguistique tchadique: synchronie dynamique et diachronie, *Proceed. of the Fifth Intern. Hamito-Semitic Congress*, H. Mukarovsky (ed), vol. 1, 199-212, Vienna.

EBERT, Karen H., 1977, Some aspects of the Kera verbal system, *Papers from the Eighth Conf. on Afric. Linguistics*, ed. by Ma. Mould and Th. J. Hinnebusch, Los Angeles, UCLA, 33-41.

— 1979, *Sprache und Tradition der Kera (Tschad), Teil 3: Grammatik*, Berlin, Reimer.

EBOBISSÉ, Carl, 1979, *Die Morphologie des Verbs im Ost-Dangaleat (Guéra, Tschad)*, Berlin, Reimer.

— 1980, L'injonctif en dangaléat de l'est, *Études sur le subjonctif en tchadique (AM Spec. Issue 4)*, H. Jungraithmayr (ed), Marburg, 41-47.

— 1987a, L'apotonie et l'apophonie dans le système verbal du dangaléat de l'est, *Langues tchadiques et langues non-tchadiques en contact en Afrique Centrale*, H. Jungraithmayr (ed), Paris, SELAF, 71-87.

— 1987b, *Les verbaux du dangaléat de l'est (Guéra, Tchad): lexiques français-dangaléat et allemand-dangaléat*, Berlin, Reimer.

FEDRY, Jaques, 1990, Verbes monosyllabiques en dangaléat, *ÉT*, 9-13.

FRAJZYNGIER, Zygmunt, 1977a, The plural in Chadic, *Papers in Chadic Linguistics*, P. Newman and R.M. Newman (eds), Leiden, 37-56.

— 1977b, On the intransitive copy pronouns in Chadic, *Papers from the Eighth Conf. on Afric. Linguistics*, Los Angeles, UCLA.

— 1982a, Another look at West Chadic verb classes, *AM* 15 (1), 25-42.

— 1982b, The underlying form of the verb in Proto-Chadic, *The Chad Languages ...*, H. Jungraithmayr (ed), Berlin, Reimer, 123-43.

— 1987, Ventive and centrifugal in Chadic, *AuÜ* 70, 31-47.

— 1989, *A Grammar of Pero*, Berlin, Reimer.

— 1993, *A Grammar of Mupun*, Berlin: Reimer.

— 2001, *A Grammar of Lele*, Stanford, CSLI Publ.

— and Erin SHAY, 2002, *A Grammar of Hdi*, Berlin, Mouton de Gruyter.

GOUFFE, Claude, 1963/66, Les problèmes de l'aspect en haoussa. I – Introduction. Le problème de l'aoriste et de l'accompli II, *GLECS* 10, 151-65.

— 1966/67, Les problèmes de l'aspect en haoussa. II – Le problème de l'inaccompli I et II, *GLECS* 11, 29-67.

— 1967/68, Les problèmes de l'aspect en haoussa III. – L'inaccompli négatif et l'ingressif, *GLECS* 12, 27-51.

HODGE, Carleton, 1977, The Linguistic Cycle, *Language Sciences* 13, 1-7, Bloomington.

HOFFMANN, Carl, 1963, *A Grammar of the Margi Language*, London, OUP.

HOSKISON, James T., 1983, *A Grammar and Dictionary of the Gude language*, Ph.D. dissertation, Ohio State University.

JAGGAR, Philip J., 1977, The nature and function of auxiliary verbs in Hausa, *Papers in Chadic Linguistics*, P. Newman and R. M. Newman (eds), Leiden, 57-87.

JARVIS, Elizabeth, 1983, Podoko verbal directionals, *Studies in Chadic and Afroasiatic Linguistics*, E. Wolff and H. Meyer-Bahlburg (eds), Hamburg, Buske, 311-28.

— 1989, *Podoko Verb Dictionary*, Yaoundé, SIL.

JUNGRAITHMAYR, Herrmann, 1963, Die Sprache der Sura (Maghavul) in Nordnigerien, *AuÜ* 47, 8-89, 204-20.

— 1966, Zum Bau der Aspekte im Westtschadohamitischen, *ZDMG* 116, 227-34.

— 1968, The Hamitosemitic present-habitative verb stem in Ron and Mubi, *JWAL* 5 (2), 71-76.

— 1968/69, Hausa, Ron, and Angas: a comparative analysis of their 'aspect' systems, *AuÜ* 52, 15-22.

— 1970, *Die Ron-Sprachen: Tschadohamitische Studien in Nordnigerien*, Glückstadt, Augustin.

— 1974, Perfektiv- (Kurz-) und Imperfektiv- (Lang-)Stamm im Aspektsystem osttschadohamitischer Sprachen, *ZDMG* Suppl., 583-95.

— 1975, Der Imperfektivstamm im Migama (‚Djonkor von Abu Telfan', Republik – Tschad), *Folia Orientalia* 16, 85-100.

— 1977, Apophony and grammatical tone in the tense system of Chadic languages, *AuÜ* 60,79-82.

— 1978, A tentative four stage model for the development of the Chadic languages, *Atti del Sec. Congr. Intern. di Linguistica Camito-Semitica*, P. Fronzaroli (ed), Florence, 381-88.

— 1983a, On mono- and triradicality in early and present-day Chadic: how reliable are reconstructions? *Studies in Chadic and Afroasiatic Linguistics*, E. Wolff and H. Meyer-Bahlburg (eds), Hamburg, Buske, 139-56.

— 1983b, Altes und neues Perfekt im Hausa und in anderen Tschadsprachen, *AuÜ* 66, 221-30.

— 1987, Zur Suffixkonjugation im Osttschadischen, *AuÜ* 70, 49-60.

— 1988a, L'intransitivité en tchadique, *ÉT*, 11-20.

— 1988b, Medium im Tschadischen?, *Afrikanistische Beiträge zum XXIV Deutschen Orientalistentag*, W. J. G. Möhlig (ed), Cologne, 75-85.

— 1990, *Lexique mokilko*, Berlin, Reimer.

— 1991, *A Dictionary of the Tangale Language (Kaltungo, Northern Nigeria)*, Berlin, Reimer.

— 1991, La femme et la mort dans quelques contes du Tchad ou La mort comme 'père dévorant', unpubl. ms.

— 1993, *Die analytische Sprachform in Afrika*, Stuttgart, F. Steiner.

— 1994, „Zweite Tempora« in afrikanischen Sprachen – Ägyptisch-tschadische Gemeinsamkeiten? *Zwischen den beiden Ewigkeiten (FS G. Thausing)*, ed. by M. Bietak, J. Holaubek, H. Mukarovsky and H. Satzinger, Wien, 102-22.

— 2003a, Altrilocality in Tangale and Tuareg: a common heritage feature?, *Motion, Direction and Location in Languages*, E. Shay and U. Seibert (eds), Amsterdam – New York, Benjamins, 123-28.

— 2003b, Prefix and suffix conjugation in Chadic, *Proc. of the 10th Hamito-Semitic (Afroasiatic) Linguistics Meeting*, P. Fronzaroli e P. Marrassini (eds), Florence.

— and Abakar ADAMS, 1992, *Lexique migama*, Berlin, Reimer.

— and Dymitr IBRISZIMOW, 1994, *Chadic Lexical Roots, vol. I and II*, Berlin, Reimer.

— and M. MUNKAILA, 1985, On the *sun*-set in Hausa, *AM* 18 (1), 63-71.

— and H. TOURNEUX (eds), 1982, Fonctionnement du verbe dans trois langues tchadiques, *AM*, Spec. Issue 6, Marburg.

KLINGENHEBEN, August, 1927/28, Die Silbenauslautgesetze des Hausa, *Zeitschrift f. Eingeborenensprachen* 18, 272-97.

— 1928/29, Die Tempora Westafrikas und die semitischen Tempora, *Zeitschrift f. Eingeborenensprachen* 19, 241-68.

LEGER, Rudolf, 1989, Mediale Verben im Tschadischen? – Eine Fallstudie anhand des Kwami, *FAB* 1 (1), 65-71.

— 2002, Verbal classes and middle verbs in the languages Kwami, Kupto and Widala, *Elements of African Linguistics – Verbal Categories*, Moscow.

— (unpubl.), Verbal classes in some Bole-Tangale languages, *Proceedings of the Maiduguri Conference 1991.*

LUKAS, Johannes, 1937, *Zentralsudanische Studien*, Hamburg.

— 1963, Der II. Stamm des Verbums im Hausa, *AuÜ* 47, 162-86.

— 1970, *Studien zur Sprache der Gisiga (Nordkamerun)*, Glückstadt, Augustin.

— 1970/71-1971/72, Die Personalia und das primäre Verb im Bolanci (Nordnigerien), mit Beiträgen über das Karekare, *AuÜ* 54, 237-86, 55, 114-39.

MCINTYRE, J. A. 1989, Is Hausa *zoo* a grade 6 verb of motion? *AAP* 19, 7-22.

— 1990, Is Hausa *jee* a grade 4 verb? *AAP* 22, 5-17.

— 1993, Das Hausa-Verb: Syntax und interne Rekonstruktion, *Beiträge zur afrikanischen Sprach- und Literaturwissenschaft*, ed. by W. J. G. Möhlig, S. Brauner and H. Jungraithmayr, Cologne, Köppe, 157-67.

MEYER-BAHLBURG, Hilke, 1973/74, Quantitative Untersuchungen zum I., II. und IV. Verbalstamm im Hausa, *AuÜ* 57, 93-101.

NEWMAN, Paul, 1971, Transitive and intransitive in Chadic languages, *Afrikanische Sprachen und Kulturen – Ein Querschnitt*, ed. by V. Six et al., Hamburg, 118-200.

— 1973, Grades, vowel-tone classes and extensions in the Hausa verbal system, *SAL* 4, 297-346.

— 1974, *The Kanakuru Language*, Leeds.

— 1975, Proto-Chadic verb classes, *Folia Orientalia* 16, 65-84.

— 1977a, Chadic extensions and pre-dative verb forms in Hausa, *SAL* 8, 275-97.

— 1977b, The formation of the imperfective verb stem in Chadic, *AuÜ* 60, 178-92.

— 1977c, Chadic classification and reconstructions, *AAL* 5 (1), 1-42.

— 1980, *The Classification of Chadic within Afroasiatic*, Leiden, Univ. Pers.

— 1989, The historical change from suffixal to prefixal reduplication in Hausa pluractional verbs, *Journal of African Languages and Linguistics* 11, 37-44.

— 1990, *Nominal and Verbal Plurality in Chadic*, Dordrecht, Foris Publ.

— and Russell SCHUH 1974, The Hausa aspect system, *AAL* 1 (1), 1-39.

NEWMAN, Roxana Ma 1976, The two relative continuous markers in Hausa, *Papers in African Linguistics in Honor of Wm. E. Welmers*, ed. by L.M. Hyman, L.C. Jacobson, and R.G. Schuh, Los Angeles, 177-90.

PARSONS, F. W., 1956, The 'mutable verb' in Hausa, *Proc. of the 23rd Intern. Congr. of Orient.*, ed. by D. Sinor, London, 381-82.

— 1960, The verbal system in Hausa, *AuÜ* 44, 1-36.

PAWLAK, Nina, 1975, The semantic problems of 'intensive' forms in Hausa verbs, *Africana Bull.* 23, 139-49.

PILSZCZIKOWA, Nina, 1957 (in Polish), *The Verbal System of Hausa; Interrelationships between the Categories of Aspect and Tense*, Warsaw, PAN.

— 1969, *The Changing Form (Grade 2) of the Verb in Hausa*, Warsaw.

SCHUH, Russell G., 1971, Verb forms and verb aspects in Ngizim, *Journ. of Afr. languages* 10, *Special Chadic Issue* (1), P. Newman (ed), 47-60.

— 1976, The Chadic verbal system and its Afroasiatic nature, *AAL* 3 (1), 1-14.

— 1977, West Chadic verb classes, *Papers in Chadic Linguistics*, P. Newman and R. M. Newman (eds), Leiden, 143-66.

— 1981, *A Dictionary of Ngizim*, Berkeley & Los Angeles, UCP.

— 1998, *A Grammar of Miya*, Berkeley, Los Angeles & London, UCP.

TULLER, Laurice, 1990, L'hypothèse inaccusative et les verbes de 'degré 3' et de 'degré 7' en haoussa, *Linguistique Africaine* 5, 95-126.

— 1997, Le "ICP" en tchadique, *Les pronoms. Morphologie, Syntaxe et Typologie*, A. Zribi-Hertz (ed), Saint-Denis : Presses Universitaires de Vincennes.

TOURNEUX, Henry, 1978, *Le mulwi ou vulum de Mogroum (Tchad). Phonologie – éléments de grammaire*, Paris, SELAF.

— 1982a, Fonctionnement du verbe dans les énoncés simples et complexes en vulum, *Fonctionnement du verbe dans trois langues tchadiques (AM, Spec. Issue 6)*, H. Jungraithmayr and H. Tourneux (eds), Marburg, 31-38.

— 1982b, Les classes verbales en mulwi (Tchad), *The Chad Languages in the Hamitosemitic-Nigritic Border Area*, H. Jungraithmayr (ed), Berlin, Reimer, 175-82.

— 1987, Peut-on parler d'extension verbale en munjuk? *ÉT*, 115-21.

— 1995, Le système aspectuel des langues dites 'kotoko', *Studia Chadica et Hamitosemitica*, D. Ibriszimow and R. Leger (eds), Cologne, Köppe, 171-79.

— , Christian SEIGNOBOS et Francine LAFARGE, 1986, *Les Mbara et leur langue (Tchad)*, Paris, SELAF.

VOIGT, Rainer M., 1989, Verbal conjugation in Proto-Chadic, *Current Progress in Chadic Linguistics*, Z. Frajzyngier (ed), Amsterdam, Benjamins, 267-84.

VYCICHL, Werner, 1990, L'origine des verbes monoradicaux en haoussa, *ÉT*, 221-28.

WOLFF, Ekkehard, 1972, *Die Verbalphrase des Laamang (Nordostnigeria)*, PhD diss., Hamburg.

— 1977a, Patterns in Chadic (and Afroasiatic?) verb base formations, *Papers in Chadic Linguistics*, P. Newman and R.M. Newman (eds), Leiden, 199-233.

— 1977b, Verb bases and stems in Migama, *AuÜ* 60, 163-77.

— 1979, Grammatical categories of verb stem and the marking of mood, aktionsart, and aspect in Chadic, *AAL* 6 (5), 161-208.

— 1982, 'Aspect' and aspect-related categories in Chadic, *The Chad Languages* ..., in H. Jungraithmayr (ed), Berlin, Reimer, 183-91.

— 1983, *A Grammar of the Lamang Language*, Glückstadt, Augustin.

— 1984, New proposals concerning the nature and development of the Proto-Chadic tense/aspect system, *Current Progress in Afro-Asiatic Linguistics*, J. Bynon (ed), Amsterdam, Benjamins, 225-39.

— 1985, The verbal aspect system in Zime-Mesme: studies on consonant-tone interference in Chadic languages III, *AuÜ* 68, 1-22.

ZIMA, Petr 1991, Le problème des formes verbales dites 'relatives' en tchadique, *ÉT*, 15-26.

On distributed predicative syntax in Western Mande

Raimund KASTENHOLZ

Johannes Gutenberg-Universität, Mainz, Germany kastenho@uni-mainz.de

Abstract

Mande languages of West Africa are known to represent a prominent case of a "Split Predicate Syntax", where "Predicate Markers" (PMs), invariant particles functioning as auxiliaries, are involved in the constitution of the clause. Inflectional marking and verbal semantics are thus "distributed", i.e. they are expressed by different elements in different syntactic positions; the systemic importance of "distributed predicative syntax" varies considerably from one language or language sub-group to the other, though: Some languages express near to all grammatical information by means of PMs for most, if not all TAM categories (e.g. Bambara, Koranko); in other languages, split predicate syntax is synchronically less prominent or even marginal (e.g. Jɔgɔ, Bɔbɔ).
Accordingly, PMs may be quite differently involved in inflectional marking. It is argued here that, in this context, Western Mande languages fall at least into two different types: Inflection-like categories are either (1) primarily marked by PMs alone, or (2) mainly on the verb. For a number of Western Mande languages, inflectional marking (i.e. to distinguish aspects like *perfective* vs. *imperfective*) is thus not predominantly with the PMs. It is suggested that, in a diachronic perspective, evidence from type (2) languages should be taken into account.

Résumé

Les langues mandé en Afrique de l'Ouest sont connues pour représenter un cas remarquable de "Syntaxe Prédicative Disloquée", où les "Marques Prédicatives" (MP), des particules invariables fonctionnant comme des auxiliaires, contribuent à la constitution de la proposition. Les flexions et la sémantique verbales sont ainsi "distribuées", c'est à dire qu'elles sont exprimées par des éléments différents dans des positions syntaxiques différentes. Cependant, l'importance de la "syntaxe prédicative disloquée" varie considérablement d'une langue ou d'un sous-groupe de langues à l'autre: certaines langues expriment presque toute l'information grammaticale au moyens des MP pour la plupart, si ce n'est toutes les catégories TAM (ex. bambara, koranko); pour d'autres, la syntaxe prédicative disloquée est synchroniquement moins importante, si ce n'est marginale (ex. jɔgɔ, bɔbɔ).
De même, les MP peuvent avoir un rôle très différent dans le marquage flexionnel. Dans cet article, on démontre que, de ce point de vue, les langues mande occidentales se répartissent en au moins deux types. Les catégories d'ordre flexionnel sont soit (1) marquées essentiellement par les MP seules, ou (2) essentiellement sur le verbe. Pour un certain nombre de langues mande occidentales, le marquage flexionnel (par ex. celui distinguant entre *perfectif* et *imperfectif*) n'est pas essentiellement assuré par les MP. Il est suggéré que, dans une perspective diachronique, les données des langues de type (2) devraient être prises en compte.

The Mande languages of West Africa, it has been argued, are part of a large contact zone in the West African Sahel/Savannah Belt (probably extending further to the East).[1] Even if the conceptualization and the extent of this linguistic area are still open to discussion, it seems acceptable to regard the Mande languages themselves as representing some kind of a sub-zone within this area.[2] By the evidence of internal structural features and of some recurrent findings and problems in comparative Mande studies, one could then be tempted to take the extreme view of reinterpreting the Mande language group as a whole, in sharp contrast to the application of the model of genetic relationship in its proper sense, as being the *result* of an ancient, long-term zone of contact-induced structural change and diffusion of lexical elements.[3] The relevant features and findings in this context are:

1. It has been observed (Kastenholz 1991/92, 1996: 82-83), at least for Western Mande languages, that (regular) sound change can only be attested in a surprisingly small number of cases, and that the type of change is repeatedly the same (Kastenholz 1989: 57). This phenomenon is connected to the fact that
2. lexical divergence is extremely high between (Western) Mande languages (see also Grégoire 1988: 103).
3. Word order in Mande is S-Aux-O-V-«Other». This word order represents a rare linguistic type, a «highly marked quirk», as Gensler (1997: 68) puts it. On the other hand, language convergence areas «may give rise to the emergence of new or rarely attested linguistic types» (Bisang, forthcoming). This argument, of course, cannot be necessarily reversed. Heine, on the other hand, identifies several *areal nuclei* in Africa, «linguistic area[s] with a relatively high concentration of recessive word order features [...].» (Heine 1976: 57). Among those is what he calls the «Mande nucleus».

The typological statement in (3) also implies that the Mande languages display a «distributed predicative syntax», i.e. that predicative functions such as inflectional marking and verbal semantics are expressed by different elements in different syntactic positions. For further studies in a variety of adjacent fields (typology in general, historical syntax, and areal linguistics), the validity of this notion for «all of Mande» needs some confirmation on the basis of data from a maximum of

[1] Cf. the «Introductory notes» to Nicolaï/Zima (2002: 5-7). Dalby's *Fragmentation Belt*, «one of the most complex linguistic areas in the world» (Dalby 1970: 170) stretches from the Central African Sahel zone to the Western Atlantic coast.

[2] Other languages, like Senufo etc., might have to be included, depending on the purpose of the study.

[3] This view is expressed here in order to open up an alternative perspective on the linguistic history of Mande. Even if contact phenomena have played a predominant role in the development of the Mande languages (which remains disputable), it would be rather erroneous to see contact-induced change as the exclusive explanatory model for the language history of Mande.

individual languages. Before discussion some differences, it is important to note, however, that some features basic to the «Mande language type» are rather uniform throughout the whole linguistic family:

(**a**) The direct object always precedes the verb. Indirect objects, locative objects, adverbs, ideophones, and depictive noun phrases *follow* the verb. The first two of these, and many of the depictive NPs, are represented as Pp-phrases. Only one object can precede the verb, and there is no difference in syntactic behaviour for nominal objects as opposed to pronominal ones. The object NP can be definite or indefinite, for languages that make that distinction. Pronouns in object position do not differ, to my knowledge, from pronouns in other syntactic functions.[4] The object noun can be modified in the same ways as the subject noun. No element can come between the object and the verb, though, and disjunctive objects are not allowed.

(**b**) Word order is invariable, to my knowledge, for all Mande languages. Also, all (Western) Mande languages, to my knowledge, do have auxiliaries preceding the object NP (see 3. above) at least for some TAM[5] categories. Certain languages, however, display the *general* structure of a «split predicate», where auxiliary-like elements convey all or most of the content we tend to expect to be grammaticalized as morphological categories on the verb, and the «lexical verb» almost exclusively contributes (lexical) semantic content to the predication.

The aim of the present article is to have a closer look at this kind of structure, its occurrence and representation with Western Mande languages.[6] In doing so, I shall refer to the «auxiliary-like elements» (see above) as *Predicate Markers* (PM, pl. PMs). The advantage is, that the grammemes in question are referred to with regard to their sentence-constituting function, and that other notions that need more discussion in a different context thus can be avoided here.

The functioning of auxiliaries as inflectional markers for certain categories is, of course, very common in a cross-linguistic perspective. What makes the «split predicate» structure of languages like e.g. Bambara (Manding) or Koranko so remarkable (apart from some more general typological characteristics), can be summed up by the following features:

---

[4] For South-western Mande languages, a specific object pronoun series is reported, but the situation is somewhat obscured by the fact that *subject* pronouns in some of these languages always seem to be fused with following PMs, at least in a diachronic perspective. I would expect that all these object pronouns can be shown to represent nothing but the «uninfluenced», i.e. non-fused, form of the general pronoun. One point in case here is that in each of these languages (Kpelle, Lɔɔma, Mɛnde etc.), these same «object pronouns» also occur in a subject position for at least one aspect or mode. Possessive pronouns are not different from general pronouns neither, if they are not fused with a genitive/associative marker.

[5] TAM = tense, aspect, mode, see list of abbreviations below.

[6] To include the Eastern Mande languages would double the task. Split predicate structure is, nevertheless, also present in Eastern Mande languages, see Bearth (1995: 89).

1. There is one PM (or rather: PM-pairing, see [2] below) per TAM-category, i.e. a PM is the only or at least a necessary inflectional marker for all categories. TAM-marking is thus exclusively operated by or in combination with PMs (there is an important conditioned exception to this, though, see 4. below). PMs follow the subject NP; they precede the object NP and/or the verb respectively.
2. Negation is expressed by negative PMs that are selected for aspect and mode, and that replace the affirmative PM in corresponding clauses (cf. Bambara examples [1]-[4] below).
3. The semantic verb is unmarked. In some cases, i.e. the progressive, aspect marking may be discontinuing, involving a PM and a verbal suffix that evolved from a postposition (cf. examples [6]-[8] from Koranko).
4. «Transitivity split» occurs for the perfective (cf. examples [8] vs. [9]-[10]), i.e. in clauses with only one argument, there is no PM in the affirmative, and the verb is marked by a suffix (-ta/-da/-ra throughout Greater Manding [GM]).

Bambara (Kastenholz 2003: 33, 43)[7]

(1) **fíɲɛ́ bɛ́ tásuma jíidi**
wind IPF fire increase
«The wind is making the fire flare up.»

(2) **fíɲɛ́ tɛ́ tásuma jíidi**
wind IPF.NEG fire increase
«The wind is not making the fire flare up.»

(3) **wùlu yé gáfe mìnɛ à ɲín ná**
dog PFV booklet seize 3ps tooth Pp
«The dog seized the booklet with its teeth.»

(4) **wùlu má gáfe mìnɛ à ɲín ná**
dog PFV.NEG booklet seize 3ps tooth Pp
«The dog didn't seize the booklet with its teeth.»

Koranko (author's field notes)

(5) **ń ná yé bàninkɛ mà ká-la**
1ps mother PROG cassava[SPM] PV peel-PROG
«My mother is peeling cassava.»

(6) **ń sí à fàà bì**
1ps HAB/PROSP 3ps kill today
«I'm going to kill him today.»

---

[7] For abbreviations, see list below.

(7) **ń sá kínɛ té-la**
1ps PROG.NEG meal/SPM cook-PROG
«I am not cooking the meal.»

(8) **kè-i dó nà-ra**
man-SPM a come-PFV
«A man came.»

(9) **káminɛ yá sùman kíi**
young_man[SPM] PFV rice plant
«The young man planted rice.»

(10) **à má nà**
3ps PFV.NEG come
«He did not come.»

A closer look at Western Mande in general reveals that languages with the above-listed criteria (1-4) only represent one of (at least) two types with regard to the role of PMs in inflectional marking,[8] albeit a prominent one.[9] For the remaining languages of this Branch, all four characteristics may be absent, i.e. inflectional systems vary considerably throughout Mande as to how inflection-like categories are primarily marked: (I) by PMs alone[10], or (II) mainly on the verb. Languages that belong to what I would like to call «Type I» as characterized above are those of a close-knit complex referred to as «Greater Manding» (and in Soninke/Bozo, see below). GM includes, besides Manding proper (i.e. the Manding dialect cluster, with varieties like Bambara, Maninka, Mandinka, Jula, and many more), Koranko and Mɔgɔfin, as well as Vai and Kɔnɔ.

Soninke and the group of Bozo languages belong to the same Type I, although there are two points in which they differ to a certain extent from GM: (1) clauses with only one argument in the PFV (affirmative) lack a PM, as in GM, but there is no inflectional marking on the verb either (see example [11] compared to [12]); (2) there is a verb form marked for IPF,[11] and this verb form combines at least with two different PMs (cf. [13]-[15]).[12] Note that in Bozo (evidence from Tigemaxo) the opposition of an unmarked verb stem vs. a marked IPF-stem has been maintained only for a certain number of lexical items (see Blecke 1996: 61-62, 70-72).

[8] The term «type» used here is not intended to imply discreteness. At the present stage of the discussion, the main function of the «types» proposed is to provide some kind of an ordering system, summarizing findings from data from a number of languages.
[9] It is «prominent» in two ways: 1. many of the relevant languages have been studied more intensively than most others of the Western Mande branch, and 2. these same languages have a wide distribution, both in geographical terms and in terms of second language function.
[10] The PROG, throughout the languages studied here, is often marked by a combination of a PM and a verbal suffix. In most cases, though, another IPF category exists in the language, either marked by a specific PM (as is the case in Koranko, see [6] above) for languages of Type I, or by a verbal suffix.
[11] This is also the case for IPF or PROG in some GM languages.
[12] **wá** for the PROG, **ná** for FUT (aspectual). The latter also combines with the unmarked verb stem. Note that there is only one corresponding NEG involving the PM **ntá**.

Soninke (Kendall et al. 1980)

(11) **yàxare ǹ sìgi**
woman DF stop
«The woman stopped.»

(12) **ń dá máaro ǹ yìga**
1ps PFV rice DF eat
«I ate the rice.»

(13) **Bíntù wá máaro ǹ yìga-na**
B. PROG rice DF eat-IPF
«Bintu is eating the rice.»

(14) **à ntá fíccè-nè**
3ps NEG vomit-IPF
«He is not vomiting/will not *vomit.»*

(15) **à ná dòlo ǹ mìnni yà**
3ps FUT wine DF drink[IPF] FOC
«He will *drink the wine.»*

The second Type (II) of languages is characterized by the fact that the function of PMs is rather marginal in clause-constituency and/or for inflectional marking. Thus, in a given variety, there are either (a) no PMs involved in clause-constituency for TAM categories that are central to the system (i.e. the role of PMs is marginal in this respect), or (b) PMs do occur in all or in an important part of the constructions, but they do not (or only secondarily) contribute to the expression of inflectional categories primarily marked on the semantic verb. Negation is not expressed by portmanteau PMs, i.e. NEG elements, if they occur in the «PM slot», are not (or to a lesser degree) specific for TAM. By a «set of TAM categories central to the system», I understand a basic opposition between an IPF with its various sub-categories (if morphologically distinct) on the one hand, and a PFV or a conceptually closely related PF/CPL on the other. Note that in many languages an additional PROG exists outside the basic dichotomy.

The individual systems of languages assigned to Type II here can differ considerably. There is a number of languages (see a) to e) below), for which central TAM categories are operated largely without PMs. Some of these languages belong to the Central Sub-branch of Western Mande (Sooso, Jɔgɔ), the others to the Northwestern Sub-branch.

(a) In Sooso, the IPF categories (PROG, HAB/PROSP), and a PF/CPL are marked by suffixes on the verb alone (cf. [16], [17], [19]). Perfective ([20]) and the subjunctive, on the other hand, are operated by PMs alone. The NEG marker **mú**, itself *not* specific for TAM, occurs *in PM position* (cf. [18]) for all categories.[13]

[13] I am not sure if the analysis of the facts is correct in this respect. There is only one form of NEG clause corresponding to the affirmative of alleged PFV and PF/CPL respectively, formally linked to the latter. Alternatively, a NEG PFV can be expressed by NEG **mú** plus the unmarked verb (cf. Friedländer 1974: 36).

Sooso (Freidländer 1976)

(16) **à xɔ̀sɛ́=sùbè dón-mà**
3ps pig=meat eat-HAB
«He eats pork.»

(17) **Fánta sèé ɲín-fe**
Fanta something cook-PRO
«Fanta is preparing food.»

(18) **à mú xɔ̀sɛ́=sùbè dón-mà**
2ps NEG pig=meat eat-HAB
«He does not eat pork.»

(19) **è xàrán.yi tìnkán.xi**
3pp read.RF learn.PF/CPL
«They have learned (how to) read.»

(20) **í bára à mè?**
2ps PFV 3ps hear
«Did you hear it/have you heard it?»

(b) In the Jɔgɔ language, inflection is primarily marked on the verb for PFV and IPF respectively. The relevant morphemes are suffixed to the verb, the IPF-suffix being fused in most phonologically conditioned environments (examples [21-24]). Only the progressive ([25]), the continuative and the hortative constructions contain a PM.[14] Negation is not marked in the PM slot, but by means of one uniform clause final element combining with all categories.

Jɔgɔ (author's field notes)

(21) **ɲàŋ=kòrà gbá-á bèkɔ̀**
woman=old tree-the fell[IPF]
«The old woman fells/is going to fell the tree.»

(22) **ɛ̀ kàkàlé fì-wɔ̀**
3ps falsehood lie-IPF
«He lies, tells lies.»

(23) **nò Mákà=tàgá jàté-rɛ̀**
3pp Mecca=walk think-PFV
«They thought about a journey to Mecca.»

(24) **ɛ̀ ɛ̀ rá sɛ̨́ ɛ̨̀-nɔ́ kó jɔ̀gɔ̀-nɛ́.**
3ps 3ps POSS thing DF-pl all lower-PFV
«He put all his things down.»

[14] The following examples are taken from the Jɔgɔ variety spoken in the vicinity of Banda town in Ghana. In another variety of this language (i.e. Wela), the PM for the progressive combines with the verb marked for IPF (see Kastenholz 2003: 35).

(25) **è wɛ́ bàgá má-rá**
3ps PRO farm make-PRO
«He is making a farm.»

(c) Seenku («Sembla»), Duun («Samogo-sien», Mali), Dzuun and Kpan («Samogo-iri» and «Samogo-guan» respectively, both in Burkina Faso). The latter three form, together with Banka (see (g) below) a group of very closely related languages (or dialects). In these varieties of «Samogo», the only PMs specific for TAM are those for FUT and SUBJ, combining with the unmarked stem of the verb.[15] Seenku has an additional, probably recent PROG, requiring a combination of a PM and a specific verbal suffix (see example [33]). Otherwise, TAM is expressed either by specific verb stems, or by a suffix. Negation in Dzuun and Kpan requires an element (unspecific for TAM) that occurs in the PM slot, combining with an additional clause final negation marker. In Duun and Seenku, on the other hand, negation is marked by a clause-final element alone.[16]

Duun[17]

(26) **ì wɔɔ mo'ɔkuje-rɔ rá'a to'o=mã rá sisa**
3pp reach[PF/PFV] witch-DF GEN dwell=place[DF] Pp now
«Now they arrived at the place [where] the witch lived.»

(27) **mu nãfã taa-ra**
1ps benefit get-IPF
«I [usually] get some benefit [out of it].»

Dzuun (Traoré, Traoré, and Solomiac 1998)

(28) **ā dzù-à keynbo-ò ʃɔ-ɔ̀ ka**
3ps farm-DF clear-PFV hoe-DF Pp_with
«He cleared the farm with the hoe.»

(29) **gadzin-nee kpìnì-ná kur-la rè**
bee-pl[DF] buzz-IPF hollow-DF Pp_in
«The bees are buzzing in the tree-hole.»

Kpan (see footnote 17)

(30) **Musa ná góoma-ma w̃**
Musa NEG speak-PFV NEG
«Musa did not speak.»

[15] It is important to note that (at least in Duun) there is (in the affirmative) an element **yɛ** (tone uncertain) that combines with the unmarked verb stem, as well as both with the IPF and the PF/PFV form of the verb under a number of conditions. This element occurs in the slot excepted for PMs, but it differs in many respects from these. Its role in clause constituency is, if at all, a minor one.

[16] The «new progressive» of Seenku, where a PM for PROG NEG combines with the clause-final element, being an exception to this rule (cf. Prost 1971: 52-54).

[17] Data for Duun and Kpan (see below) are from H. Tröbs' field notes, kindly put at my disposal.

Seenku (Prost 1971)

(31) **à ci ɲe**
3ps house build[PF/PFV]
«He built/has built a house»

(32) **mini kwò ta-won**
woman[pl] 'to' cook[IPF/HAB]
«The women prepare the 'to'»[18]

(33) **n sin jo mi-ne**
1ps PROG water drink-PROG
«I am drinking water.»

(d) The Jɔ (or Jɔwulu) language, too, is often referred to as «Samogo». It does not belong to the same cluster of closely related languages discussed above under (c), though. Jɔwulu marks PFV, PRO and FUT on the verb (the former two by means of suffixes, the latter tonally). PRO and FUT do combine with PMs specific for the respective category. This is, to a certain extent, some kind of a double marking system, but verb forms (in central categories) are *always* marked for TAM, which implies that PM-marking is secondary for inflection. Negation is marked by a clause final element alone.

Jɔwulu (Carlson 1993)

(34) **ʃōrō ki ʃɛ̰̀ɛ̰̀ ki tɛ́rí-ì siná ŋū**
man DF meat DF cut-PFV knife with
«The man (has) cut the meat with a knife.»

(35) **má-a ǹ tɛ́rí**
1ps-FUT 3ps cut[FUT]
«I shall cut it.»

(36) **mí-í ǹ tɛ́r-ra**
1ps-PROG 3ps cut-PROG
«I am cutting it.»

(e) Central to the TAM system of Bɔbɔ is a dichotomy of tonally marked verb stems for the IPF and the PFV respectively (examples [37]-[38] below). PMs have the secondary function of differentiating several sub-categories of the IPF, i.e. they operate on clauses (of the type of ex. [38] below) that are grammatical without them (but less specific for aspect). Among the meanings specified by PMs are PRO, HAB and PROSP (see ex. [39-40]).

---

[18] 'To' is a dish made from boiled and pounded millet.

Bɔbɔ (Prost 1983)

(37) **à nānɛ̄ kìmì**
3ps chicken steal[PFV]
«He stole/has stolen a chicken.»

(38) **à nānɛ̄ kìmī**
3ps chicken steal[IPF]
«He steals a chicken.»

(39) **à tī nē ɲòn jōó**
3ps PRO ? to eat[IPF]
«She is eating 'to'.» (See footnote 18)

(40) **lākuɔ̄.nē tīɛ́ sànēmā tàā**
blacksmith.pl HAB bracelet[pl] make[IPF]
«The blacksmiths make bracelets.»

(f) Jeri is lexically and phonologically closely related to Jɔgɔ. Quite similar to what has been described for that latter language (see (b) above), the basic distinction of TAM is operated by the selection of an unmarked verb stem (PFV, PF, and SUBJ) vs. a marked one by suffixation (general IPF, PROSP). Unlike Jɔgɔ, this verb stems interact with a PM for the IPF (and for some more marginal categories, see table 1 below). Negation, as in Jɔgɔ, is clause final.[19]

Jeri (Tröbs 1998)

(41) **a a kpuru si kara-nɛ**
1pp IPF leather FOC sew-DER
«We sew leather.»

(42) **na a kɛlɛmugu sa- ŋɔ i ma**
1ps IPF twenty lay/DER-PRSP 3ps Pp
«I am going to add twenty (i.e. 100 Francs CFA).»

(43) **ni na kenɛ**
3pp 1ps insult
«They insulted me.»

(44) **na wa taga**
1ps PF go
«I'm gone.»

The following Table is added here in order to illustrate in which respect the systems of the two closely related languages Jeri and Jɔgɔ differ (only the affirmative is shown). Details for Jeri are from Tröbs (1998: 163-164), those for Jɔgɔ are based on the author's field notes.

[19] In a different view, Jeri could probably be excluded from Type II, for reasons rather similar to those stated for the South-western languages below.

	Jeri	Jɔgɔ (Banda)	Jɔgɔ (Wela)
PFV	V	V-rɛ	
PF/STRS[20]	wa … V	V-rɛ wɛ́	
SBJ	a … V	rá … V	
IPF	a … VDER	V-wɔ	
PRSP	a … VDER- ŋɔ	V-wɔ	
PROG		wɛ́ … V-ra	wɔ́ … V-wɔ
CONT	a ri … VDER		

Table 1: Jeri and Jɔgɔ compared[21]

(g) In Banka, a language of the «Samogo» cluster (cf. (c) above), inflectional marking for the IPF and the PF/PFV respectively is clearly with the verb, too.[22] In contrast to what has been described for the other «Samogo» varieties, Banka has an additional PM – the *same* one for both categories, grammaticalized from a copula (existential) – that combines with these inflectionally marked verb forms (examples [41]-[43]). The PM is formally weak (at least in the variety studied by the author). It consists of lengthening of the vowel of the preceding element (i.e. in the subject NP). Alternatively, a (newly acquired) PM mɛ̄ is used (compare examples [41] and [42]).[23] It is remarkable that, for both contrasting categories, the PM *cannot* occur in clauses with one argument (subject) only (cf. ex. [44]). Negation, similar to Dzuun and Kpan (see above), requires a negative marker that precedes the PM, combined with an additional clause final element (ex. [45]).

Banka (author's field notes)

(41) **tãã-ri-ì** **je-an** **ker-la** ***or***
woman-RF.pl-PM song-RF sing-IPF
«The women are singing (a song).»

(42) **tãã-ri** **mɛ** **je-an** **ker-la**
woman-RF.pl PM song-RF sing-IPF
«The women are singing (a song).»

(43) **ī-ì** **mur-li** **buo**
3pp-PM knive-RF.pl take_out[PF]
«They took out knives.»

---

[20] PF has been analyzed by Tröbs (1998: 141-143) for Jeri, STRS is assumed for Jɔgɔ by the present author.

[21] The copulas **a**, **wa**, **wɛ́** and **wɔ́** respectively follow the subject NP. An object NP precedes the verb. A structure for the Wela variety of Jɔgɔ is only shown where it differs from the Banda variety.

[22] On the other hand, there are specific PMs combining with an unmarked verb stem for FUT and SUBJ. In these cases, negation is marked clause-finally only.

[23] This element seems to be a recent loan from Jula/Bambara, and the two PMs seem to be used in free variation. The choice made might be conditioned by sociolinguistic factors, though.

(44) **ŋgár-lán tὲὲ-ná**
rain-RF drip-IPF
«It is drizzling.»

(45) **kuri ɲan na, ɲɛ rán mɛ ɲu-an jii má**
yesterday evening Pp 1pp NEG PM dance-RF dance/PF NEG
«Yesterday night, we did not dance.»

Although the individual languages of the South-western Branch of Mande could probably be assigned to either Types I or II as proposed above, they are presented separately here.[24] For these languages, the answer to the question whether inflectional marking is predominantly with the PMs, or with the verb word, seems disputable either way. In the following, Bandi is meant to represent the Mɛnde/Bandi/Loko language cluster.[25]

(a) In Bandi, as in all South-western languages, special pronoun series are selected for TAM. The pronouns of these series either combine the functions of subject *and* of PM, when the subject is pronominal, or they follow the nominal subject, in which case their function is reduced to that of a PM.

For the IPF, the relevant series seems to be the result of the fusion of an original simple pronoun, and a PM ***a**.[26] In clauses with a pronominal subject, the addition of a simple pronoun, preceding the fused one, distinguishes a PROG from a HAB reading of the construction (examples [46]-[47]). With nouns or complex NPs as subject, this distinction cannot be made formally. The IPF also seems to have a PROSP reading in any case (and a modal one, cf. [47]). There is a different PM (not fused) for a new (?) PROG (cf. [48]), and another series of pronouns probably fused with a PM ***(w)ɔ** for FUT. Inflectional marking for the three afore-mentioned categories is operated by the relevant PMs (fused with the pronoun for two categories) alone, the semantic verb remains unmarked.

Bandi (Heydorn 1941)

(46) **ɲá ŋga li**
1ps 1ps/IPF leave
«I am leaving», «I'm going to leave.»

(47) **a ndɔ i bɔle**
3ps/IPF palm wine DF drink
«He usually drinks palm wine», «He is going to drink palm wine», «He may drink palm wine.»

[24] Given the fact that these languages display common features – depending on the view taken – both with Type I and with Type II languages, I hesitate to regard them as being representative of another Type (IIII).
[25] The TAM systems of these three languages are very similar in most points central to our argumentation. In Mɛnde, though, the element (PM?) lɔ́ has a much wider combinatory use than in Bandi. This phenomenon needs further research.
[26] This reconstructed PM probably was grammaticalized from an existential copula *ga/(ɣ)a, as found in Lɔɔma.

(48) **ɲá lɔ li**
1ps PROG leave
«I am leaving.»

In opposition to this, there is a group of (conceptually connected) categories that share the following characteristics: (1) they all select the same pronoun series, (2) this series is distinct from those mentioned above for the IPF etc., (3) it is not transparent, i.e. the pronouns do not seem to be analyzable as being the result of some fusion with a PM, (4) inflectional marking is primarily with the verb (the selection of the pronoun series being classified as a secondary process here):

(49) **ŋgi va- ŋgɔ**
1ps[SJ] come-PF
«I have come.»

(50) **wu va-i**
2pp[SJ] come-PFV
«You (pl.) came.»

(51) **i ha-i**
3ps[SJ] die-PFV
«He died.»

(52) **i ha-a**
3ps[SJ] die-STRS
«He has died/is dead.»

Negation is operated by an element **i** (for IPF and FUT) or **aa** (for PF, PFV, and the «new PROG») respectively. They are not portmanteau morphemes, but add to (and fuse with) the pronoun selected from the relevant series. The following table is meant to summarize the situation in Bandi. SP means «subject pronoun», **-a** or **-ɔ** respectively represent the (probable) PMs that fused with the SP.

	affirmative	negative
IPF	(P) SP-a V	SP-ɛi V
PRO	P lɔ V	SP-aa V-ma
FUT	SP-ɔ V	SP-ɛi V
PF	SP V- ŋgɔ	SP-aa V-ŋgɔ
AOR[27]	SP V	
STRS	SP V-a	
PFV	SP V-(n)i	SP-aa V-(n)i

Table 2: Bandi

Given the assumption that the «subject pronouns» for the second set of categories (in Table 2) do not contain or represent a PM, we can say that in Bandi, inflection

[27] «Aorist» is the label applied by Heydorn (1941).

is marked on the verb for certain categories, and it is marked by PMs alone for others. Moreover, this is true for the IPF/PFV dichotomy central to the system.

(b) In Lɔɔma, a PM **kà/ɣà** (< a local, or existential [?] copula) is required for all IPF subcategories, and for FUT. In the variety described by Prost (1967), it combines either with the unmarked verb stem (FUT, cf. [53]), with a suffixed stem (IPF, with a PROG and a PROSP reading, cf. [54]-[55]), or with a secondary, modifying PM (PROG[28] and HAB, examples [56]-[57]) and the unmarked stem. In case of a pronominally expressed subject, the PM is fused with the pronoun (example [55]).

Lɔɔma

(53) **Folomo ɣà kálé i ɓɛ**
Folomo PM fish DF hunt
«Folomo will fish.»

(54) **Folomo ɣà kálé i ɓɛ-zù**
Folomo PM fish DF hunt-IPF
«Folomo is going to fish», «Folomo is fishing.»

(55) **dà kálé i ɓɛ-zù**
2ps/PM fish DF hunt-IPF
«You are fishing.»

(56) **ázánù i ɣà na ɓáɣá i ɣílí**
woman DF IPF PROG rice DF cook
«The woman is preparing the rice.»

(57) **gílé i ɣà da dǫ́go i na zɔlɔ wɔmɔ̃**
dog DF IPF HAB child DF POSS excrements lick
«The dog (usually) licks the baby's excrements.»

The rendering of the function of **ɣà** varies in the above examples. The reason for this is that, although one might be tempted to regard **ɣà** as a PM marking the IPF, this is not easy to correlate with its meaning of FUT in [53].[29] Also, **ɣà** is not obligatory in clauses like (57). In other Lɔɔma varieties, the PM for HAB is primary (i.e. not a modifying one; see Table 3, Heydorn).

For all «completive» categories, including the PFV (ex. [60]-[61]), the semantic verb is marked for TAM, no PMs are involved. Pronominal subjects are, however, selected from a series reserved for these categories. It is impossible to say at the present state of the analysis if this could be the result of the fusing of pronouns with another PM, or not (but see Bandi above for a similar case).

---

[28] Prost's analysis (or rather, the translations offered) suggest that the Lɔɔma variety he describes has an additional construction that exclusively expresses PROG (as opposed to the IPF with – at least – two readings).

[29] It is, of course, possible that FUT is just not the most appropriate label for the category concerned.

(58) **zílé gi súó i ɓɔ́lé-a**
python DF animal DF swallow-PF
«The python has swallowed the animal.»

(59) **Folomo.ni dí-ve dósó i ma**
Folomo-pl go-STV hunt DF Pp
«The Folomos are gone hunting.»

(60) **másà gí ʑ̨á moimoi séí-ni**
chief DF woman many settle-PFV
«The chief married many women.»

(61) **ge la lí-ni dɔ́wɔ́ i wogi**
1ps NEG go-PFV market DF yesterday
«I did not go to the market yesterday.»

Negation in Lɔɔma (as in Kpelle, see below), is expressed by a negative element (**tá/lá**) not specific for TAM, i.e. used for all categories. This element follows the subject NP (like a PM), and in IPF categories, it replaces the PM. Thus, one could argue that PMs, after all, are only marginally involved in inflection marking in Lɔɔma. Table 3 gives an overview, with some dialectal variation as described by Heydorn [HD] (1970).

	Prost		HD	HD Wu./Bo.	HD Giziga
PRSP/PRO	**ɣà .. V-zù**	PRO	**ɣà … V-zù**	**ɣà … V**	**ɣà sá … V-zù**
PRO	**ɣà na … V**				
FUT	**ɣà … V**	FUT	**ɣà … V**		**ɣà … V-sɛi**
HAB	**(ɣà) da … V**	HAB	**jé … V**		

	Prost		HD
PF	**V-(g)a** or **V-(g)a-ve**	PF	**V-(g)a**
STRS	**V-ve**		
STAT	**V-ve**	STAT	**V-vὲ**
PFV	**V-ni**	PFV	**V-ni**

Table 3: Lɔɔma[30]

(c) The Kpelle language has a number of categories that are marked by the combination of a PM with a suffixed (or tonally changed) verb. The PMs are all similar in form (**á** < ***ká/gá, káà** and **áà**), and so are the suffixes (see Table 4). The difference between the alleged two PMs (**á** vs. **áà**)[31] is not always apparent in my material.[32]

---

[30] HD = Heydorn, a Liberian variety of Lɔɔma not identified; HD Wu./Bo. = Lɔɔma as spoken in Wubɔmai and Bode (Liberia); HD Giziga = Giziga dialect of Lɔɔma (Liberia).

[31] **káà** only occurs as a reinforcing secondary element with the fused pronoun (incorporating **á**) in the PROG, it seems.

[32] Cf. the fused pronoun forms in (62) and (64), of which one (62) is supposed to be 1pp plus **-á**, the other (64) 1pp plus **–áà**.

Comparing the central categories, IPF (represented by the sub-categories PROG and HAB) is operated by a/the PM and a marked verb stem (suffix **-ì** for the PROG, HAB with low tone marking), PFV has verbal (tonal) marking alone. The PM (in its form **áà**) also occurs with the STAT (combined with a **-nì** suffix to the verb),[33] the RES, and (in its form **á**) for the PF. (Tonal) marking on the verb, on the other hand, is the same for the opposing categories HAB and PFV. The NEG element occurs in the PM slot. It is not (or only minimally) specific for TAM: its form is **fa** for the HAB, **fe** for all other categories.

Kpelle

(62) **kwa pá-ì**
1pp+PROG come-PROG
«We are coming.»

(63) **kú fé pá-ì**
1pp NEG come-PROG
«We are not coming.»

(64) **kwa kpὲlεε=woo ɓò**
1pp+HAB Kpelle=language speak[HAB]
«We speak Kpelle.»

(65) **kú fa kpὲlεε=woo ɓò**
1pp NEG Kpelle=language speak[HAB]
«We do not speak Kpelle.»

(66) **kú ɓá mìi**
1pp rice eat[PFV]
«We ate rice.»

	affirmative	*negative*
PRO	SP-a V-ì	P fe v-ì
	SP káa V-i	
HAB	sp-aa V-`	P fa V-`
STAT	SP-aa V-nì	P fe V(-nì)
PFV	P V-`	P fe V-ní
PF?	SP-a V	?
RES	SP-âa V	P fe níì V-nì
STAT/ADJ	P Vstat-ì	

Table 4: Kpelle

For all South-western Mande languages, the question whether inflectional marking is primarily operated by PMs or by suffixes to (or tonal changes on) the verb, rises some problems. In Bandi, when concentrating on the central dichotomy, both

[33] It is not clear to the present author if this clause type is restricted to stative verbs; if so, it could be regarded as a form of the IPF.

views are probably defendable, i.e. either (1) a basic opposition between a PM **–a** for the IPF and a zero-PM for the PFV; or (2) a basic opposition between a suffixed verb stem for the PFV, and an unmarked stem for the IPF. The alternatives are quite similar for Lɔɔma (see Table 3 above). In the case of Kpelle, it seems rather difficult to assign a primary function either to the PM or to the verbal markers. In this language, the combination is essential. In all three languages, the recurrent PM-forms **á**, **áa**, **kà**, **ɣà**, etc. are grammaticalized from an existential/locative copula common to all of South-western Mande, hence the formal closeness or identity of PM(s) in Kpelle for IPF categories on one hand, and for the PF and RES on the other.

Such PMs derived from existential or locative copulas are very frequent throughout Western Mande. Individual languages differ as to the functions covered by these elements, though. In Table 5 below the occurrence of an «existential» PM in the PFV and the IPF,[34] as opposed to no PM or PMs of different origin, is shown.

	IPF	*PFV*
Type I languages	EXT	Pp
Banka	EXT	EXT
other Type II languages[35]	Ø	Ø
South-western Mande	EXT	Ø

Table 5: Occurrence and origin of PMs in Western Mande[36]

Instead of a conclusion, I would like to add the following observations: (1) Only in Type I languages, where a PM derived from an existential copula for the IPF opposes a PM of different origin for the PFV, inflectional marking is predominantly and near to exclusively with the PMs. The occurrence of undisputable «portmanteau-PMs», i.e. of PMs that combine the functions of aspect marking and polarity, is restricted to this Type, too.[37] (2) From comparative evidence, the situation encountered in South-western Mande languages can either be explained (a) by loss of PM for the PFV (probably on the basis of a structure similar to that of Banka), or (b) by assuming that, even at an earlier stage, no PM was involved in sentence constituency for that category.[38] Loss of the PM (derived

[34] Note that (1) in some languages (i.e. in Banka), we rather have a category that covers PF *and* PFV, and that (2) some languages, again, have an IPF *and* a PROG different from the former (as is the case for Jɔgɔ), or distinct PMs etc. for HAB, PROG, and/or PROSP rather than a basic IPF.

[35] Jeri is excluded here.

[36] EXT: PM for the relevant category has been grammaticalized from an existential/locative copula; Pp: the PM has been grammaticalized from a postposition (for this view, see Creissels 1997, Kastenholz 2003, and Tröbs 2004). Ø (zero) absence of PM.

[37] There are, however, PMs in many other languages (one case would be Banka) for the subjunctive and other modal categories that are selected for polarity.

[38] Note that the structure of a one-argument predication in the affirmative PFV («transitivity split») in Type I languages resembles much what is generally encountered for the PFV in Type II or in South-western languages (i.e. no PM involved, inflection is marked by a verbal suffixes).

from a copula) for the IPF, or practically simultaneous PM-loss for both categories, would account for the structure of Type II languages as lined out above in Table 5. In any case,[39] this would imply that, at a previous stage, PMs in these languages (i.e. South-western and those of Type II) did not make a *major* contribution to the expression of inflectional-type categories.

List of abbreviations

1ps	1st person singular
3ps	3rd person singular
3pp	3rd person plural
ADJ	adjective
AOR	aorist
AUX	auxiliary
COP	copula
CONT	continuative
CPL	completive
DER	derived stem
DF	definiteness
DO	direct object
EXT	existential
GEN	genitive marker
GM	Greater Manding (Manding-Koranko-Vai/Kɔnɔ)
HAB	habitual
IPF	imperfective
NEG	negative, negation
NP	noun phrase
P	pronoun (simple pronoun in South-western Mande)
PF	perfect
PFV	perfective
PM	predicate marker
Pp	postposition
PROG	progressive
PROSP	prospective
PV	pre-verb
RF	reference-marking element
SJ	subject
SP	subject pronoun (from series selected for TAM in South-western Mande)
SPM	specifier morpheme
STAT	stative
STRS	stative/resultative
SUBJ	subjunctive
TAM	tense, aspect, mode
V	verb

[39] Assuming that PMs not specific for TAM are more liable to be deleted than those highly marked for inflectional categories.

Bibliography

BEARTH, Thomas, 1995, Nominal periphrases and the origin of the predicative marker in Mande languages – an alternative view, *Afrikanistische Arbeitspapiere* 41, 89-117.

BISANG, Walter, Forthcoming, *Linguistic areas, language contact and typology – some consequences from the case of Ethiopia as a linguistic area.*

BLECKE, Thomas, 1996, *Lexikalische Kategorien und grammatische Strukturen im Tigemaxo (Bozo, Mande),* (Mande Languages and Linguistics/Langues et Linguistique Mandé, 1), Köln, Köppe.

CARLSON, Robert, 1993, A sketch of Jɔ: A Mande language with a feminine pronoun, *Mandenkan* 25, 1-109.

CREISSELS, Denis, 1997, Postpositions as a possible origin of certain predicative markers in Mande, *Afrikanistische Arbeitspapiere* 50, 5-17.

DALBY, David, 1970, Reflections on the classification of African languages, with special reference to the work of Sigismund Wilhelm Koelle and Malcolm Guthrie, *African Language Studies* 11, 147-171.

FRIEDLÄNDER, Marianne, 1976, *Lehrbuch des Susu,* Leipzig, VEB Verlag Enzyklopädie.

GENSLER, Orin, 1997, Grammaticalization, typology, and Niger-Congo word order: Progress on a still-unsolved problem, *Journal of African Languages and Linguistics* 18, 57-93.

GRÉGOIRE, Claire, 1988, An attempt to reconstruct labial consonants in Mandé, *Phonological reconstruction, problems and methods*, edited by Marc Dominicy and Juliette Dor, (Belgian Journal of Linguistics, 3), Pp. 101-155, Bruxelles, Université.

HEINE, Bernd, 1976, *A typology of African languages, based on the order of meaningful elements,* (Kölner Beiträge zur Afrikanistik, 4), Berlin, Reimer.

HEYDORN, Richard, 1941, Die Sprache der Bandi im nordwestlichen Liberia, *Zeitschrift für Eingeborenen-Sprachen* 31,2: 81-114; 31,3: 188-217.

HEYDORN, Richard, 1970, Grammar of the Lɔma language, with some Kɔnɔ words in the vocabulary, *Afrika und Übersee* 54,1/2: 77-99.

KASTENHOLZ, Raimund, 1989, Voyelles nasales et consonnes prénasalisées en position médiane dans les langues mandé centrales, *Mandekan* 18, 43-60.

KASTENHOLZ, Raimund, 1991/92, Comparative Mande studies: state of the art, *Sprache und Geschichte in Afrika* 12/13, 107-158.

KASTENHOLZ, Raimund, 1996, *Sprachgeschichte im West-Mande. Methoden und Rekonstruktionen,* (Mande Languages and Linguistics/Langues et Linguistique Mandé, 2), Köln, Köppe.

KASTENHOLZ, Raimund. 2003. Auxiliaries, grammaticalization, and word order in Mande, *Journal of African Languages and Linguistics*, 24,1: 31-53.

KENDALL, Martha B., with Mamadou Soumare, Saloum Soumare, and Charles Bird, 1980, *Soninke. Grammar Handbook,* (Peace Corps Language Handbook Series), Brattleboro/Vt, Experiment in International Living.

Nicolaï, Robert, and Petr Zima (eds), 2002, *Lexical and structural diffusion,* (Corpus, les Cahiers, 1), Nice, Université.

PROST, André, 1967, *La langue loghoma. Esquisse grammaticale, suivie de textes et d'un glossaire,* (Documents Linguistiques, 13), Dakar, IFAN.

PROST, André, 1971, *Eléments de sembla. Phonologie, grammaire, lexique (Haute-Volta, groupe mandé),* Lyon, Afrique et Langage.

PROST, André, 1983, Essai de description grammaticale du dialecte bobo de Tansila, Haute-Volta, *Mandenkan* 5, 3-101.

TRAORE, Ali, Fabé Traoré, and Paul Solomiac, 1998, *Dzùùngoo dzuɔn tsùnfyɛɛ́ ɲàn ko à sɛbɛun'n kur'la. Lexique orthographique dzùùngoo-français,* Ouagadougou, SIL.

TRÖBS, Holger, 1998, *Funktionale Sprachbeschreibung des Jeli (West-Mande),* (Mande Languages and Linguistics/Langues et Linguistique Mané, 3), Köln : Köppe.

TRÖBS, Holger. 2004. Zur Entstehung von Perfektiv-Markern im Manding (West-Mande), *Sprache und Wissen in Afrika*, edited by Raimund Kastenholz and Anne Storch. pp. 279-301. Köln: Köppe.

Logophoric Pronouns in the Southern Bole-Tangale Languages

Rudolf LEGER & Ulrike ZOCH Lerud@em.uni-frankfurt.de

Johann Wolfgang Goethe-Universität, Frankfurt, Germany

Abstract

In this paper, the characteristic features of the pronominal systems in the southern Bole-Tangale languages are examined from a synchronic and comparative view, paying special attention to logophoricity. The languages dealt with are chiefly Kwami, Kupto, Tangale, Pero and Widala, but also some references are made to Bole and Hausa. There is a dichotomy between the geographical northern and southern Bole-Tangale-languages which can be observed not only by the difference of the grammatical gender in nouns, but also in the closely related pronominal systems. Gender levelling and the appearance of logophoric pronouns in the southern languages can be explained by historical contacts between the Chadic and surrounding Adamawa/Benue-Congo languages. It can be presumed that not the morphological forms of the pronouns but rather the idea of expressing logophoricity by using special pronouns is contact induced.

Résumé

Dans cet article, les traits caractéristiques des systèmes pronominaux des langues bole-tangale septentrionales sont examinés d'un point de vue synchronique et comparatif, en insistant particulièrement sur la logophoricité. Les langues étudiées sont le *kwami*, le *kupto*, le *tangale*, le *pero* et le *widala*, mais on fait également référence au *bole* et au *hausa*. Il existe une dichotomie entre les langues bole-tangale du nord et du sud, différence qui peut être observée non seulement dans le genre grammatical nominal, mais également dans les sytèmes pronominaux étroitement apparentés. L'alignement du genre et l'apparition de pronoms logophoriques dans les langues du sud peuvent être expliqués par des contacts historiques entre les langues tchadiques et les langues Adamawa/Benoué-Congo voisines. On peut supposer que ce ne sont pas les formes morphologiques des pronoms qui sont nées du contact, mais plutôt l'idée d'exprimer la logophoricité par des pronoms.

This paper discusses the characteristic features of the pronominal systems in the southern Bole-Tangale languages from a synchronic and comparative view, paying special attention to logophoricity.

The languages dealt with are chiefly Kwami, Kupto, Tangale, Pero and Widala, but also some references are made to Bole and Hausa. The classification of these languages (after Crozier & Blench (1992: 124-125)) can be seen in the following chart:

Chadic
- West-Chadic
  - Sub-branch A
    - Bole-Angas major group
      - Bole group
        - Northern: **Bole**, Bele, Kirfi, Deno, Galambu, Gera, Geruma, Maha, Ngamo, Karekare
        - Southern: **Kwami, Kupto, Tangale, Pero, Widala-Kholokh**

These languages were chosen for two reasons. The first reason is their geographical distribution, since a transfer line can be made visible from the northernmost to the southernmost located representative of this group, i.e. from Bole to Widala-Kholok. The second reason is a typological one, which specifically relates to the phenomenon of 'gender levelling'. In the geographically northern languages, like Bole, Kwami and Kupto, we observe grammatical gender distinction in nouns (as well, of course, as in pronouns). The nouns do not show any overt gender marker, neither tonological nor morphological.

Examples:

	masculine		feminine	
Kwami	*shìlìm*	shadow, soul	*shòlòm*	west, evening
	kùrè	fence	*lúgó*	well
	bàrà	hunt	*ʔàlà*	grass
	píllì	offence	*díndì*	story, fable
Kupto	*bàrbátè*	wasp	*wúyó*	hole
	túlúm	hyena	*fáhá*	arm, wing
	yèɗɗè	dog	*kúngú*	leopard

In the southern languages, however, like Tangale, Pero, Piya and Widala, the grammatical gender distinction is in almost all cases levelled in favour of the feminine gender. See the following examples. For Pero and Tangale they are taken from Frajzyngier (1989) and Jungraithmayr (1991) in their original orthography.

	elbow	knee	saliva
Kwami	*kùngìlì (m)*	*pùrùm (m)*	*ʔìllé (m)*
Kupto	*gùnkúllì (m)*	*fúrúm (f)*	*ʔìllék (f)*
Widala	*gùŋlì (f)*	*pùrì (f)*	*ʔìllèk (f)*
Pero	*kúŋlì (f)*	*púrùm (f)*	*élèc (f)*
Tangale	*kurgundûm (f)*	*purum (f)*	*elis (f)*

(Leger 1998: 204ff)

This gender levelling may be explained as a result of intensive historical contacts with the surrounding Benue-Congo languages, since the languages Kushi, Tangale and Widala are spoken on the southern fringe of the Chadic belt. In addition to this phenomenon the intensive contact between the Chadic and the Benue-Congo languages, and here particularly the Adamawa languages, can be demonstrated by a considerable amount of common vocabulary as well as by the same vowel harmony system found in Tangale and the neighbouring Adamawa language Waja (Kleinewillinghöfer 1990, Jungraithmayr 1991).

For the pronominal system, however, the grammatical gender of a noun is of utmost importance, as the gender of a noun is reflected by the pronouns (subject and object pronouns resp.) in case of substitution.

Kwami	*módő fàadíjì* The guinea-corn (m) is sold	*shófí ɓèlíshì* The tree (f) is broken
	yí fàadíjì It (m) is sold	*tè ɓèlíshì* It (f) is broken
Widala	*vrò tèelòw* The tree (f) is broken	*càw pìlòw* the guinea-corn (f) is sold
	tè tèelòw It (f) is broken	*tè pìlòw* It (f) is sold

As we can see from the examples cited above the difference of gender is clearly visible in the third person singular.

The following chart shows the complete paradigms of the «simple» subject pronouns in the languages under discussion:

		Bole	Kwami	Kupto	Tangale	Pero	Widala
Sg.	1.	*ǹ*	*nè*	*nè*	*na/n*	*nì*	*nè*
	2. m	*ká*	*kè*	*kè*	*ka*	*kà, ké*	*khè*
	2. f	*shí*	*shì*	*shì*	*sị*	*cì*	*cì*
	3. m	*(íshí)*	*yì*	*yì*	*mbẹ́ẹndám*	*cákkà*	*càkhù*
	3. f	*(ítá)*	*tè*	*tè*	*mbáastám*	*tè*	*tè*

		Bole	Kwami	Kupto	Tangale	Pero	Widala
Pl.	1.	*mú*	*mìn*	*mùn*	*mịn*	*mínù*	*mùn (excl.)*
							khàmmè (incl.)
	2.	*màá*	*mà*	*mà*	*ma*	*mà*	*mà*
	3.	*(màté)*	*yìn*	*wùn*	*mbíindám*	*cínù*	*cùnù*

The languages Kupto and Widala show peculiarities, in that the latter differentiates between inclusive and exclusive in the first person plural. Furthermore both languages have developed their own pronominal set for the second future and subjunctive respectively. In surveying this kind of development we should take into account the fact that the original pronominal sets (as shown in the following chart) have been extended by special TAM-marking morphemes, to the extent that in Kupto an *a*-morpheme and in Widala an *n*-morpheme is added.

		Kupto second future	Widala subjunctive
Sg.	1.	*nàa*	*nèn*
	2. m	*kàa*	*khèn*
	2. f	*shàa*	*cìn*
	3. m	*yàa*	*càkhùn*
	3. f	*tàa*	*tèn*
Pl.	1.	*mùnà*	*mùnùn/khàmmèn*
	2.	*màa*	*mèn*
	3.	*wùnà*	*cùnùn*

Some examples may illustrate this:

Kupto	*nè kù fuɗɗè*	future
	I will wash (things)	
	nàa (rò) fuɗɗè	second future
	I will wash (things) later	
Widala	*khè dìttòw lòlòw*	perfect
	You (m) plucked cotton	
	gòddá khèn dìttù lòlòw	subjunctive
	It is better, you pluck cotton	

In many respects the pronouns of the third person are an exception. It can generally be stated, that the pronouns of the third persons – as far as they really do exist – often follow their own rules.

Regarding Hausa perfect the hypothesis is widely accepted (Newman/Schuh 1974), that in Proto-Hausa the preverbal subject pronouns did not need to be used, even when there was no nominal subject – which finally led to ambiguity. To define gender and number, free pronominal forms were used. This usage became obligatory in the course of time so that to guarantee the symmetry in the pronominal set, the first and second persons also adopted the characteristic morphological and/or tonological features of the free pronouns. That there were «holes» in the system can be further illustrated by taking a glance at Bole, as Bole does not have true preverbal pronouns in the third persons. In the perfect paradigm there is no use of any third person pronouns – but there is no need for disambiguation as gender and number are marked in the verbal stem.

Example:

Bámói ʔyór-wò
B. stop-Perf.-PM
Bamoi (m) stopped

*(ítá) ʔyòr-**ák**-kò*
3.f stop-Perf-**F**-PM
she stopped

*(màté) ʔyòr-**án**-gò*
3.pl stop-Perf-**PL**-PM
they stopped

In future and progressive a stand-in morpheme *a* is used; gender and number can be optionally specified by the use of the absolute pronouns.

Example:

à sòor-à
3agr. fall-VN
he/she/they will fall

íshí à jìi ngòr-á kôm
he 3agr. ProgM tie-VN cow
he is tying a cow (Gimba 2000)

Only in Kwami and Kupto are the ordinary pronouns employed in all contextual situations. In Tangale, Pero and Widala, however, special pronouns have emerged which not only allow differentiation of gender and number, but additionally mark logophoric reference. Logophoricity presupposes «logocentric verbs» in the main clause, «which can be distinguished on a largely semantic basis. The set of logocentric verbs centrally includes verbs of reporting, and thus the dependent clauses in which logophoric pronouns are licensed are archetypically contexts of reported speech» (Stirling 1993: 52). The class of these verbs may differ slightly from language to language. Tangale and Pero will serve as examples. In the former case the class of logocentric verbs comprises verbs like «saying, thinking, believing,...», in Pero, however, the class of these verbs is restricted to «saying» only. After such verbs, the normal case is to employ a morphologically different pronoun to mark identity between the subjects of the main and the dependent clause. The use of the same, regular/ordinary pronoun in the dependent as well as in the independent clause, however, indicates the non-identity of the subjects.

Starting from the most complete model of a logophoric system we can refer to Mupun, a Plateau-Chadic language of the Angas-group (Frajzyngier 1993). In Mupun the logophoric system has three sets of pronouns of the third person. In the first set there is no coreference between the subjects of the dependent and the independent clause. In the second set co-reference with the speaker is marked. In the third set coreference with the addressee is expressed.

This fully-fledged system is shown in the following chart:

		noncoreference	coreference with the speaker	coreference with the addressee
Mupun	3. Sg m	*wù(r)*	*ɗì*	*gwàr*
	3. Sg f	*wà(r)*	*ɗè*	*páa*
	3. Pl	*mo*	*ɗu*	*nuwa*

Examples:

noncoreference:

wu/wa/mo	*sat*	*nəə*	***wu/wa/mo***	*ta*	*dee*	*n*	*Jos*
he$_i$/she$_i$/they$_i$	say	COMPL	he$_j$/she$_j$/they$_j$	stop	stay	PREP	Jos

He$_i$ … said that **he$_j$** … stopped over in Jos

coreference with the speaker:

wu/wa/mo	*sat*	*nəə*	*ta*	***ʔdi/ʔde/ʔdu***	*dee*	*n*	*Jos*
he$_i$/she$_i$/they$_i$	say	COMPL	stop	he$_i$/she$_i$/they$_i$ LOG	stay	PREP	Jos

He$_i$ … said that **he$_i$** … stopped over in Jos

coreference with the addressee:

n-sat	***n-wur***	*nə*	***gwar***	*ji*
1Sg-say	PREP-3Sg	COMPL	3SG LOGADDR	come

I told **him$_i$** that **he$_i$** should come.

In case the addressee and the subject of the dependent clause are not identical the pronouns of the first set, i.e. the pronouns of noncoreference, have to be used:

n-sat	***n-wur***	*nə*	***wur***	*ji*
1Sg-say	PREP-3Sg	COMPL	3Sg	come

I told him$_i$ that he$_j$ should come.

The use of the plural form of the coreferential set indicates that the subject of the main clause is part of the subject of the dependent clause:

wu/wa *sat nə n nas* ***mo***
he$_i$/she$_i$ say COMPL 1Sg beat them$_j$
he$_i$ ... said that I beat **them$_j$**

wu/wa *sat nə n nas* ***ɗun***
he$_i$/she$_i$ say COMPL 1Sg beat them$_i$
LOG
he$_i$/she$_i$ said that I beat **them$_i$**
(Frajzyngier 1993)

Looking closer at logophoric pronouns of the languages of the southern Bole-Tangale group we find remarkable deviations from the fully developed system as shown above. These deviations consist of lacking one of the pronominal sets, employing morphologically composed pronouns to indicate disjoint reference and using functionally anti-logophoric pronouns.

The following examples from Pero, Tangale and Widala demonstrate this:

In Pero, coreference with the speaker is not morphologically expressed unlike coreference with the addressee, which can be seen from the following chart:

		noncoreference	coreference with the speaker	coreference with the addressee
Pero	3. Sg m	*cákka*		*péemò/u*
	3. Sg f	*tè*		*péejè*
	3. Pl	*cínù*		

noncoreference/coreference with the speaker:

As noncoreference/coreference with the speaker can not be clearly indicated, the ordinary pronoun is used in any of these cases.

coreference with the addressee:

péemè *tók-nà* ***cákkà*** *n wàt-tù áɗɗò róccò-ì*
2plREP killVent 3m Consec come-Vent eat liver-Def
(**he$_i$** told **him$_j$**) **he$_j$** killed animals and **he$_i$** would come and eat the liver.
(Frajzyngier 1989, translation Leger/Zoch)

In Tangale special pronouns which indicate disjoint reference are morphologically composed of two elements denoting «person» (*pee-*) + demonstrative (*-ndam*) and the old inherited pronouns are used only when coreference with the speaker is expressed.

It is interesting to note that these logophoric forms of pronouns are cognate with the «classical» personal morphemes in Common Chadic (Jungraithmayr 2002 Ms.)

		noncoreference	coreference with the speaker	coreference with the addressee
Tangale	3. Sg. m	*mbę́ęndám*	*yi*	*pę́ęmọ́*
	3. Sg. f	*mbáastám*	*ta*	*paazę*
	3. Pl.	*mbíindám*	*yini*	*piimo*

noncoreference:

mbę́ęndám *yịmgọ ka* ***mbę́ęndám*** *nęgọ ka* ***mbę́ęndám*** *nga kịna*
he$_i$ thought that **he**$_j$ said that **he**$_k$ had money
(personal communication with Mairo Kidda)

coreference with the speaker:

(mbíindám) káa ***yin*** *pará wọrọp*
(They$_i$) said that they$_i$ were looking for a woman.

(mbáastám)	*káa*	***ta***	*yáaz*	*ụk*	*mọ*
	say	she	do-PROG	likeness	DEM

(**She**$_i$) said **she**$_i$ is doing like this. (Jungraithmayr 2002)

Widala is a special case. In this language coreference with the speaker is expressed by using the same ordinary pronouns in the dependent as well as in the independent clause. Disjoint reference, however, is indicated by employing morphologically modified pronominal forms. Therefore we could consider the system as anti-logophoric. The following chart shows these particularities:

		noncoreference	coreference with the speaker	coreference with the addressee
Widala	3. Sg. m	*càkhì*	*càkhù*	*pèemò*
	3. Sg. f	*mòtò*	*tè*	*pèeyè*
	3. Pl.	*yèelè*	*cùnù*	*pìimè*

noncoreference:

càkhù *tèkkòw* ***càkhì*** *wèeyòw ʔìndè*
he$_i$ said **he**$_j$ saw a dog.

coreference with the speaker:

càkhù *tèkkòw* ***càkhù*** *wèeyòw pàyàl*
he$_i$ said **he**$_i$ saw a star.

coreference with the addressee:

*càkhù tèkkòw **(pèemò,) pèemò** wèeyòw náabìlà.*
he told (**him$_i$**) that **he$_i$** saw a rainmaker.

*càkhù tèkkòw **(pèemò) càkhì** wèeyòw ʔìndè.*
he told (**him$_i$**) that **he$_j$** saw a dog.

As we hope to have demonstrated in our presentation there is a dichotomy between the geographical northern and southern Bole-Tangale-languages which can be observed not only by the difference of the grammatical gender in nouns, but also in the closely related pronominal systems. On the one hand Kupto, like Hausa, has a second set of pronouns for far future and in Widala an *n*-morpheme is attached to the pronominal elements in subjunctive. On the other hand, gender levelling which goes in favour of the feminine gender is observed in the geographical southern located languages Widala, Pero and Tangale. The last phenomenon might be explained by historical contacts between the Chadic and surrounding Adamawa/Benue-Congo languages. Under this aspect we also subsume the appearance of the logophoric pronouns, which can be attributed to that long-lasting linguistic contact. Here it can be presumed that not the morphological forms of the pronouns but rather the concept or idea of expressing logophoricity by using special pronouns is contact induced. It should be emphasized nevertheless that each language has followed its own way. This can be explicitly observed in Tangale where the inherited pronouns have undergone a transformation so that their use has been limited to logophoric reference.

We are quite aware that there are some questions we cannot sufficiently explain:

(1) Why, for example, do the geographically southern and not the closely related geographically northern languages display the feature logophoricity?
(2) What triggers the innovation of developing logophoricity?
(3) Why does Widala display a typologically highly marked anti-logophoric system?
(4) Will traces of logophoricity also be found in still yet unknown or insufficiently described languages of the Chadic or Adamawa family?

Abbreviations

3agr.	stand-in morpheme to indicate agreement with third person
COMPL	complementizer
Consec	consecutive
Def	definite
DEM	demonstrative
F	feminine
LOG	logophoric pronoun, indicates coreference with speaker
LOGADDR	logophoric pronoun, indicates coreference with addressee
Perf.	Perfect(ive) stem
PL	plural
PM	Perfect(ive) morpheme
PREP	preposition
PROG	progressive
ProgM	progressive morpheme
Vent	ventive
VN	verbal noun

Selected Bibliography

CROZIER, D. H. & R. M. BLENCH, 1992, *An Index of Nigerian Languages*, Abuja / Ilorin / Dallas.

FRAJZYNGIER, Zygmunt, 1985, *A Pero-English and English-Pero Vocabulary,* Berlin.

FRAJZYNGIER, Zygmunt, 1985, Logophoric Systems in Chadic, *Journal of African Languages and Linguistics* 7, 23-37.

FRAJZYNGIER, Zygmunt, 1989, *A Grammar of Pero,* Berlin.

FRAJZYNGIER, Zygmunt, 1993, *A Grammar of Mupun,* Berlin.

GIMBA, Alhaji Maina, 2000, *Bole Verb Morphology,* Ms. Gimba dissertation.

JUNGRAITHMAYR, Herrmann, 1991, *A Dictionary of the Tangale Language,* Berlin.

JUNGRAITHMAYR, Herrmann, 2002a, *The emergence of new pronouns in Tangale*, Ms.

JUNGRAITHMAYR, Herrmann, 2002b, *Síndi. Tangale Folktales,* Köln.

KLEINEWILLINGHÖFER, Ulrich, 1990, Aspects of Waja vowel hamony and Tangale-Waja common vocabulary, *Frankfurter Afrikanistische Blätter* 2, 93-106.

LEGER, Rudolf, 1994, *Eine Grammatik der Kwami-Sprache,* Köln.

LEGER, Rudolf, 1998, Grammatical Gender in some Southern Bole-Tangale Languages - Kwami, Kupto, Kushi and Piya, *Afrika, Society, Culture and Languages. Institute of Africa Studies Moscow,* 204-216.

NEWMAN, Paul & RUSSELL G. Schuh, 1974, The Hausa Aspect System, *Afroasiatic Linguistics* 1/1, 1-39.

RONCADOR, Manfred von., 1992, Types of Logophoric Marking in African Languages, *Journal of African Languages and Linguistics* 13, 163-182.

STIRLING, Lesley, 1993, *Switch-Reference and Discourse Representation,* Cambridge.

A Note on Kanakuru Tense/Aspect/Mood (TAM)

Paul NEWMAN

Indiana University pnxxpn@indiana.edu

Abstract

Kanakuru, the south-easternmost language belonging to the West branch of Chadic is structurally very similar to Hausa, the north-westernmost West Chadic language. Kanakuru is a strict SVO language. It indicates TAM by overt TAM markers combined with distinct preverbal pronoun paradigms, sometimes accompanied by inflection in the verb form itself or by the use of a verbal noun in place of the finite verb. The only exception is the imperative, which uses a bare verb with no preverbal marker or subject pronoun. Negation is indicated by a discontinuous negative marker **w(o) ... u**, reminiscent of Hausa **ba(a) ... ba**. The perfect is obligatorily replaced by a corresponding "second perfect" TAM in relative clauses or when a focused or interrogative element occurs to the left of the verb. This second perfect is also required in the negative whether focus or relativization is present or not.

Résumé

Le *kanakuru*, langue de la branche occidentale du Tchadique située le plus loin au sud-est, est structurellement très similaire au *hausa*, langue du Tchadique occidental située le plus loin au nord-ouest. Le *kanakuru* est une langue strictement SVO. Elle indique le TAM par des marqueurs TAM combinés avec des paradigmes de pronoms préverbaux spécifiques, en conjonction avec des flexions sur la forme verbale elle-même, ou avec un nom verbal à la place de la forme finie du verbe. La seule exception est l'impératif, qui utilise un verbe nu sans marque préverbale ni pronom sujet. La négation est indiquée par une marque négative discontinue **w(o) ... u** qui rappelle le **ba(a) ... ba** du *hausa*. Le parfait est obligatoirement remplacé par un "second parfait" dans les propositions relatives ou quand un terme focalisé ou interrogatif figure à gauche du verbe. De même, ce second parfait apparaît obligatoirement à la forme négative, indépendamment de la focalisation ou de la relativisation.

Kanakuru is a member of the Chadic language family (Newman 1990). It belongs to the West Branch (the branch that includes Hausa), within which it is most closely related to Tangale (Jungraithmayr, Galadima, and Kleinewillinghöfer 1991), and other languages of the so-called Bole group (see Lukas 1970/71-1971/72, Schuh 1978). It is spoken south of the Biu Plateau in Borno State and Adamawa State, making it the southeastern most West Chadic language. Other languages in the area are either Chadic languages belonging to the Biu-Mandara branch, such as Bachama and Ga'anda, or non-Chadic Adamawa-Ubangi languages, such as Lala and Longuda. The following sketch is based on data drawn from my Kanakuru grammar published some thirty years ago (Newman 1974).

1. TAM marking is accomplished by a combination of the following: (a) distinct «weak subject pronoun» paradigms placed between the nominal subject (if any) and the verb; (b) an overt TAM marker before the weak subject pronoun, found in some TAMs only (e.g., the subjunctive, the future, and the past continuous/ habitual); (c) segmental and/or tonal modification in the form of the verb itself, most notably replacement of the final vowel of the verb by **-a**; and (d) replacement of the finite verb by a related present participle/verbal noun. Examples:

(a)	**támyén**	**wə̀**	**nái**	**gwá**	cf.	**támyén**	**wə̀n**	**nái**	**gwá**
	women	they(pf)	drink	water		women	they(cn)	drink	water
	Women drank water.					*Women are drinking water.*			

(b)	**...bə̀là**	**kà**	**wúpè**	**gám**
	sjn	you	sell	ram
	... that you sell a ram			
	à-kò	**wúpè**	**gám**	
	fut-you	sell	ram	
	You will sell a ram.			
	jí-kò	**wúpè**	**gám**	
	pcn-you	sell	ram	
	You used to sell ram(s).			

(c)	**wónò**	**mə́n**	**wùpà**	**gám**
	yesterday	we(2pf)	sell	ram
	YESTERDAY we sold a ram.			
	támyéníi-mè	**wə́n**	**nàa**	**gwá**
	women-these	they(2pf)	drink	water
	THESE WOMEN drank water.			

(d)	**gúnyò-i**	**shèe**	**pór-má**	cf.	**gúnyò-i**	**à**	**pòrò-tó**
	girl-the	she(cn)	exit-ing		girl-the	pf	exit-her(icp)
	The girl is going out.				*The girl went out.*		

(In some paradigms, the third person singular weak subject pronouns are zero. In that case, the perfect, which is usually indicated by the bare pronoun, is realized as /**à**/.)

2. The basic word order is SVO, e.g.,

lówò-i	**à**	**tàɗè**	**kílé-ì**	**Múusá**	**shìi**	**níimè**	**mətəkà**
boy-the	pf	break	pot-the	Musa	he(cn)	repair	car
The boy broke the pot.				*Musa is repairing a car.*			

3. Negation is indicated by a discontinuous marker **w(o)**- ... **-u**, where **w(o)**- appears immediately preceding the weak subject pronoun and **-u** appears at the end of the sentence. (The tone of **w(o)**- is normally polar to what follows it and the tone of **-u** is normally polar to what precedes it; but the actual realization is quite complex and not essential to the discussion here.) Examples:

wó-nàa	**pór-má-ù**	**Báshà**	**w-à-tò**	**shír**	**áyìm-ú**
neg-I(cn)	exit-ing-neg	Basha	neg-fut-she	steal	money-neg
I am not going out.		*Basha will not steal money.*			

Most TAMs (e.g., the continuous and the future) appear both in the affirmative and the negative. The perfect, however, is obligatorily replaced in the negative, by a distinct TAM, the «2nd perfect» (2pf), e.g.,

wò-mən	**wùpà**	**gám-ù**	cf.	**mə**	**wùpè**	**gám**
neg-we(2pf)	sell	ram-neg		we(pf)	sell	ram
We did not sell a ram.				*We sold a ram.*		

In the negative subjunctive (which also serves as the negative of the imperative), a special prefix **bò-** incorporates the initial negative marker, e.g.,

bò-nò	**táɗé-ù**	cf.	**bəlà**	**nà**	**táɗé**
nsjn-I	break-neg		sjn	I	break
Let I break (it).			*I should break (it).*		

bò-kò	**póró-kó-ù**	cf.	**pòr-kó**
nsjn-you	exit you(icp)-neg		exit-you(icp)
Don't go out!			*Go out!*

4/5. In Kanakuru, the range of TAMs (= conjugational forms) includes the subjunctive. Mood (e.g., indicative vs. non-indicative) does not exist as a distinct and contrastive category. The only exception is the Imperative. This is special command form that is indicated primarily by replacing the verb-final vowel by **-u** and by the absence of the weak subject pronoun, e.g.,

kàpú	**dəlù mətəkà-i**	**pòr-shí**
Plant (it)!	*Push the car!*	*Go out (you-f)!*

As indicated above, negative commands are not indicated by the imperative, but rather make use of the negative subjunctive conjugational form.

6. The TAMs fall into two major classes depending on whether the verbal element appears as a finite verb or as a verbal noun (= present participle). The first group, labeled aux_1, includes the perfect, the «2nd perfect», the subjunctive, and the negative subjunctive. The second group, labeled aux_2, which corresponds more or less to «imperfective» TAMs in other Chadic languages, includes the continuous, the future, and the past continuous/habitual. Here are some examples, where **-má** (or **-mái**, with the anaphoric marker **-i** attached) is the verbalizing suffix:

aux_1	**aux_2**
mə dəlè we(pf) push *We pushed (it).*	**mən dəl-má-i** we(cn) push-ing-it *We are pushing (it).*
bəlà nà tá-nó sjn I go-me(icp) *I should go.*	**à-nò táa-má** fut-I go-ing *I will go.*
wò-shée àyà wúná-ù neg-she help them-neg *She did not help them.*	**jí-tò áy-má-wù** pcn-she help-ing-them *She used to help them.*

7. There is a syntactically conditioned alternation between the neutral perfect and the so-called 2nd perfect. This latter is required in relative clauses and in sentences with a focused element to the left of the verb. Examples:

gúnyò-i jì náa bèelà rá girl-the that I(2pf) choose her *the girl whom I chose*	cf.	**nà bèelè ré** I(pf) choose her *I chose her.*
məní mən kòa wúná us we(2pf) catch them *WE caught them.*	cf.	**mə kói wúní** we(pf) catch them *We caught them.*

Question words occurring to the left of the verb condition shift to the 2nd perfect; question words found to the right, which are perfectly normal in Kanakuru, do not, e.g.,

məndái káa ɓálè what you(2pf) say *What did you(plural) say?*	cf.	**kə ɓálè məndái** you-pl (pf) say what *What did you(plural) say?*

As indicated earlier, the 2nd perfect is also required in non-relative, non-focused sentences in the negative, e.g.,

wò-náa bèelà rá-ù
neg-I(2pf) choose her-neg
I didn't choose her.

Abbreviations

2pf	2nd perfect
cn	continuous
fut	future
icp	intransitive copy pronoun
ing	«ing» (verbal-noun suffix)
neg	negative
nsjn	negative subjunctive
pcn	past continuous
pf	perfect
sjn	subjunctive

References

JUNGRAITHMAYR, Herrmann, in collaboration with Njeno Andirya GALADIMA, and Ulrich KLEINEWILLINGHÖFER, 1991, *A Dictionary of the Tangale Language (Kaltungo, Northern Nigeria),* (Sprache und Oralität in Afrika, 12.) Berlin, Dietrich Reimer.

LUKAS, Johannes, 1970/71-1971/72, Die Personalia und das primäre Verb im Bolanci (Nordnigerien), Mit Beiträgen über das Karekare, *Afrika und Übersee,* 54, 237-286, 55, 114-139.

NEWMAN, Paul, 1974, *The Kanakuru Language,* (West African Language Monographs, 9.) Leeds, Institute of Modern English Language Studies, University of Leeds and West African Linguistic Society.

NEWMAN, Paul, 1990, *Nominal and Verbal Plurality in Chadic,* (Publications in African Languages and Linguistics, 12.) Dordrecht, Foris Publications.

SCHUH, Russell G., 1978, *Bole-Tangale Languages of the Bauchi Area (Northern Nigeria),* (Marburger Studien zur Afrika- und Asienkunde, Serie A, Afrika, 13.) Berlin, Dietrich Reimer.

TAM Verbal Paradigms in the West African Sahel as Areal (Sprachbund), Genetic and Sociolinguistic Features. (Where are we 75 years after Klingenheben?)

Petr ZIMA

Charles University, Faculty of Humanities, Praha zimap@cesnet.cz

Abstract

Since A. Klingenheben's 1929 paper, a general feeling has developed, according to which substantial parts of the TAM verbal/predicate systems in various language groups of the West African Sahel share certain structural and typological similarities, if not identities, disregarding their different origins, and present/past geographical locations. The paper proposes that these structural, typological (and sometimes also formal) similarities may be grouped into three complexes, i.e. Split Predicate (or SP+/– Aux) vs Verbal Stem (VS) TAM marking, the Modal dichotomy of contrasting Indicative vs. Non-indicative appearing to have strong ties with the different types of Polarity, i.e. the dichotomy of contrasting Positive vs. Negative paradigms, and last but not least, the syntactic alternation of Neutral vs. Focussed TAM paradigms. Regarding all these three complex categories, the questions of their distribution, origins (roots) and present dynamics should be formulated and answered, if possible.

Résumé

L'hypothèse formulée par A. Klingenheben en 1929 concernant les ressemblances possibles des systèmes de fonctions et de morphèmes aspecto-temporels et modaux qui affectent plusieurs langues de l'Afrique occidentale d'origines génétiques différentes est actuellement renforcée par des données récemment analysées. Dans cet article, on propose de regrouper ces ressemblances en trois ensembles : (i) les marques aspecto-modales portées soit par le radical verbal, soit par un morphème ou un auxiliaire indépendant ; (ii) l'opposition modale indicatif/non-indicatif dont l'expression est souvent associée avec celle de la polarité positive/négative ; (iii) et enfin l'alternance syntaxique entre paradigmes +/– focalisés. L'auteur pose les questions de l'origine, de la distribution et du dynamisme de ces trois ensembles de phénomènes.

1.1. Beyond any doubt, the great German linguist August Klingernheben has laid the foundations of areal research in TAM paradigms of languages in West Africa. When comparing the verbal systems of Hausa and Vai he wrote: «*Diese auffälige Übereinstimmung, ja fast völlige Identität des Systems der Aktionsarten im Hausa und im Vai lässt sich nicht aus einer Urverwandschaft der beiden Sprachen erklären, da diese ja, wie schon oben erwähnt, zwei ganz verschiedenen Sprachfamilien angehören. Die Übereinstimmung ist ja auch nicht eine materielle, d.h. eine solche die sich auf den Sprachstoff selbst bezöge, wenn sie auch zum Teil in der verwendung semasiologisch gleicher Sprachelemente besteht, sondern eine solche des Systems, der Psychologie.*» (1929: 257-8). And in stressing the hypothetical and preliminary character of this research, he does not exclude extending such a comparison beyond the limits of Hausa and Vai: «*Es braucht wohl kaum gesagt zu werden, dass der obige Erklärungsversuch nur als Hypothese gewertertet werden will. Zu ihrer Fundierung genügt natürlich nicht die Untersuchung der verbalen Kategorien des Hausa und Vai, sondern es müssten auch die übrige westafrikanische Sprachen herangezogen werden.*» (ibid.: Footnote 1). Disguised within the liminary context of this footnote, he even suggests that similarities may affect not only the functional patterns, but also the forms.[1] In our time, we are unlikely to share much of Klingenheben's methodological orientation, but the essentials of his more than 70 years old observations about certain similarities in TAM/Verbal paradigms affecting structures and forms of languages from often quite different genetic families or branches in West Africa now appear clearer than in Klingenheben's time.

1.2. Before the early 1960's, most serious research on the verbal paradigms in this area was restricted to the confines of the genetic limits of language families. Intensive research in Chadic within its Afro-Asiatic genetic context opened the field for comparative research and reconstruction of the verbal paradigm development with particular attention to TAM functions and formal paradigms in Chadic in general, Hausa being, for obvious reasons, one of the most analysed structures within this family. Similar attempts in another genetical phylum, Niger-Congo, were focused mainly on Mande, and on certain areas of Benue–Congo, Fula being one of the most investigated language structure, in this respect within the Atlantic branch. As for the Songhay and Saharan complexes, the external genetic affinities of these complexes being questionable for longer periods, attempts at reconstructions of their verbal piece dynamics were usually operated at their lower-level genetic contexts: thus dialects or relatively recent offsprings within a broad cluster of languages were mostly object of such studies in the case of Songhay, or limited groups of closely related languages in the case of Saharan. Klaus Schubert (1971) was, to my knowledge, the first linguist to re-open a sort of transgenetic approach to the verbal paradigms in the Sahel, in the post-

[1] «Eine eingehende Vergleichung benachbarter Sudansprachen mit dem Hausa wird zeigen, dass dieses den Sudansprachen mit den psychologischen Kategorien vereinzelt auch Elemente des Sprachstoffes selbst entlehnt hat.» (1929: 258, Footnote 1).

Klingenheben period. Later, since the mid-1990's, an adaptation of the very concept of Sprachbund for the African conditions, and its broadening took place (Zima 1998, Cyffer, 2000, 2002, Nicolaï, forthcoming), the TAM paradigms and functions being one of the main preliminary: hence the study of the TAM systems opens a new approach towards understanding Sprachbund as a bundle of isoglosses running not only within given genetic confines (as it does in classical dialectology and «language geography»), but also across the genetic language frontiers in the Lake Chad area, and beyond its present limits into the major parts of the Sahel belt.

1.3. A general feeling therefore develops that substantial parts of the TAM verbal/predicate systems in various language groups of the West African Sahel share certain structural and typological similarities, if not identities, disregarding their different origins, and present/past geographical locations. We propose that these structural, typological (and sometimes also formal) similarities may be grouped into three complexes, as follows:

1.3.1. Split Predicate (or SP+/–Aux) vs. Verbal Stem (VS) TAM marking systems. Recently, particular varieties in patterns of such «split predicate» TAM paradigms in several types of Mande language systems were analysed, and these constructions characterised as a situation «in which auxiliary-like elements (Predicate Markers) convey all or most of the content we tend to expect to be grammaticalised as morphological categories on the verb, and the «lexical verb» almost exclusively contributes (lexical) semantic content to the predication.» (Kastenholz, in this volume). In this paper, we would like to show that

- typologically similar or even identical patterns exist in the Sahel, far beyond the genetic limits of Mande;
- these different patterns may often be linked with marking the morphosyntactic tense/aspect contrast of Perfective vs. Imperfective, and with that of the syntactic contrast Transitivity vs. Intransitivity;

1.3.2. the modal dichotomy of contrasting Indicative vs. Non-indicative often appears to have strong ties with the different types of Polarity, i.e. the dichotomy of contrasting Positive vs. Negative paradigms;

1.3.3. last but not least, there is the phenomenon of the syntactic alternation of Neutral vs. Focalised TAM paradigms (in certain Hausaist traditions this dichotomy is labelled as that of Relative vs. Non-Relative Verbal forms);

1.3.4. regarding all these three complex categories, the questions of their distribution, origins (roots) and present dynamics should be formulated and answered, if possible.

2. There are basically two typologically different systems of TAM marking in most language systems of the West African Sahel, one using formal TAM exponents expressed in the verbal stem (the so-called *VS TAM system*), the other expressing all (or in certain types some) TAM categories by complex exponents standing usually after the subject, and often formally disconnected from the verbal predicate (the so-called *Split Predicate* or *PVP+/–Aux System*). Apart from Mande, the dynamics of the relationship between the two types of predicate markers has also been analysed in Chadic and Hausa, where the relationship between these two types of predication has also been used as one of the features of diachrony, the Chadic languages with the prevailing VS TAM marking being considered as «early stage» development, while Hausa (with certain other languages of the same group) with its prevailing Split Predicate marking of certain tense/aspect/mode categories being diachronically considered the «late-stage» development (Jungraithmayr, 1989). Different dynamic stages of development of both types of systems and various transitional stages/subtypes of this dichotomy exist in both Chadic and Mande languages: before analyzing their common parallels, similarities and difference, we should have in mind two methodological caveats:

2.1. there are no classical genetic ties between these two complexes, both of them belonging even at their highest, i.e. most ancient levels to different macro-families of languages of completely different origins. Chadic is a branch of Afroasiatic, while Mande appears to be (despite certain doubts) a relatively ancient branch of Niger-Kordofan. However, data collected by Mukarovsky (1987) and certain other authors probably indicate strong mutual interference between them, relatively ancient in its nature;

2.2. in the contemporary West African Sahel, direct immediate areal contacts between these two language blocks are relatively limited in their intensity and space (such contact and interference cases as that of the Boko/Busa cluster contacts with Hausa and Chadic as described by Ross MacCallum Jones, 1998, being rather exceptional). Hence mass language interference may hardly be suspected to take place, today.[2] Thinking in areal terms, it should be stressed at this point, however, that Songhay as a language complex is geographically «inserted» between these two blocks, currently forming a sort of territorial language link/or barrier between them;

2.3. it should be stressed, moreover, that Songhay as a language cluster shares essential structural similarities of the split-predicate TAM paradigms typology with both certain sections of Mande and Chadic. Thus, Bambara (and perhaps most of what Kastenholz calls «Great Manding»), and Hausa (and certain other Chadic languages), together with most of the Songhay cluster form a sort of areal typological «Split Predicate Sahel Belt». For details see Table 1.

---

[2] This obviously does not exclude the possibility that such mass contacts and interference existed in the past, the present geographical distribution of the Chadic and the Mande complex in the Sahel may differ from that of the past.

Table 1

	Timbuktu	Zarma	Bambara	Hawsa
Ipf Pos Ind Intr	S *go/o* Verb	S *gà* TP Verb	S *bè* V	S *sunàà* VN
Ipf Ng Ind Intr	S *si* V Verb	S *sí* Verb	S *tè* V	S *baasàà* VN
Ipf Pos Ind Tr	S *go/o* V O	S *gà* TP O V	S *bè* O V S	*sunàà* VN gcAt / VN O
Ipf Neg Indic Tr	S *si* V O	S *sí* O V	S *tè* O V	S *baasàà* VN gcAt / VN O
Pf Indic Pos Intr	S V	S V	S V Suf Pf	S *sun* V
Pf Ind Neg Intr	S *na* V	S *mánà* V	S *ma* V	S *bà sù* V ba
Pf Pos Ind Tr	S V O	S *nà* O V	S *ye* O V	S *sun* V GrSuf O
Pf Neg Ind Tr	S *na* V O	S *mánà* O V	S *ma* O V	S *bà sù* V GrSuf O ba
Subj Pos Tr	S *ma* V O	S *mà/má* O V	S *ka* O V	S *sù* V GrSuf O
Subj Neg Tr	S *ma si* V O	S *mà/mási* O V	S *kana* O V	S *kadàsù* V GrSuf O

Note: all three compared language structures display certain marginal irregularities of their «split-predicate systems»: thus, typologically speaking, the verbal suffix of progressive constructions in Bambara, and the marking of intransitivity/transitivity of those parts of the paradigm which is supposed to use VN forms, display a similarity with the different types of object marking in Hawsa using the tonal, quantitative and qualitative variation of the final syllable (symbolised by *grsuf,* meaning grade-suffix in our Table 1). For details of Mande see Kastenholz in this same volume, for Songhay see Nicolaï-Zima, 1997, for Hawsa see Zima (2002, and forthcoming).

If at least certain languages of the Atlantic stock together with languages of the Saharan stock could be added to such a «split predicate typology», such a belt would thus spread from the Western Coast to the Lake Chad region.

2.4. As for the languages and clusters analyzed in Table 1, the distribution of different varieties of the split-predicate (+/–Aux) vs. verbal stem TAM marking appears in many cases to be linked with the opposition perfective x imperfective and transitive x intransitive. While the perfective x imperfective contrast appears to be expressed in most languages of the Sahel belt, its links with the transitivity vs. intransitivity differ from one language complex to another.

As for many Mande languages and for the Songhay cluster, the TAM paradigm markers of intransitivity/transitivity operate mostly in or close to the Aux complex of the Split Predicate expressing tense/aspect/mode at the same time. Hausa (and certain selected Chadic languages typologically close to it) also tends to distinguish the present-day perfective x imperfective and other aspect/tense/mode contrasts mostly within the Aux components (Predicate Markers) of the split predicative constructions: the traditional concept of the so-called Subject-Pronoun complex has been developed for this purpose by the school of F. W. Parsons. On the other hand, various markers linked with the verbal stem (VS) are used for marking transitivity x intransitivity, together with other markers expressing the nature of structural links between the verb and its complements in a more general way. Details of such operations concerning the tonal structure of the predicate, together with the quantity, and (in certain cases) even the quality of the final vowel or other features of the last syllable of the predicate were elaborated within the context of the concept of the «grade system», and reformulated in the successive periods.[3] In general, however, one might formulate a hypothesis that while both the perfective x imperfective and the transitive x intransitive contrasts are preferred to be expressed by the Aux complex of the split-predicative pattern in many Mande languages and Songhay, the type displayed in Hausa and in typologically close Chadic languages separates the features of tense/aspect (and mode), connected more with the split predicate Aux markers from those of transitivity/intransitivity expressed in the verbal stem.

One of the reasons for such a difference may be inherent in the fact that the two types of predication are also closely linked with the SAuxOV and SAuxVO word order, the former being characteristic for major areas of Mande and Songhay clusters, the latter being shared by Hausa and several other Chadic languages typologically close to it. In fact, it has been stressed on several occasions that the traditional dividing line between the predicative, exocentric (verbal) constructions, and the nominal (endocentric) constructions appears much less clear in many languages of the West African Sahel area than elsewhere. It is worth mentioning that certain authors analyse particular language systems of this area even without recognising any essential analytical need to distinguish between verb and noun (N. Tersis for Zarma Songhay in 1981). Hence the S AuxOV and the SAuxVO types could be analysed as possibly derived from two varieties of attributive constructions: one displaying the pattern Head +/– Marker + Attribute, the other displaying the pattern Attribute +/– Marker + Head.[4] This seems to be confirmed by the fact that the dividing line between the present distribution of the S Aux O V type, and that of the S Aux V O type is to a certain extent parallel with the present dividing line between the distribution of the constructions Attribute +/– Marker + Head, and that of Head +/– Marker + Attribute. All these facts may support the thesis that a special African areal subclass of nomino-verbal morphemes, labelled *stabilisers* by various members of the London school several decades ago, was at the origin of the differentiation of the predicate and non-predicative constructions types in the whole Sahel area, and perhaps far beyond its limits (for details see Zima, 1998). If this hypothesis is correct, it might explain some of the different structural features of the two main types of predication disseminated in particular complexes of languages within the Sahel Sprachbund.

---

[3] See Parsons (1960), Zima (1972). Even P. Newman who proposed an alternative analysis of Hausa in terms of verbal vowel-classes in 1973, has recently accepted the Hausa grade-system, as developed by Parsons «as a reasonably sound synchronic basis for organising the various morphological classes of verbs in Hausa» (2000: 677).

[4] The whole earlier discussion about the possible diachronic development of the SOV versus SVO constructions in Mande and in Niger-Congo (see Heine-Reh, 1984, Claudi, 1993, etc.) presumes thus, explicitly or implicitly, that clear transitional links between attributive and predicative constructions must have existed in these structures.

3. Polarity and modality

3.1. While the aspect/tense contrasts of perfectivity vs. imperfectivity are distributed in at least two main types of paradigms affecting various areas and genetic families of the Sahel, the same is valid for mode and polarity (i.e. the opposition of the positive x negative verbal paradigms). Turning to Table 1 again, we realise that mode as a grammatical category (displayed mostly as the opposition of indicative vs. non-indicative) is far from being an analytically «pure» grammatical category in most documented language structures of the Sahel. A sort of indicative vs. non-indicative binary modal contrast is inherent in the TAM verbal predication markers of such genetically different languages as Bambara, Songhay and Hausa. Further analysis reveals that the TAM systems in these languages may be typologically subdivided from this point of view into two sets of paradigms: one set of TAM forms expresses tense/or aspect (or both), but all its paradigms are indicative or modally neutral in their character; the paradigms of the other set, however, may be modally characterised as non-neutral, non-indicative. In general, EITHER *tense-aspect* OR *mode* is explicitly marked in each set. Whether we accept the analytical position that mode is not marked if tense-aspect is (which is the analytical solution preferred in the present paper), or vice versa, i.e. that aspect is unmarked when the non-indicative mode is functional (an option preferred for Songhay by Heath 1999: 155), we must accept the thesis that tense-aspect and mode markers are in a sort of complementary distribution, in most of these language structures.

3.2. Moreover, in most language structures summarised in Table 1, many (though not all) positive and negative TAM exponents are also complementary in their distribution, i.e. there are separate sets of positive and negative paradigms for particular TAM functions. This is the phenomenon of the so-called «suppletivity» of the TAM negation, observed already earlier in other languages of the Sahel. As for the Mande languages, D. Creissels first analyzed this particular typological feature. He contrasted the «classical» typology of negation where «*la phrase négative se réalise par la simple adjonction d'un morphème de négation à la phrase positive correspondante*» (1997: 3) to what he calls «*la situation typologiquement exceptionnelle du mandingue (qui se retrouve à des degrés divers dans d'autres langues de la famille mandé*» .., «*où la négation s'exprime par des modifications des formes verbales dans lesquelles il n'est pas possible d'isoler un morphème de négation s'ajoutant à ce qui autrement serait une forme verbale positive.*» (1997: 4) This suppletive distinction of positive and negative verbal paradigms, though not obligatory, but frequent in Mande, was commented on and analyzed by Kastenholz: «*The dominant strategy in Mande languages is to mark negation in post subject position of the clause, either making use of different complementary negative auxiliaries for different TAM categories, as in Bambara... or of additional negation markers where the corresponding affirmative does not require an auxiliary, as in Sooso...*» (2002: 96).

3.3. The broader existence of a suppletive character of the TAM negation in various Sahel language structures of different genetic origins, was also analyzed in Zima (1998: 144ff). Hausa and Songhay, the two genetically unrelated but geographically and sociolinguistically close languages of the Sahel, offer excellent, though partly differing typological patterns of this phenomenon. In the core (central, well-grammaticalised) indicative perfective and imperfective TAM paradigms, the analyzed feature appears to be fully operational in both languages. If we abstract from certain particular features of Hausa which (unlike Songhay) operates in both the perfective and the imperfective paradigm, the distinction between the so-called neutral/non-relative, non-focalized, and the focalized/relative forms (for details see further in Para 4), the typological symmetries between the two genetically unrelated, but geographically and sociolinguistically close language systems are clear, as illustrated in Table 2.

Table 2 - Suppletive Negation of Central/Core Verbal TAM Indicative Paradigms: Hausa and Songhay

		Hausa
PfApos	1S	*naa tàfi*
	3Pl	*sun tàfi*
PfBpos	1S	*na tàfi*
	3Pl	*sukà tàfi*
Pf Neg	1S	*bàn tàfi ba*
	3Pl	*bà sù tàfi ba*
Ipf APos	1S	*inàà zuwàà*
	3Pl	*sunàà zuwàà*
Ipf B pos	1S	*nakèè zuwàà*
	3Pl	*sukèè zuwàà*
Ipf Neg	1S	*baa nàà / bân zuwàà*
	3Pl	*baa sàà / suàà zuwàà*

		Songhay (Timbuktu)	Songhay/Dendi
PfPos	1S	*ay koy*	*á kpéỳ?*
	3Pl	*i koy*	*ŋ̀ kpéỳ*
PfNeg	1S	*ay na koy*	*á ná kpéỳ*
	3Pl	*i na koy*	*ŋ̀ ná kpéỳ*
Ipf Pos	1S	*ay go koy*	*áà kpéỳ*
	3Pl	*i go koy*	*ŋ̀ŋ̀ kpéỳ*
Ipf Neg	1S	*ay si koy*	*ású kpéỳ*
	3Pl	*ay si koy*	*ŋ̀ sú kpéỳ*

In both systems, that of Hausa and Songhay, the two main TAM paradigms (the perfective and the imperfective) contrast the positive and the negative functions in a suppletive way, the positive TAM exponents being formally different from the negative ones. Notwithstanding a certain dialectal variation, in both language structures, these differences concern either suprasegmental or segmental features, or both.

In Hausa, differences of positive and negative exponents of perfective and imperfective concern more the suprasegmental features of the pronominal part of the TAM complexes, the main segmental structure of the negative exponent being derived in both cases from *BA (though the suprasegmental variation of this latter base is, however, also subject to variation in different paradigms of negatives). However, the general suppletivity of negation is perfectly clear in both the perfective and the imperfective paradigm.

In Songhay, there are two distinct exponents of negatives, displaying different dialectal varieties of *MANA/*NA and *SI/SU. The former is used in negatives of perfective, the latter is used in negatives of the imperfective paradigm. In both paradigms of Songhay, i.e. perfective and imperfective, the polarity contrasts of positive/negative paradigms is expressed thus in a suppletive way, although this feature is much clearer in the imperfective paradigm: in the perfective, the surface contrast of a zero morpheme in the positive and the *na/ná* surface exponent of the corresponding negative paradigms might also be interpreted as a sort of zero + *na/ná* agglutination. It should be added, however, that this phenomenon of suppletivity between the negative and positive indicative verbal forms concerns mainly those «core» or «central» areas of the split predicate TAM verbal systems of both Hausa and Songhay. The further we get from the central, more or less grammaticalised pairs of perfective-imperfective TAM verbal forms, towards less gramaticalised peripheric «periphrastic» TAM verbal paradigms (such as various sorts of progressives, ingressives, or other «phasal» constructions that exist in both language systems), the weaker the features of suppletivity between their positive/negative paradigms, if they appear at all (for details see Zima, forthcoming).

3.4. Contrasting various geographically close but genetically unrelated language structures as those analysed in Table 1 reveals that the usage of a sort of suppletive type of negation, is to some extent always linked with the indicative modality. In this respect, there is an opposition between most fully grammaticalised *indicative* TAM paradigms contrasted to the *non-indicative ones*. While the suppletive negation (polarity) affects most central indicative forms, the subjunctive, non-indicative paradigms express negation typologically in the classical way, combining positive subjunctive forms with the agglutination of a sort of negative particle, as can be observed in Table 3. It is possible that whole sets of negative TAM paradigms link with the differing functional aspects of predication in particular types of clauses within complex sentences. This is an idea developed by Güldemann (1996) for the Bantu structures.

Table 3 : Classical Negation of Non-Indicative / Subjunctive Forms

	Hawsa	Songhay (Timbuktu)	Songhay/Dendi
Subj Pos	*ìn/nà tàfi*	*ay ma koy*	*áŋ́ kpéỳ*
	sù tàfi	*i ma koy*	*mmá kpéỳ*
Subj Neg	*kadà ìn/nà tàfi*	*ay ma si koy*	*áŋ́ sú kpéỳ*
	kadà sù tàfi	*i ma si koy*	*mmá sú kpéỳ*

In Songhay, the subjunctive agglutinates one of the negative markers (that of the imperfective) into the full positive paradigms, and thus the *ma-má* positive exponent of non-indicative modality is combined with the *si/sí/sú* negation.[5]

In Hausa, the only partly non-indicative *sù* paradigm displays the negative exponent *+kada/kar/kaC* (unknown for other, indicative paradigms), adding it in a classical (agglutinative) way in front of the positive non-indicative *sù* paradigm. It should be added that according to P. Newman (1971), this type of negation is an innovation in Hausa, speaking in internal, Chadic comparative terms.

This essential distinction between the suppletive forms of negation in most central, or core «indicative» paradigms, and the non-suppletive, «agglutinative» forming of negatives in the marginal or peripheric (and hence periphrastic, and relatively less grammaticalised and most frequently more recent in origin) indicative TAM paradigms, as well as in most «non-indicative» TAM paradigms is typologically shared not only by both genetically unrelated, but geographically close languages of the Sahel-Songhay and Hausa, but further data confirm the existence of comparable structural interdependence in various other languages of the Sahel, genetically unrelated with either Chadic or Songhay, as e.g. Pular (see Abdurahmane Diallo, 2000: 186) or Kanuri (see N. Cyffer, 1974: 99). This certainly stresses the links existing in the respective TAM systems between modality and polarity (negation type), in general.

4. Syntactic alternation of TAM's : independent x relative vs. neutral x focalised : the category of focality

4.1 Although the analysis of the verbal systems of the Sahel area languages in terms of such traditional categories as tense-apect-mode has a relatively long tradition, towards the end of the 19th century doubts started to appear about whether certain differences between verbal paradigms estimated previously in terms of the categories of tense-aspect-mode only were not, in fact, due to other factors, such as the syntactic character of the clause in which the given paradigm appears. Hausa was among the first language systems where differences between the so-called «relative» vs. «non-relative» verbal paradigms were distinguished. Although certain misunderstandings and shortcuts between the TAM-based and

[5] For details about the Hausa TAM system see Zima, 2002. As for the situation in Songhay, see e.g. Nicolaï-Zima, 1997. See also Heath, 1999: 155.

«relative/non-relative» based concepts of the character of particular Hausa verbal paradigms have survived for longer periods, since Klingenheben's (1929) time, there has been no doubt that only the verbal forms belonging to the so-called *sukà* and *sukèè* sets (labelled B in terms of our Table 2) are accepted as correct in Hausa relative clauses, and in certain other types of syntactic environments. Only since the 1960's has the structural existence of two functionally different types of verbal paradigms in Hausa been accepted, the difference between them being defined in terms of different syntactic distribution. While the strictly tense-aspect-mode-defined paradigms are in mutual contrastive distribution, their occurrence being subject to rules of tense/aspect, modality and polarity contrasts, the choice or alternates between the so-called relative vs. non-relative verbal paradigms has in most cases little, if anything, to do with the above defined contrasts (the only exception being perhaps the so-called «narrative» usage of the *sukà* paradigm). Thus the so-called A-type paradigms *sun* and *sunàa* («neutral, non-relative» in traditional Hausaists' terminology) are mutually in complementary distribution with the B-type paradigms *sukà and sukèe* («relative» in traditional Hausaists' terminology), the choice between them being subject to syntactic contexts. Hence the concept of a *syntactically conditioned alternation of particular varieties of certain TAM paradigms* for Hausa was coined (Zima, 1967). Already at that stage, the original concept of the *relative x non-relative* contexts as syntactic factors conditioning this alternation was broadened. Hence, the syntactically conditioning contexts of the «relative» B alternates were extended to *WH- questions and to emphatic constructions. A decade later, the major role of the *FSP* (Functional Sentence Perspective) in the concepts of the Prague Linguistic School (to become later and more widely known in terms of FOCUS-TOPIC/FOCALISATION-TOPICALISATION) in syntactic conditioning of this alternation in Hausa and in many Chadic languages was recognised (Zima, 1991). Possible broader links with comparable phenomena in Chadic were discussed (Frajzyngier, 1987), and possibilities to find correlations within other branches of this whole major genetic phylum, and even Afroasiatic approached (Jungraithmayr, 1994, Aikhenwald, 1987). In its present concept, we might label this syntactically defined, but morphologically manifested verbal category as that of *focality*, as functional contrasts between particular types of questions, emphatic constructions and relative clauses on one hand and all other types of syntactic environments on the other hand, may be defined in its terms of focalised/focussed x neutral (non-focalised/non-focussed).

4.2. This category of focality apparently exists as a fully operational part of the structures in various other languages of the area, genetically unrelated to Chadic or even to Afroasiatic. D. W. Arnott's first definition of its functioning in Fula as early as in 1965 was fully supported by the analysis performed by Koval'-Nyalibouly (1983), and relations with comparable phenomena in other Atlantic languages are now established (Gottschligg, forthcoming). Analytical descriptions of typologically comparable phenomena in such languages as Ibibio or Ibo have also been published (Essien, 1988, 1991; Emenanjo, 1991) and most recently, Cyffer (2000, 2002) has brought evidence that this alternation exists even in Kanuri, though affecting its system in a less intensive way than that of Hausa, Fula and related languages. According to this author, the Kanuri system displays this phenomenon in perfective TAM verbal paradigms only. Moreover, it affects only the focused constructions of subject and direct-object, while indirect object and adverbial phrase focusing remain outside this pattern (2002: 39).

4.3. Structurally, it should be added that languages with this syntactically conditioned alternation of verbal TAM paradigms in its full operation, i.e. affecting both the perfective and imperfective verbal paradigms (as e.g. Hausa and Fula[6]) avoid this alternation in negative constructions. Thus, they offer two pairs of syntactically conditioned paradigms for the fully grammaticalised TAM categories in the positive contexts against one single paradigm for their negative counterparts. One can say that the contrast between the focalised/focussed and the non-focalised/focussed syntactic functions is not operative in the negative sections of the verbal systems, and hence the operation of focality as a morphosyntactic category is neutralised in the negative. Hence, clear structural links between the two categories (that of focality and that of polarity) thus must exist. In this sense, Caron formulated a hypothesis of his own for Hausa that «*l'opération de négation est du même ordre que l'opération de subordination. Elle implique un préconstruit positif repris et sur lequel porte l'opération de négation.*» (1990: 40).

4.4. The distribution of this typological pattern in languages of at least two (or even three, if partly affected Kanuri is taken into account) genetically distinct great phyla contacting and interfering one with another in the Sahel over long periods of time has confirmed an evident conclusion that this phenomenon is also to be conceived as one of the Sprachbund distinctive features affecting many, but not all Sahel areas (Zima, 1998). Although available data are far from complete, one may perhaps summarise in a preliminary way, at the present moment, that this syntactically conditioned alternation affects a wide belt of the Sahel, starting from Berber in the North West, Atlantic languages in the West (with the Fula Diaspora bringing it, in a secondary way, perhaps far to the East into the Hausaland and the Lake Chad area). Moreover, several comparable phenomena illustrate its diffusion far to the southeast from the Sahel (Ibo, Ibibio). As no comparable features have as yet been discovered either in the Mande or the Songhay complexes, this might support the thesis about their special position on the «Sprachbund» maps of the Sahel, at least in a negative (exclusive) way.

[6] See e.g. Arnott, 1970: 290; Zima, 1967: 196.

5. Problems of Interplay: Split predicativity, Modality, Polarity, Focality (plus or minus one)

While the detailed picture of the distribution of all these typological features which we may summarise as split-predicativity vs. verbal stem predicativity, polarity (suppletivity vs. non suppletivity of negation), modality and focality of the TAM complexes in the Sahel is still far from complete, the mutual links of these categories appear clearer today than in A. Klingenheben's time. Three more general analytical questions arise in this context, that of the present-day structural links in particular language systems, that of their contemporary distribution, and that of their possible roots/origins.

5.1. While the link between split predicativity, polarity and modality appears to affect a broad belt of languages spoken in the Sahel (including several Mande, Fula/plus or minus certain other Atlantic languages, Songhay, Hausa/plus or minus certain Chadic, and Kanuri), focality as a TAM exponent concerning category is operational in a geographically more restricted zone, most of the Mande and Songhay block being unaffected by it. On the other hand, most language structures displaying focality integrate its operation within the context of modality and polarity (and to some extent even that of the split predicativity). In other words, the operation of the whole of the categorial complex appears to display two areal varieties in the Sahel: one is richer and more extended (including focality plus split predicativity, modality and polarity), while the other is restricted to split predicativity, modality and polarity.

5.2. It is possible that the origins and roots of such phenomena are embedded in a particular cluster/branch or family of languages definable in genetic terms, and hence we face phenomena which are of an either Afro/Asiatic, Niger/Congo, vs. Niger/Kordofan, or Saharan origin. If this is true in general, we might suppose that such phenomena only later became the object of structural diffusion in the Sahel (and possibly beyond its limits). This may concern either the whole complex or only certain parts of it.

5.2.1. As for the typological links between modality and polarity, interesting typological similarities of negation-types concerning language structures of various genetic origins spoken in the Sahel are shared with the Bantu cluster, as suggested already by C. Meinhof (1906: 64). Most recently, the Bantu linguistics has produced rich inventories of comparative data on these structural phenomena (Kamba-Muzenga, 1981) and broader stimuli for theoretical thinking about them (T. Güldemann 1996, 1999). In other words, most patterns of the Bantu situation concerning polarity and modality are typologically comparable with the situation in several genetically unrelated languages of the West African Sahel analysed above: if such phenomena are confirmed in other Niger-Congo languages, and especially those distributed in Central and West Africa today, then hand in hand with their relatively frequent distribution in the Mande complex, but with the relatively more restricted frequency of their distribution in the Saharan and Chadic complexes, one may contemplate the idea of their original Niger-Congo genetic roots. Hence the penetration of such phenomena into Songhay, Kanuri, Hausa and certain other structures would appear to be a secondary consequence of contact and interference, i.e. the Sprachbund phenomena.

5.2.2. On the other hand, the distribution of focality as a grammatical category is stretched over wider areas of present-day Afroasiatic, even into Berber, and perhaps far beyond the geographical confines of Africa. As the Sahel distribution of this category is more restricted than that of the modality/polarity and even split-predicativity, one cannot exclude the hypothesis that the genetic roots of this category are still to be located somewhere within the Afroasiatic macro-family, the present distribution in several genetically non-AA languages being a consequence of subsequent language contacts and interference, and hence also Sprachbund phenomena.

5.3. Apart from questions of the possible genetic origins/roots of the areal TAM Sprachbund features, other factors may be considered to have played their role in the development of such a TAM Sprachbund in the Sahel, and perhaps far beyond its limits. If, in fact, the whole set of languages concerned in the Sahel is analysed not only in terms of their purely linguistic diachrony and typological synchrony, but also in terms of their social functions, one tendency appears: most (though not all) of the languages concerned have served as the «lingue franche» in different periods of their development, i.e. as languages of wider, inter-community communication (Bambara, Songhay, Hausa, even Kanuri, etc.). The fact that several languages of quite different genetic origins that display such features have or had served in lingua franca functions, may thus favour the alternative hypothesis.

6. Conclusion, perspectives

As functional analogies affect parallels in whole functional morphosyntactic categories in so many languages of different genetic origins, typological structures and social roles in the Sahel, it is often very difficult, if not sometimes impossible, to decide

- what are the limits of this bundle of distinctive features characteristic for this TAM-defined Sahel (and Sahara?) Sprachbund;
- where did their diffusion start from;
- whether their diffusion really originated from the emblematic substrates into the non-emblematic superstrates or the other way round: several different cases analysed here might suggest that while the former direction appears more frequent, the latter cannot be altogether excluded; hence the entire concept of metatypy, as formulated by Ross and others, should be given

further analytical attention, and perhaps revision. Classical and non-traditional areas (such as the African Sahel, Autralia, New Guinea or Amerindian languages) might enable more reliable generalisations and represent a real challenge for areal and general linguistics.

References

AIKHENVALD, A. I., 1987, *Strukturno-typologitcheskaya klassifikatsya berberskih yazykov,* Moscow.

ARNOTT, D. W., 1970, *The Nominal and Verbal Systems of Fula,* Oxford.

BEARTH. T., 1995, Nominal Periphrasis and the origin of the predicative marker in Mande languages, *Afrikanistische Arbeitspapiere,* 41-117. Köln.

CARON, B., 1990, La négation en haoussa, *Linguistique Africaine,* 4:31-46, Paris.

CLAUDI, U. 1993, *Die Stellung von Verb und Objekt in Niger-Kongo-Sprachen,* Köln.

CREISSELS, D., 1997, Une tentative d'explication de particularités typologiques de la négation en mandingue, *Mandenkan,* 32: 3-22, Paris.

CYFFER, N., 1974, *Syntax des Kanuri,* Hamburg.

CYFFER, N., 2000, Areale Merkmale im TAM System und in der Syntax der saharanischen Sprachen, *Mehr als nur Worte Afrikanistische Beiträge zum 65. Geburtstag von Franz Rottland,* R. Vossen, A. Mietzner, A. Meissner (Eds.), 159-182, München.

CYFFER, N., 2002, The Lake Chad: a new Sprachbund Boundary? *Lexical and Structural Diffusion*, R. Nicolaï and P. Zima, Editors, 27-44, Nice-Praha.

DIALLO, A., 2000, *Grammaire descriptive du pular du Fuuta Jaloo,* Frankfurt a. M.

EMENANJO, E. M., 1991, *The Tense System in Igbo*, Essien (ed), 129-144.

ESSIEN, O. E., 1988, The nature of tense in African languages, *Archiv orientálni 59*, 1-11, Praha.

ESSIEN, O. E. (ed), 1991, *The Tense Systems in Nigerian Languages and English (Afrikanistische Arbeitspapiere No 27)*, Koeln.

FRAJZYNGIER, Z., 1987, The relative clauses in Proto-Chadic, *Proceedings of the 4th Intern. Hamito-Semitic Congress,* Jungraithmayr, H. - Mueller, W. W. (eds), 425-450, Amsterdam.

GOTTSCHLIGG, P., forthcoming, Dialectal Variance, Standardisation and the Development of a Written Language: the Case of Fula, *African languages in global society*, Th. Bearth *et al* (eds).

GOTTSCHLIGG, P., forthcoming, *Elaboration and simplification in Fula verbal morphology*.

GOUFFE, C., 1971, Une corrélation typologique dans quatre langues de l'Afrique Occidentale: les fonctions de *N, *Afrika und Übersee 54,* 286-302.

GÜLDEMANN, T., 1996, *Verbalmorphologie und Nebenpredikationen im Bantu*. Bochum.

GÜLDEMANN, T., 1999, The Genesis of Verbal Negation in Bantu and its Dependency on Functional Features of Clause Types, *Bantu Historical Linguistics*, J.-M. Hombert and L. M. Hyman (eds), 545-587, Stanford.

HEATH, J., 1999, *A Grammar of Koyra Chini. The Songhay of Timbuktu*. Berlin.

HEINE, B., Reh, M., 1984, *Grammaticalization and Reanalysis in African Languages,* Hamburg.

JONES, R. M. C., 1998, *The Boko-Bussa Language Cluster*. München.

JUNGRAITHMAYR, H., 1989, Is Hausa an early or late stage Chadic language? *Current Progress in Chadic Linguistics,* Zygmunt Frajzyngier (ed), 251-266, Amsterdam-Philadelphia.

JUNGRAITHMAYR, H., 1994, Zweite Tempora in Afrikamischen Sprachen - Aegyptisch-Tschadische Gemeinsamkeiten? *Zwischen den beiden Ewigkeiten*, Bietat-Holaubek-Mukarovsky-Satzinger (eds), 102-122, Festschrift G. Thausig, Wien.

JUNGRAITHMAYR, H., NICOLAÏ, R., IBRISZIMOW, D., 1997, The West-Central Sudan and Savanna «Sprachbund», *Langues et Contacts de Langues en Zone Sahelo-Saharienne,* Baldi, S. (ed), 109-128, Napoli.

KAMBA-MUZENGA, J. G., 1981, *Les formes verbales négatives dans les langues bantoues,* Tervuren.

KASTENHOLZ, R., 2002, «Samogo» language island, and Mande-Senufo interference phenomena, *Lexical and Structural Diffusion*, R. Nicolaï and P. Zima, Editors, 91-109, Nice-Praha.

KASTENHOLZ, R., forthcoming, *TAM verbal paradigm systems in Western Mande: An overview.*

KLINGENHEBEN, A., 1929, Die Tempora West Afrikas und die semitischen Tempora. *Zf f. Eingeborenen-Sprachen 19*, 241-268, Berlin.

KOVAL' A. I., NYALIBOULY, B. A., 1983, Glagolnoye spryazhenie v Fula i ego svyaz ssintaksitcheskim urovnyem, *Voprosy afrikanskogo yazykoznaniya,* N. V. Gromova (ed), 74-101, Moscow.

LACROIX, P., 1969, L'ensemble songhay-jerma: problèmes et thèmes de travail, *Actes du 8ème Congrès de W.A.L.S.*, 87-95, Abidjan.

MEINHOF, C., 1906, *Grundzüge einer vergleichenden Grammatik der Bantusprachen,* Berlin.

MUKAROVSKY, H. G., 1987: *Mande-Chadic. Common Stock. A Study of Phonological and Lexical Evidence,* Wien.

NEWMAN, P., 1971, Hausa negative markers, *SAL 2,* 183-195.

NEWMAN, P., 1973, Grades, vowel-tone classes and extensions in the Hausa verbal system, *SAL 4,* 297-346.

NEWMAN, P., 2000, *The Hausa Language. An Encyclopaedic Reference Grammar,* New Haven and London.

NICOLAÏ, R., 1981, *Les dialectes du songhay,* Paris.

NICOLAÏ, R., forthcoming, *Songhay-Mande Convergence Area? Facts, Questions, Frames.*

NICOLAÏ R., 2003, *La force des choses ou l'épreuve 'nilo-saharienne',* Köln.

NICOLAÏ, R. - Zima, P., 1997, *Songhay,* Muenchen.

PARSONS, F. W., 1960, The verbal system in Hausa, *Afrika und Übersee 44,* 1-36.

ROBERT, S., 2000, Le verbe wolof ou la grammaticalisation du focus, *Topicalisation et focalisation dans les langues africaines*, B. Caron (ed.), 229-267, Louvain: Peeters.

SCHUBERT, K., 1971, Zur Bedeutung und Anwendung der Verbalparadigmen im Hausa und Kanuri, *Afrika und Übersee 55*, 1-49, 208-227; *56*: 90-118.

TERSIS, N., 1981, *Economie d'un système: Unité et relations syntawiques en Zarma (Niger)*, Paris.

TRÖBS, H., 2003, On the origin of some predicative markers in imperfective constructions in Manding, *Mandenkan No 38,* 1-9.

ZIMA, P., 1967, On syntactic alternation of verbal forms in Hausa, *MIO 13,* 188-198. Berlin.

ZIMA, P., 1972, *Problems of Categories and Word-Classes in Hausa,* Praha.

ZIMA, P., 1991, Le problème des formes dites «relatives» en tchadique, *Etudes tchadiques: La phrase complexe,* Jungraithmayr, H. et Tourneux, H. (eds), 15-26, Paris.

ZIMA, P., 1998, Stabilizers expressing existence, identification and localization in African languages and their roles in the dynamics of their systems, *Language and Location in Time and Space*, Zima, P. and Tax, Vl. (eds), 131-149, München.

ZIMA, P., 1998a, Localisation, Space and Time in Languages of Different Types and Regions, *Language and Location in Time and Space*, Zima, P. and Tax, V. (eds), 3-10, Muenchen.

ZIMA, P., 2002, Hausa TAM markers analysed in their dialectal, genetic and areal context, *Lexical and Structural Diffusion*, R. Nicolaï and P. Zima, Editors, 265-282, Nice-Praha.

ZIMA, P., forthcoming, *Songhay negation in its areal contexts*

PRINTED ON PERMANENT PAPER • IMPRIME SUR PAPIER PERMANENT • GEDRUKT OP DUURZAAM PAPIER - ISO 9706
N.V. PEETERS S.A., WAROTSTRAAT 50, B-3020 HERENT